A
CROSS-SECTION
OF RESEARCH
IN MUSIC
EDUCATION

Edited by
Stephen H. Barnes
University of Tulsa

UNIVERSITY
PRESS OF
AMERICA

LANHAM • NEW YORK • LONDON

Library of Congress Catalog Card Number: **81-43496**

CONTENTS

Preface   v

Suggestions for Evaluating Research
Articles in Music Education   1

A CROSS-SECTION OF RESEARCH IN MUSIC
EDUCATION   7

Student Perceptions of Characteristics of
Effective Applied Music Instructors
HAROLD F. ABELES   9

Development and Validation of a Music
Education Competency Test
HERSCHEL V. BEAZLEY 20

Grade/Age Levels and the Reinforcement
Value of the Collative Properties
of Music
SUSAN R. EISENSTEIN 29

The Roots of Music Education in Baltimore
JAMES L. FISHER 45

Relationship of Selected Factors in Trumpet
Performance Adjudication Reliability
HAROLD E. FISKE, JR. 60

Theories of Affective Response to Music
MARY FRIEDMANN 71

Fray Pedro de Gante: Pioneer Music Educator
GEORGE HELLER 94

i

Conformity Behavior Reflected in the
Musical Preference of Adolescents
    HOWARD G. INGLEFIELD 105

A Case Study of a Chromesthetic
    PAUL A. HAACK & RUDOLF E. RADOCY 119

Selected Indexes of the Academic and
Professional Preparation of Music
Supervisors in Canada
    ESTELLE R. JORGENSEN 128

Expressive Qualities in Music Perception
and Music Education
    DAVID S. LEVI 146

An Experimental Study of a Keyboard
Sight-Reading Test Administered to
Freshmen Secondary Piano Students at
The Ohio State University
    JERRY LOWDER 163

A Study of Two Approaches to Developing
Expressive Performance
    DAVID J. MARCHAND 174

Duties and Activities of Music Supervisory Personnel in California
    LAWRENCE J. McQUERREY 186

Inconsistencies in the Writing of
James L. Mursell
    DONALD E. METZ 195

The Story of W. Otto Miessner:
Visionary of What Might Be
    SAMUEL D. MILLER 203

ii

A Multivariate Analysis of Factors in the
Backgrounds of Wyoming Adults Related to
Their Attitudinal Levels Concerning Music
ROBERT F. NOBLE 228

The History and Development of the
American Institute of Normal Methods
MELVIN C. PLATT 248

A Longitudinal Investigation of the Rhythm
Abilities of Pre-School Aged Children and
A Final Report on a Three-Year Investigation
of the Rhythmic Abilities of Pre-School
Aged Children
EDWARD RAINBOW 259

Philosophy in Music Education:
Pure or Applied Research?
ABRAHAM A. SCHWADRON 275

The Effect of the Television Series,
Music, on Music Listening Preferences
and Achievement of Elementary General
Music Students
PATRICIA K. SHEHAN 285

The Use of Videotape Recordings to
Increase Teacher Trainees' Error
Detection Skills
MELANIE STUART 299

Appendices

    I. On Writing a Critical Review
        CARROLL L. GONZO 307

   II. About the Authors 321

Index of Methods Used in Collecting
and Analyzing Data 325

iii

PREFACE

This text is designed to serve as a supplementary resource for courses in methods of research in music education. The evaluation of appropriate research studies is an indispensable part of these courses. By evaluating research studies, the student learns to differentiate between good practices which he or she will wish to emulate, and poor practices, which should be avoided. The student also learns that research studies must be evaluated before conclusions stated by the author can be accepted.

Class discussions of research studies are of optimum value if all students have the opportunity to study the research in question. Textbooks written for courses in research in music typically do not supply original research studies for class evaluation. In addition, most libraries carry the research articles in the form of bound journals in the "reserve" section of the library. The articles contained therein are therefore not permitted to be removed from the library for either longterm individual study or simultaneous group analysis.

To meet the needs of professors and students alike, this anthology has been prepared. In all, twenty-three articles are presented. They have been selected from four journals: the <u>Journal of Research in Music Education</u>, the <u>Bulletin</u> of the Council for Research in Music Education, <u>Contributions to Music Education</u> (the research publication of the Ohio Music Educators Association), and the <u>Bulletin</u> of Historical Research in Music Education. The articles selected represent the four modes of inquiry in the discipline: descriptive, experimental, historical, and philosophical. Each article is reprinted in its entirety.

Herein, research is considered to be the formal, systematic, and intensive process of carrying on a scientific method of analysis. Since many students will find this statement to be too abstract, the following characteristics are offered as a clarification:

    1. Research is directed toward the solution of a problem. It attempts to answer a

question, substantiate a hypothesis, or
determine new relationships between variables, objects, or phenomena.

2. Research is more than information retrieval;
it is not the simple gathering of information. It emphasizes the development of
generalizations, principles, and/or
theories.

3. Research involves gathering new data from
primary sources or using existing data for
a new purpose. Merely reorganizing or re-
stating what is already known is not
research. In short, to be designated as
"research", it must generate new knowledge.

4. Research is based on empirical evidence. It
rejects revelation and dogma as methods of
establishing knowledge.

5. The researcher attempts to eliminate bias in
his/her work. There is no attempt to persuade or to prove an emotionally held conviction.

Methods of research endeavor in music education
include:

1. The descriptive, in which a subject or a
condition is systematically described.

2. The experimental, in which an independent
variable is manipulated by the researcher
to determine what can result under carefully
controlled conditions.

3. The historical, in which a chronological
account of a subject using primary sources
(where possible) is given.

4. The philosophical, in which an objective
speculation or theory about music, aesthetics, or the teaching-learning process
in music is formulated.

The term "cross-section" in the title indicates
that the articles are intended to be typical of those
being published rather than as models to be emulated
uncritically. Articles included herein provide a

variety of research designs, subjects, methods of data-gathering, and methods of analyzing data.

Students enrolled in research methods classes vary widely with respect to their preparation in statistics. Therefore, the articles selected include those that can be understood with no background in statistics, some which require a fairly high degree of statistical sophistication, and a majority which require an intermediate-level of understanding of statistical theory and computations.

The articles included are reprinted exactly as originally published. The point in so doing is to present the student with exactly the same problem in interpreting the research that he or she would encounter if the original source had been consulted.

The book begins with an introductory section "Suggestions for Evaluating Research Articles in Journals of Music Education." It provides guidelines relating to the many judgments required to determine the adequacy and competency of the research report.

There are two appendices. Appendix I is a reprint of an article by Carroll L. Gonzo entitled, "On Writing a Critical Review." Appendix II is an "About the Authors" section supplying the reader with the authors' current academic, institutional affiliation and title.

An invaluable index listing the methods used in collecting and analyzing the data concludes the text.

Grateful appreciation is expressed to the authors and to the journals for their permission to reprint the articles in this text.

SUGGESTIONS FOR EVALUATING RESEARCH ARTICLES IN JOURNALS OF MUSIC EDUCATION

The student or practitioner turning to the research literature for suggestions or assistance in solving a problem needs to determine whether the conclusions reached in the research report are correct. The basis for determining the correctness of the conclusions involves a careful evaluation of the competency and adequacy of the research report.

Erwin Schneider and Henry Cady have formulated criteria for the evaluation of research reports based on a model proposed by Deobald Van Dalen. These are presented below in question form under four main headings: (1) The Problem, (2) The Method of Attack, (3) The Analysis of Data, and (4) The Conclusion.

1. The Problem

Was the logic of the problem analysis sound?
Were the hypotheses or questions posed in agreement with the known facts and compatible with well-tested theories?
Were the hypotheses testable and the questions of the type that would lend themselves to an objective treatment?
Were the purposes of the study possible of attainment?

2. The Method of Attack

Was an adequate, detailed explanation of the methods, techniques, and tools used to test the deduced consequences given?
Were the procedures the most appropriate for testing the particular consequences?
Were the assumptions that underlie the use of the data gathering device(s) fully met in the study?
Would the techniques, methods, and tools employed produce relevant, reliable, valid, and sufficiently refined data to justify inferences drawn from them?
Did the report accurately describe where and when the data were gathered?

1

Did the research report describe precisely the
number and kinds of subjects, objects, and
materials used in the investigation?

A. Historical Studies

Was most of the report based upon the employ-
ment of primary resources?
If secondary sources were used, did they contribute the less significant data rather
than the crucial evidence for the solution
of the problem?
Were the source materials examined critically
for authenticity and credibility?
Were words and statements from earlier documents correctly interpreted?

B. Descriptive Studies

Was the design adequate in scope, depth, and
precision in order to obtain the specific
data required?
Had every possible precaution been taken to
establish observational conditions, frame
questions, design observational schedules,
record data, and check the reliability of
witnesses and source material so as to
avoid collecting data that were faulty?
Were the specific items the observer was to
note describing a condition, phenomenon,
event, or process clearly defined, and a
uniform method provided for recording
precise information?
Were the categories for classifying the data
unambiguous, appropriate, and capable of
bringing to light likenesses, differences,
or relationships?
Does the study reflect a superficial analysis
of surface conditions, or does it probe
into inter-relationships and/or causal
relationships?

C. Experimental Studies

Was the possibility of hidden factors, other
than the experimental variable, considered
as an explanation of the obtained results?
Did the investigator randomize the variables
that he/she did not want to influence the
results?

Did the investigator consider the possibility of unconscious signaling or of previous practice as an influence upon the results?
Did the investigator take into account all significant characteristics necessary to obtain equivalence of groups?
Was the law of the single, independent variable obeyed in traditional designs?
Were all assumptions underlying the use of statistical techniques met in the design?
Were there any conditions biasing the experimenter or the subjects in the experiment?

D. Philosophical Studies

Were the premises for the construction of the argument stated clearly and concisely?
Were the premises based on contemporary knowledge rather than subjective speculation?
Were the processes leading to the conclusions acceptable in terms of proper logic?
Were inferences drawn within reasonable and logical limits of the semantics used?
Were the conclusions commensurate with the logic and the initial premises?

E. Sampling

Was the sample sufficiently representative of the population to permit the investigator to generalize the findings?
Was the sample an adequate one in kind and number?
Were there any conditions biasing the selection of the sample?
Was the control group as representative as the experimental group?
Were the techniques of pairing or matching the subjects valid?
Did the sample satisfy the assumptions underlying the use of the statistical procedures?

F. Tests and Measures

Were the tests employed appropriate for the abilities of the subjects, time limits, sex, social class, etc.?

Were qualified judges chosen to rate various
phenomena?
Were there any items or factors in the tests
or measures that might limit the extent or
type of the subject's response?
Were the materials pretested before use?

G. Questionnaires and Interviews

Was each question sharply delineated to
elicit the specific responses required as
data?
Did the questions adequately cover the deci-
sive features of the needed data?
Were the questions colored by personal or
sponsorship bias, loaded in one direction,
or asked at an improper time?
Did each question afford a sufficient number
of alternative answers to permit the respondent an opportunity to express himself/
herself accurately?
Were stereotyped, prestige-laden, or super-
lative words or phrases used that biased
the response?
Were multiple-choice responses randomly
arranged to reduce the likelihood of systematic errors?
Were the materials pretested before use?

3. The Analysis of Data

Was the analysis objectively stated and free from
opinions and personal prejudices?
Were broad generalizations made without sufficient
evidence to support them?

4. The Conclusions

Were the conclusions justified by the data
gathered?
Were the conclusions qualified to show the limits
within which they apply?

Sources

Schneider, Erwin H., and Cady, Henry L. "Evaluation
and Synthesis of Research Studies Relating to
Music Education," Cooperative Research Project
No. E-01ʳ. The Ohio State University, 1965.

Van Dalen, Deobald B. <u>Understanding Educational
Research</u>. 4th ed. New York: McGraw-Hill
Book Co., Inc., 1979.

A CROSS-SECTION OF RESEARCH IN MUSIC EDUCATION

STUDENT PERCEPTIONS OF CHARACTERISTICS OF EFFECTIVE APPLIED MUSIC INSTRUCTORS*

Harold F. Abeles

Abstract

The lack of a satisfactory instrument for evaluating applied music instruction stimulated this research. A four-factor (rapport, instructional systemization, instructional skill, and musical knowledge), 30-item rating scale for systemizing student evaluations of applied faculty was developed. The facet-factorial scale development procedure was employed. The study produced a scale that seems appropriate to employ in the evaluation of applied faculty. The interjudge reliability estimates for the scale are sufficiently high (.88 to .96) and the relationship with an appropriate criterion variable, student performance, seems acceptable (.60).

Key Words: instrumental instruction, statistical analysis, teaching ability, teaching method, test development, testing.

In recent years many institutions of higher education and several school systems across the country have begun systematic evaluation of their faculties' teaching ability. In assessing teaching competence, several sources of information are usually examined. These may include self evaluation, colleague evaluations, and in most cases, student evaluations.

The evaluation of faculty in music departments often presents special problems because of the diverse instructional techniques that are employed in teaching music. Forms that have been developed to aid in systemizing student evaluations of classroom instruction seem inappropriate when examining the unique student-teacher interaction that takes place in the applied

---

music lesson. Having the student evaluate an applied faculty member on such characteristics as, "The instructor is a very thorough lecturer," or "The lectures are easy to become interested in," would seem to have little relevance to successful applied instruction. In order to develop a form that is more valid for the applied teaching situation, a study was undertaken during the spring 1973 semester at the School of Music of the University of North Carolina at Greensboro. A facet-factorial approach to scale development was employed.(1)

Scale Development

In order to obtain items for an applied faculty rating scale that would reflect the behaviors that applied music students viewed as affecting the applied teaching environment, 75 undergraduate and graduate students were asked to write a one- or two-page essay describing "an applied teacher who stands out most in your mind." The students were asked to include both the good and bad characteristics of the teacher. A content analysis of the essays by the researcher produced 123 statements descriptive of applied teachers. To better conceptualize the 123 statements, three members of the applied faculty and the researcher organized the statements into five categories. The categories were the following: rapport, communication technique, musical knowledge, musical understanding, and performing ability.

The 123 statements were randomly placed in a five-option likert-type rating scale format. Response options ranged from "highly agree that the statement is descriptive [of the applied teacher]" to "highly disagree that the statement is descriptive." Approximately 35 percent of the statements were phrased negatively. The following are examples of statements included on the initial rating instrument: (1) He treats the student with respect for his musical taste. (2) His teaching is innovative. (3) I have never heard him perform. (4) He is unable to demonstrate what he wants. (5) The student learns a great deal about teaching from him.

The 123-item rating scale was then employed in a trial evaluation of ten applied faculty. The 93 undergraduate and graduate students who participated in the evaluation were asked to describe as accurately as possible their present applied instructor employing

10

the response scale and statements of the evaluation instrument.

To examine empirically the a priori organization of the statements, a factor analysis was performed on the results of the trial evaluation. The number of factors to be rotated was determined by the scree test(2) and subjective judgment. A four-factor solution yielded the most meaningful interpretation and was the solution used for later scale development.

To produce a scale of practical length that reflected this structure, 30 items were selected from the original 123-item pool based upon the item factor loadings. Of the items chosen, 23 had relatively high factor loadings on the factor they were selected to define and had relatively low correlations with the other three factors. The remaining seven items selected for the 30-item Applied Faculty Student Evaluation Scale (AFSES) had relatively high loadings on several factors and high communalities. This group of seven items was labeled general instructional competence. Both positive and negative statements were selected from the item pool.

To obtain some initial information on the interjudge reliability of the 30-item AFSES, 17 brass students were asked to use the rating scale to evaluate four applied brass faculty members. Estimates of the interjudge reliability for the factor scores as well as the total score were obtained. To examine the relationship of the AFSES scores with other applied faculty variables, additional data were obtained. The four members of the brass faculty were asked during the brass applied jury playing examinations to evaluate each of the 17 brass students employing a Performance Rating Scale (PRS). Each brass faculty member also completed a Colleague Teacher-Description Scale (CTDS) for the other three brass faculty. Correlations were obtained between the AFSES scores for each faculty member, the PRS scores of his students, and the CTDS scores.

Further investigation of the psychometric characteristics of the AFSES was facilitated by the trial implementation of faculty evaluation procedures during the fall 1973 semester. A total of 64 undergraduate and graduate students evaluated eight applied faculty members from the voice, piano, string, and wind divisions. Estimates of interjudge reliability

11

and measures of the relationship between the AFSES scores and the CTDS for the eight faculty members were obtained.

Results

The final 30-item form of AFSES was based on a four-factor orthogonal rotation of the 123-item trial evaluation form. The resulting four factors agreed somewhat with the a priori organization developed. The items on the AFSES rapport and musical knowledge factors were originally classified in these categories, respectively. The items on the AFSES instructional systemization and instructional skill factors were all initially classified as communication technique. The seven general instructional competence items were classified in several different a priori categories. The 30 items selected for the AFSES appear in Table 1 grouped under the factors that they were selected to measure. This factor matrix, produced by a factor analysis of the brass faculty evaluations forcing a four-factor structure, is similar to the matrix produced by the factor analysis of the 123-item trial evaluations, thus lending support to that organization of the items.

Interjudge reliability coefficients were obtained for the students who evaluated the four brass faculty. A KR21 procedure was employed, providing a measure of judge homogeneity or agreement for the four AFSES subscales and the total score. Additional judge homogeneity measures were obtained from the evaluations of eight applied faculty during the fall of 1973. Table 2 lists the interjudge reliability estimates for both evaluations.

To examine the relationship of the AFSES with other measures of applied faculty competence, CTDS forms were obtained for faculty members who participated in the trial evaluations. In addition, the students of each of the brass faculty during the spring 1973 semester were evaluated during their jury examinations employing the PRS. The four brass faculty served as judges. The alpha reliability estimate of the CTDS was .93. The Hoyt Analysis of Variance interjudge reliability coefficient for the PRS employing four judges was .90.

TABLE 1

VARIMAX FOUR-FACTOR MATRIX OF THE AFSES

Items	Factors			
	1	2	3	4
1. Rapport				
He does not instill a feeling of confidence in his students	.68	.21	.27	.26
His enthusiasm is infectious and inspiring	.66	.22	.48	.15
He encourages the student to express himself	.73	.18	.23	.14
He brings out the best in his students	.74	.13	.44	.22
He is too overbearing	.74	.18	.22	.14
He shows a genuine interest in the student outside the lesson	.73	.42	.09	.14
He is patient and understanding	.71	.26	.16	.23
2. Instructional Systemization				
He gives explicit directions regarding what to practice	.09	.60	.15	.06
Music is chosen to strengthen the student's weaknesses	.34	.56	.00	.16
Analysis is part of his approach to a new piece of music	.07	.58	.15	.18
He is absent-minded and forgetful, and never seems to remember what music the student is working on each lesson	.11	.65	.01	.09
He outlines his system of teaching for the student, so the student knows where he is heading	.40	.56	.11	.11
3. Instructional Skill				
His explanations are clear and concise	.31	.18	.60	.17
His method of teaching gives the student insight into teaching as well as performing	.37	.13	.72	.08
He is flexible, and his instruction begins at the student's own level of proficiency	.54	.08	.57	.17

13

TABLE 1--Continued

VARIMAX FOUR-FACTOR MATRIX OF THE AFSES

Items	Factors			
	1	2	3	4
He is unable to diagnose technical problems	.30	.26	.49	.06
He is able to correct technical difficulties	.02	.18	.68	.15
4. Musical Knowledge				
He has a knowledge of different musical styles and performance practices	.16	.08	.26	.66
He has to refer to references in order to answer basic questions	.13	.01	.03	.64
He knows little music outside his own interests	.29	.09	.01	.63
He has a knowledge of the repertoire	.16	.23	.02	.67
He has a knowledge of good performing editions of music in his field	.07	.00	.02	.53
He has a knowledge of reference materials to which the student can refer	.29	.16	.11	.51
5. General Instructional Competence				
He "talks down" to his students	.55	.13	.43	.16
He is reluctant to admit a mistake	.41	.12	.41	.48
His teaching includes criticism and correction mixed with compliments and praise	.56	.45	.30	.18
He has difficulty communicating his ideas	.42	.37	.48	.00
He is aware of current professional musical activity	.19	.02	.43	.51
He instills a sense of responsibility which is needed to get the work done	.35	.36	.43	.34
He has an accurate perception regarding the student's ability	.60	.12	.44	.06

TABLE 2

INTERJUDGE RELIABILITY ESTIMATES FOR THE AFSES
TOTAL SCORE AND SCALE SCORES (10 JUDGES)

Score	Spring 1973	Fall 1973
Total (30 items)	.96	.88
1. Rapport (7 items)	.71	.94
2. Instructional System-ization (5 items)	.56	.73
3. Instructional Skills (5 items)	.67	.71
4. Musical Knowledge (6 items)	.80	.89
5. General Instructional Competence (7 items)	.72	.88

The zero order correlation coefficients between the AFSES scores and both the PRS and CTDS scores appear in Table 3. Coefficients for both the AFSES total and factor scale scores are provided. Inspection of the table indicates a moderately strong relationship (.60) between the AFSES scores and the student performance ratings, while a moderately weak, negative relationship appears to exist between the AFSES scores and the CTDS scores. The instructional skill subscale seems to have the strongest relationship (above .70) with the PRS scores.

Discussion

In the development of the AFSES the factor structure produced by the student evaluations of applied faculty is of some interest. This four-factor structure was similar to the a priori grouping of items, with one interesting exception: the absence of the original performance ability items from the 123-item pool. This seems due to the consistently high rating all the applied faculty received on these items, thus producing almost no item variance. From these results one might conclude that students may suffer from a "halo effect" and are unable to discriminate among the performing abilities of applied faculty.

15

TABLE 3

ZERO-ORDER CORRELATION COEFFICIENTS BETWEEN THE AFSES SCORES
AND THE CTDS AND PRS CRITERION SCORES

	Factor 1	Factor 2	Factor 3	Factor 4	General Competence	Total Score	PRS Score	CTDS Score
Factor 1 (Rapport)								
Spring 1973		-.24	.62	.57	.98	.65	.49	-.41
Fall 1973		.76	.63	-.12	.90	.87		-.33
Factor 2 (Instructional Systemization)								
Spring 1973			.57	.59	-.21	.55	.05	-.23
Fall 1973			.84	-.06	.86	.91		-.04
Factor 3 (Instructional Skill)								
Spring 1973				.81	.47	.98	.70	-.42
Fall 1973				.29	.66	.89		-.33
Factor 4 (Musical Knowledge)								
Spring 1973					.41	.89	.16	-.32
Fall 1973					-.18	.19		-.18

TABLE 3--Continued

ZERO-ORDER CORRELATION COEFFICIENTS BETWEEN THE AFSES SCORES
AND THE CTDS AND PRS CRITERION SCORES

	Factor 1	Factor 2	Factor 3	Factor 4	General Competence	Total Score	PRS Score	CTDS Score
General Instructional Competence								
Spring 1973						.49	.45	-.14
Fall 1973						.87		-.04
Total Score								
Spring 1973							.60	-.34
Fall 1973								-.18
Performance Rating Scale								
Spring 1973								-.31
Fall 1973								
Colleague Description- Teaching Scale								
Spring 1973								
Fall 1973								

17

The interjudge reliability estimates for the total score on the AFSES seem sufficiently high to allow the scale to be used in the assessment of applied faculty. The subscale reliability estimates do not seem adequate to use the subscales for evaluation purposes, although an examination of subscale scores might aid applied faculty in identifying their strengths and weaknesses.

The study also examined the relationships between various other measures of applied faculty competence and the AFSES scores. The results seem to indicate a negative relationship exists between the AFSES student evaluations and CTDS colleague evaluations. These results, confirmed by both data collections, contradict results reported in prior investigations that have examined the relationship between student evaluations and colleague evaluations of classroom instruction.(3) Evaluation of classroom instructors in the School of Music obtained concurrently with the AFSES data yielded a strong positive (.79) relationship between student and colleague measures. This may suggest that while faculty and students agree on criteria for good classroom instruction, they seem unable to agree on criteria for good applied instruction.

It has often been suggested that teachers be evaluated by the success of their students. The moderately strong (.60) relationship between the AFSES scores and the PRS scores of brass student performances seem to support this position. In addition, the relationship lends support to the criterion-related validity of the AFSES, although the lack of random assignment of students to instructors confounds the result.

The study produced a scale that seems to be appropriate to employ in the evaluation of applied faculty. The interjudge reliability estimates for the total score are satisfactory, and the relationship with an appropriate criterion variable, student performance, seems acceptable. There are three areas of this study that warrant further examination:

1. The relationship between the AFSES and other measures of applied faculty competence, such as colleague evaluations, performing ability, and training and experience.

2. The AFSES subscale and total score reliability as a function of the number of response options employed.

3. The ability of applied students to discriminate among musical performances of faculty members.

References

(1) Harold F. Abeles, "A Facet-Factorial Approach to the Construction of Rating Scales to Measure Complex Behaviors," Journal of Educational Measurement, Vol. 10, No. 2 (Summer 1973), pp. 145-151.

(2) Raymond B. Cattell, "The Scree Test for the Number of Factors," Multivariate Behavioral Research, Vol. 1 (1966), pp. 245-276.

(3) Robert C. Wilson, Evelyn R. Dienst, and Nancy L. Watson, "Characteristics of Effective College Teachers as Perceived by their Colleagues," Journal of Educational Measurement, Vol. 10, No. 1 (Spring 1973), pp. 31-37.

DEVELOPMENT AND VALIDATION OF A MUSIC EDUCATION COMPETENCY TEST*

Herschel V. Beazley**

Abstract

The purpose of the study was to develop and validate a competency test in music education. The resulting Music Education Competency Test (MECT), pilot form, provided information on a student's proficiency in selected singing, conducting, keyboard, and rehearsal skills. Three validity studies were conducted in order to obtain evidence on the relationship of MECT scores to (1) the student's course grades, academic status, and teacher rating; (2) students entering as freshmen as opposed to those entering as transfer students; and (3) students with piano as the principal instrument as opposed to voice or orchestral instruments. One hundred and twenty-five undergraduates at the University of Illinois took one of the test forms. Results indicated that: (1) seniors score better than freshmen on the singing and conducting subtests; (2) instrumentalists score better than vocalists on the conducting subtest; and (3) students' scores on the conducting and diagnostic rehearsal skills subtests correlate significantly with instructors' ratings in corresponding areas.

Decisions concerned with adjusting the process of teacher education must be based on valid data.

---

*Copyright (c) 1981 by the Music Educators National Conference. Reprinted by permission of Herschel V. Beazley and the Journal of Research in Music Education, Vol. 29, No. 1 (Spring, 1981), pp. 5-10.

**This article is based on the author's doctoral dissertation, The Development and Validation of a Competency Test in Music Education (University of Illinois at Urbana-Champaign, 1978).

Competency-Based Teacher Education (CBTE) is a data-based system for training teachers, which is committed to such decision making (Houston & Howsam, 1972). Most approaches to CBTE attempt to identify and specify competencies assumed essential for successful teaching, and then to focus instruction upon the individual's development and refinement of these competencies.

Durmond (1971) pointed to the need for valid data in designing a competency-based curriculum and assessing student skill proficiency. Bunda and Sanders (1979) recently summarized methodological problems of testing in competency-based programs. They identified primary measurement issues including reliability procedures, standard setting models, instrument quality indexes, and validity and generalizability processes.

Many competency-based teacher education programs will focus on the identification of essential skills, the development of lists of competencies as course objectives, and the organization of the curriculum around identified objectives. Music teacher educators need to go beyond this "input stage" to develop assessment procedures that yield valid and reliable data for use as part of the total evaluation of the undergraduate student's progress.

During the past decade Colwell (1970) drew attention to the need for the systematic measurement of student achievement in relation to the stated objectives of the music curriculum. Lawrence (1974) suggested constructing and using tests that measure student competency in terms of performance criteria, and Miller (1976) reported the need for tests that measure student proficiency on generic music skills.

Researchers at Syracuse University are currently developing observation forms as part of the evaluation of a competency-based approach to teaching conducting. The observation forms (Madsen & Harbrough, in press) assess the level of student proficiency on prespecified conducting skills. Initial studies (Yarbrough, Wapnick, & Kelly, 1979, pp. 103-104) indicate that reliability estimates of .89 and above have been obtained using these forms with undergraduates in basic conducting classes.

Braswell (1980) found many CBTE programs in

music to be underdeveloped in the area of evaluation. One attempt to remedy this situation was made at the University of Illinois. Upon initiating a CBTE curriculum in music, the Illinois faculty recognized that if undergraduates were to be held accountable for meeting prespecified music skills, then a test must be constructed to accurately assess skill proficiency. Since the systematic measurement of music skills taught in CBTE programs is a relatively unexplored area, test development in this field is needed. Therefore, the purpose of this study was to develop and validate a test that would measure the skill proficiency of senior undergraduates in music education on a selective list of senior-level music competencies.

Procedure

The Music Education Competency Test (MECT), pilot form, was developed and validated to provide information on a student's proficiency in selected singing, conducting, keyboard, and diagnostic rehearsal skills. Three validity studies were conducted to obtain evidence on the relationship of MECT scores to (1) the student's course grades, academic status, and teacher rating; (2) students entering as freshmen as opposed to those entering as transfer students; and (3) students with piano as the principal instrument as opposed to voice students or students with an orchestral principal instrument. The test was administered individually to each student in one 45-minute session. Proficiency levels were recorded on Likert-type five-point rating scales that generated scores for singing, conducting, keyboard, and diagnostic rehearsal skills. The singing, conducting, and keyboard subtests required the students to make a music response; these tests were administered to each student individually. Written responses were required on the diagnostic rehearsal skills subtest.

The content for the test grew out of the identification of music skills assembled from an examination of professional literature, doctoral dissertations on music teacher training and assessment, and course outlines and examinations used in undergraduate music courses. Fifty-two skills were identified, verified through field observation, and approved by the music education faculty at the University of Illinois. Broad task categories were generated to

22

summarize the competencies needed within a given domain. From the broad categories, competency statements were written that provided specific tasks, in behavioral terms, reflective of the original skills list.

A table of specifications (Gronlund, 1976) was constructed according to the content organization of the curriculum. The test content reflected the relative emphasis contained in the table.

The pilot form of MECT evolved from the sequential construction, administration, and analysis of two exploratory forms. Over a six-month period 125 undergraduates at the University of Illinois took one of the test forms. Six graduate students served as judges, administering MECT pilot form to 94 undergraduate music education majors consisting of 45 choral and 49 instrumental majors. Each judge underwent two training sessions devoted to the test's construction, validation procedures, and the format of the rating scales.

Results

Interjudge reliability estimates of .96, .98, and .95 were computed using the odd-even split-half Spearman-Brown formula (Guilford, 1954) on the singing, conducting, and keyboard subtests, respectively. Intrajudge reliability was computed using the test-retest method (Kerlinger, 1973). The six judges rated videotape performances of 10 students. Four days later, the same tapes were viewed again and each student was scored. Estimates of .99, .89, and .95 were obtained on the singing, conducting, and keyboard subtests. Reliability of the content analysis procedures used to score written responses to the diagnostic rehearsal skills test was verified by having selected music faculty independently rate answers obtained on exploratory forms.

Content validity was asserted on the basis of the previously described content sampling procedures. Criterion-related validity was assessed on the basis of group differentiation accomplished by the test score, the correlation of student test scores with instructor rating, and the correlation of scores with the student's grade point average. The criterion-related validity studies using group differentiation employed the following criteria in

23

grouping students: academic status, transfer/non-transfer status, and curriculum specialization.

A one-way analysis of variance (Kerlinger, 1973) was conducted upon MECT subtest scores earned by each of the four groups: freshmen, sophomores, juniors, seniors. The analyses indicated significant differences on the singing subtest, $F(3,90) = 3.188$, $p < .05$, and on the conducting subtest, $F(3,90) = 13.986$, $p < .01$. The mean score earned by the seniors on both subtests was greater than that earned by the freshmen (see Table 1). Students near the completion of the four-year undergraduate curriculum were expected to have refined the competencies being tested more than those who had just entered the program. Results of these analyses suggest that certain MECT subtests were valid in identifying students who had had more in-depth experiences and that these subtests were measuring senior-level music competencies.

TABLE 1

GROUP MEANS AND STANDARD DEVIATIONS EARNED BY
FRESHMEN AND SENIORS ON MECT CONDUCTING
AND SINGING SUBTEST

	Conducting			Singing		
	n	$\overline{X}$	SD	n	$\overline{X}$	SD
Freshmen	26	53.0	13.08	26	79.5	14.48
Seniors	20	83.2	8.97	20	90.1	10.25

A one-way analysis of variance also was conducted upon MECT subtest scores earned by transfer and nontransfer students. None of the obtained F ratios was significant ($p < .05$). When all students were grouped according to major (choral or instrumental) and a one-way analysis of variance conducted upon MECT scores, the resulting F ratio was significant ($p < .05$) for both the singing and the conducting subtests. It was not significant on the keyboard and diagnostic rehearsal skills subtests. Multiple Scheffé comparisons (Hays, 1973) disclosed that there was no statistically significant difference among the mean scores earned by the curriculum specialization groups on the singing subtest. Data on the conducting subtest, however, indicated that the mean conducting subtest scores earned by instrumental majors was significantly different from that earned by choral majors (see Table 2). Having piano as the principal instrument had no significant differences on test scores for either group.

TABLE 2

F VALUES OBTAINED USING THE SCHEFFÉ METHOD TO MAKE ALL POSSIBLE PAIRWISE COMPARISONS OF MEAN SCORES EARNED BY CURRICULUM SPECIALIZATION GROUPS ON THE CONDUCTING SUBTEST

	A	B	C
B	2.225		
C	4.926*	2.771	
D	5.717*	3.673*	1.017

Note. Curriculum specialization groups are identified as follows: A = instrumental; B = instrumental majors, piano principal; C = choral majors; D = choral majors, piano principal.
* $p < .05$

The results of analyses dealing with the non-transfer students and the students with piano as principal instrument should be accepted with caution. The number of examinees in these groups represents smaller sample sizes than were represented in the other groups.

To assess criterion-related validity, using instructors' rating as criterion, instructors in music methods, conducting, group piano, and class voice or applied voice rated the 94 examinees according to their ability in each area. When each rating was correlated with a student's corresponding test score, two of the four correlations were significant. The product-moment correlation (Hays, 1973) computed between conducting test scores and instructor's rating was $r = .250$, $p < .05$.

To assess criterion-related validity using grade point average (GPA) as criterion, a Pearson product-moment correlation was computed between

MECT subtest scores and various partitionings of
each examinee's GPA. The singing subtest scores
correlated .887 with conducting GPA, and .251 with
applied music GPA. The scores on the conducting
subtest correlated .873 with student teaching GPA,
and .343 with conducting GPA. Correlation coefficients on the keyboard subtest scores were .675
with student teaching GPA, .249 with academic music
GPA, and .248 with conducting GPA. The diagnostic
rehearsal skills subtest scores correlated .500 with
student teaching GPA, .413 with conducting GPA, .361
with overall GPA, and .359 with academic music GPA.
These coefficients represent the strongest correlations obtained.

Discussion

The Music Education Competency Test, pilot
form, was developed at the University of Illinois,
but future studies should determine the content
validity of MECT at other institutions. More research is needed to replicate the correlational
studies reported in this investigation, using a
larger sample.

Measurement is at the heart of competency-
based programs. The findings in this study indicate
that a valid and reliable test can be developed to
measure the music skill proficiency of undergraduates
in such programs. The procedures used in constructing competency tests afford music teacher
educators the opportunity to (1) clarify long- and
short-range instructional goals; (2) detail and
delimit those music skills effectively acquired in
a campus setting as opposed to those better acquired
in a field-based setting; and (3) continuously evaluate the curriculum by examining test results in
light of course content and overall curriculum
effectiveness. A carefully constructed competency
test may also prove helpful in providing advanced
placement information on music students entering the
upper-division level of the teacher education
program.

Finally, it is important to emphasize the need
for studies that will help develop and refine the
technical base underlying competency test construction. This technology is needed by test developers
in music as well as specialists in other fields. It

is hoped that the present study will provide an impetus toward these research efforts and advance the application of valid assessment procedures in competency-based music programs.

References

Braswell, J. Competency-based Curricula in Higher Education. Paper presented at the meeting of the Music Educators National Conference, Miami Beach, Fla., April 1980.

Bunda, M. A., and Sanders, J. R., eds. Practices and Problems in Competency-based Measurement. Washington, D.C.: National Council on Measurement in Education, 1979.

Colwell, R. J. The Evaluation of Music Teaching and Learning. Englewood Cliffs, N.J.: Prentice-Hall, 1970.

Durmond, W. J. "Comments on Achieving the Potential of PBTE." Achieving the Potential of Performance-based Teacher Education. Washington, D.C.: American Association of Colleges for Teacher Education, 1971.

Gronlund, N. Measurement and Evaluation in Teaching, 3rd ed. New York: Macmillan, 1976.

Guilford, J. Psychometric Methods, 2nd ed. New York: McGraw-Hill, 1954.

Hays, W. Statistics for the Social Sciences, 2nd ed. New York: Holt, Rinehart and Winston, 1973.

Houston, R., and Howsam, R. B., eds. Competency-based Teacher Education: Progress, Problems, and Prospects. Chicago: Science Research Associates, 1972.

Kerlinger, F. N. Foundations of Behavioral Research, 2nd ed. New York: Holt, Rinehart and Winston, 1973.

Lawrence, G. "Delineating and Measuring Professional
    Competencies." Educational Leadership 31
    (January 1974):298-302.

Madsen, C. K., and Yarbrough, C. Competency-based
    Approach to Music Education. Englewood
    Cliffs, N.J.: Prentice-Hall, in press.

Miller, S. D. "CBTE in Music." Proceedings, 50th
    Anniversary Meeting, National Association of
    Schools of Music. Washington, D.C.: NASM,
    1976.

Yarbrough, C.; Wapnick, J.; and Kelly, R. "Effect of
    Videotape Feedback Techniques on Performance,
    Verbalization, and Attitude of Beginning Con-
    ductors." Journal of Research in Music
    Education 27 (1979):103-104.

GRADE/AGE LEVELS AND THE REINFORCEMENT VALUE OF THE COLLATIVE PROPERTIES OF MUSIC*

Susan Rachel Eisenstein**

Abstract

The objective of this investigation was to determine whether complex or redundant music conditions as found in form, dynamics, rhythm, and multiple combination of elements have different reinforcement values at developmentally crucial grade and age levels. Sixty-four subjects from second, third, fifth, and sixth grade classrooms participated in the study. Two measurements were obtained for each subject: (1) the number of seconds spent attending to complexity and redundancy as found in each of the four music components; and (2) choice frequencies between complexity and redundancy in each of the music components. Both measurements employed the same music stimuli--appropriately manipulated tone row music. The results indicated that second and third graders listened to more of the complex and redundant music conditions than fifth and sixth graders. No differences were apparent either in complexity and redundancy conditions or between any grades in choice.

Key Words: age, attitudes, fundamentals, grade level.

An important issue in music education is the ability to identify the controlling variables of music selection. Such variables include the

---

*Copyright (c) 1979 by the Music Educators National Conference. Reprinted by permission of Susan R. Eisenstein and the Journal of Research in Music Education, Vol. 27, No. 2 (Summer, 1979), pp. 76-86.

**This article is based on the author's doctoral dissertation, "Grade/Age Levels and Free-Operant Music Selection of Collative Properties of Music" (Columbia University, 1977).

components of music, teacher behavior, discrimination learning, and conditioned reinforcement learning variables. With the identification and isolation of what it is in music that children learn, the profession can order the objectives of learning.

Research has demonstrated that changes in music selection are sensitive to environmental contingencies that control behavior, such as teacher approval/disapproval (Dorow, 1977; Greer, Dorow, Wacchaus, & White, 1973), disc jockey and peer approval (Tanner, 1976), and participation in school music productions (Randall, 1975).

It has also been theorized that one factor that influences the reinforcement value of music listening is the degree of complexity in aesthetic stimuli (Berlyne, 1960; Dember & Earl, 1957; McMullen, 1973, 1974a, 1974b). Bragg and Crozier (1974), and Crozier (1973) found that subjects listened longer to more complex sound sequences as opposed to redundant sound sequences. This finding has some corroboration in the work of Duke and Gullickson (1970), Overmier (1962), and Simon and Wohlwill (1968). For these latter researchers the controlling variables of interest in music selection are believed to be brain processes and brain structures. They see music selection behavior as the overt indication of hedonic value and as a consequence of arousal-raising and arousal-reducing stimulus properties. Hence, music selection is a function of hedonic value or primary reinforcement mechanisms (of the brain) based on responses to stimulus organization that is theorized to be naturally reinforcing.

The purpose of the present study was to investigate the effect of complexity and redundancy conditions (as found in music form, dynamics, rhythm, and multiple combination of elements) on music selection and free choice. The objective of the investigation was to determine whether complex or redundant music conditions have different reinforcement values at developmentally crucial grade and age levels. The questions investigated were: (1) will there be a differential effect on free-operant listening time or free-operant choice between complex and redundant music conditions as they may be applied in form, dynamics, rhythm, and multiple combination elements? and (2) will there be a grade or age level differential effect on free-operant listening time or free-operant choice between complex and redundant music conditions as they may be applied in form, dynamics, rhythm, and multiple combination elements?

Method

Sixty-four subjects were randomly selected, half from second and third grade classes, and half from fifth and sixth grade classes, from a metropolitan New York City parochial elementary school. Subjects were randomly drawn from one of two age groups: primary level (second and third grades) and upper level (fifth and sixth grades). Primary level students had an age range of 7 to 9.5 years and upper level students had an age range of 10 to 12.5 years. These two levels of subjects were included in this study so as to investigate the developmental or potential developmental phenomenon associated with complex and redundant music stimulus organization. The grade levels were chosen because previous research (Greer, Dorow, & Randall, 1974) found that the time between third and fourth grade appeared to be a pivotal time in terms of music taste.

A counterbalanced experimental design was used for the presentation of music conditions (Winer, 1971). All subjects received all treatments. The dependent measurement was time spent listening or free-operant music selection time, and choice. The independent variables were (1) complexity and redundancy in the music conditions of form, dynamics, rhythm, and combined elements and (2) grade and age levels. There were two age levels by four conditions (form, dynamics, rhythm, combined elements) with two subcell stimulus properties (complexity and redundancy).

Tape loops were recorded and played back on a Wollensak 3M reel-to-reel tape recorder (model 6250) and a Panasonic reel-to-reel tape recorder (model RS-780s). A Seth Thomas electronic metronome model number E962-105 was used to insure accurate and consistent performance of pitch duration at a tempo of one beat per second ($\quad = 60$). Music stimuli were recorded from an electronic organ. A pair of Philmore headphones (no. SP3) and a pair of Baldwin headphones (no. 300B) provided audio reproduction of the tape loops (one for each tape recorder, rotated across observations, alternated for subjects, to account for possible variability in the accuracy of

31

the headphone components). The dependent measurement was recorded by two Chateau stopwatches (1/10) and by pencil and paper instrumentation. To account for possible variability in the accuracy of the instrumentation, stopwatches were rotated across observers and alternated for free-operant listening time complexity/redundancy sessions.

Data and reliability observers, trained in behavioral observation techniques, were used to collect data. Reliability was taken on 88% of the total sessions because both data and reliability observers could simultaneously be present for these sessions. Duration recording (Hall, 1971) was used to measure the amount of time each subject spent listening to each sound contingency. Event recording (Hall, 1971) was used to measure choice behavior between complexity and redundancy in each of the four music components. Free-operant listening time was measured from the initial depression of the play button on the tape recorder, by the subject, to the depression of the stop button on the tape recorder, by the subject. Choice behavior was measured by circling the appropriate complexity or redundancy symbol for each music component on the same chart used for recording subject free-operant listening time. Subjects indicated choices by pressing appropriate tape recorder play buttons marked either "first" or "second." The Pearson product-moment coefficient of reliability (Winer, 1971) for interobserver reliability for free-operant listening time was $r = .99$.

Eight sound contingencies consisting of tone row music stimuli varied in complexity and redundancy in form,(1) dynamics, rhythm, and combination of elements were recorded on a master tape. From the master tape eight test tapes were made, each containing a tape loop of a different music condition, each in both a complexity and redundancy arrangement. After 15 seconds the tape loop repeated itself. Construction of the tape loops was necessary as free-operant selection listening time was a dependent measure, and some extension of each music stimulus was necessary. All music selections used for the tape loops were taken from a tone row composition, <u>Wie Bin Ich Froh! No. 1 in Drei Leider, Opus 25</u> by Webern that was chosen by randomly selecting from tone row composition literature (see Figures 1 and 2).

Figure 1

Webern: Wie Bin Ich Froh! No. 1 in Drei Lieder, Op. 25

Through-composed
(abcd)

Procedure

All subjects were tested individually. Each
subject was taken into a room by the experimenter and
seated at a table on which the tape recorders and
headphones were located. The experimenter then gave
the following instructions.

This is part of a music workshop. You will
hear a music tape and then another music tape.
There will be a few music tapes that you will
listen to. After listening to each music tape
you are to press one of the two tape recorder
play buttons in front of you. Now I will show
you how to do this so that you will know what
to do when it is your turn. (Experimenter (E)
presses subject's (S) hand on each tape recorder's play button.) See, this starts the

33

tape so that you can listen to it. If you
press the play button marked "first" (E points
to the button) you will hear the first music
tape again, and if you press the play button
marked "second" (E points to the button) you
will hear the second music tape again. Ready?
Let's begin. (E helps S adjust headphones.)

The experimenter then presented 15 seconds of each
paired complexity and redundancy music stimuli to the
subject one at a time. Each tape loop stimulus was
presented according to a random predetermined order.
Paired complexity and redundancy conditions were rotated. After listening to each paired complexity and
redundancy music stimulus the subject was told "now
you choose." The subject indicated a choice of
complexity over redundancy or redundancy over complexity for each music component by pressing the play

Figure 2

Webern: Wie Bin Ich Froh! No. 1 in Drei Lieder, Op. 25

p=pitch group

34

button on the appropriate tape recorder. The choice was recorded by the observers on a chart.

After the subject made a choice and this choice was recorded the experimenter said:

> You can now listen to each music tape for as long as you want to listen to it. When you are finished listening press to stop button so that you can listen to another tape. Listen to only one music tape at a time. Now I will show you how to do this so that you will know what to do when you want to listen to different tapes. (E presses S's hand on each tape recorder's stop button.) See, this stops the tape so that I will know that you want to listen to another one. (After ascertaining that S understood the procedure E helps place headphones on the S again.) Ready? You can listen now. Press the play button of whichever tape recorder you want to.

Results

Free-Operant Listening Time
For this study, α = .05. Results of the two-way analysis of variance (Winer, 1971) for the music component form revealed significant differences between grades (see Table 1) and no significant differences between complexity and redundancy.

TABLE 1

SUMMARY OF TWO-WAY ANALYSIS OF VARIANCE FOR FORM
(4 GRADES x 2 CONDITIONS)

Source of Variation	SS	df	MS	F
Between Subjects	268867.42	63		
A (Grades)	48519.43	3	16173.14	4.40
				p < .05
Subjects within groups	220347.99	60	3672.47	
Within subjects	6370312.78	64		
B (Complexity/ Redundancy)	36.54	1	36.54	0.00NS
AB	4114.30	3	1371.43	0.01NS
B x subjects within groups	6366161.94	60	106102.69	

The Newman-Keuls multiple range test for ordered pairs of means was used to ascertain differences between pairs of grades for form. Statistically significant differences between grades three and six, two and six, and two and five were found (see Table 2).

Results of the two-way analysis of variance applied to the music component multiple combination elements revealed statistically significant differences between grades (see Table 3) and no statistically significant differences between complexity and redundancy.

Applied to multiple combination elements, the Newman-Keuls multiple range test for ordered pairs of means revealed statistically significant differences between grades two and six, and three and six (see Table 4).

No overall statistically significant differences for the music components of dynamics and rhythm were found. However, differences between grades for rhythm were statistically significant at the probability level $p < .10$.

There were differences under complexity conditions between grades three and six, three and five, two and six, two and five, and five and six in free-operant listening time. As for form and multiple combination elements, the lower grade levels listened more than the upper grade levels. No overall statistically significant differences for all redundancy conditions were found. However, the F statistic for between grade differences was $F = 2.37$, $df = 3$, $p \leq .10$.

The results of the present study showed that students found form and multiple combination elements (form, dynamics, and rhythm combined) to be more reinforcing than dynamics and rhythm.

Free-Operant Choice Behavior
A two-way (two conditions x four grades) Chi-Square test for four independent samples used to analyze the free-operant choice behavior data revealed no significant differences between grades in any of the paired-comparison choices between complexity and redundancy for any of the music components; form ($\chi^2 = 5.24$, $df = 3$, N.S.), dynamics

TABLE 2

SUMMARY OF NEWMAN-KEULS MULTIPLE RANGE TEST FOR FORM

Grade Level Comparison	Means Lower Grades	Means Upper Grades	SD Lower Grades	SD Upper Grades	Signif-icance Level	Direction
Third vs. Sixth	74.48	31.68	55.05	20.86	$p < .05$	Third > Sixth
Third vs. Fifth	74.48	39.70	55.05	27.92	N.S.	
Second vs. Third	73.94	74.48	72.51	55.05	N.S.	
Second vs. Sixth	73.94	31.68	72.51	20.86	$p < .05$	Second > Sixth
Second vs. Fifth	73.94	39.70	72.51	27.92	$p < .05$	Second > Fifth
Fifth vs. Sixth	39.70	31.68	27.92	20.86	N.S.	

TABLE 3

SUMMARY OF TWO-WAY ANALYSIS OF VARIANCE FOR MULTIPLE COMBINATION
ELEMENTS: (4 GRADES x 2 CONDITIONS)

Source of Variation	SS	df	MS	F
Between subjects	236637.52	63		
A (Grades)	38214.77	3	12738.26	3.85 $p < .05$
Subjects within groups	198422.75	60	3307.05	
Within subjects	5570910.80	64		
B (Complexity/Redundancy)	536.57	1	536.57	0.01 N.S.
AB	409.91	3	136.64	0.00 N.S.
B x subjects within groups	5569964.40	60	92832.74	

TABLE 4

SUMMARY OF NEWMAN-KEULS MULTIPLE RANGE TEST FOR MULTIPLE COMBINATION ELEMENTS

Grade Level Comparison	Means Lower Grades	Means Upper Grades	SD Lower Grades	SD Upper Grades	Significance Level	Direction
Second vs. Sixth	71.84	29.80	70.86	22.52	$p < .05$	Second > Sixth
Second vs. Fifth	71.84	40.72	70.86	36.00	N.S.	
Second vs. Third	71.84	65.44	70.86	34.57	N.S.	
Third vs. Sixth	65.44	29.80	34.57	22.52	$p < .05$	Third > Sixth
Third vs. Fifth	65.44	40.72	34.57	36.00	N.S.	
Fifth vs. Sixth	40.72	29.80	36.00	22.52	N.S.	

(χ^2 = 3.27, df = 3, N.S.), rhythm (χ^2 = .51, df = 3, N.S.), and multiple combination elements (χ^2 = 3.61, df = 3, N.S.). Thus the four grades did not differ in the frequency with which they chose between complexity and redundancy in any of the music components.

Discussion

Results showed that when differences occurred in free-operant listening time, second and third graders listened to more of the music regardless of complexity or redundancy conditions than fifth and sixth graders. Thus, younger students listened more to the available sound contingencies than older students. The data indicated that the tone row music stimuli presented were less reinforcing for the upper graders than the lower graders.

Results also indicated that second, third, fifth, and sixth graders did not differ significantly in the frequency with which they chose between complexity and redundancy in form, dynamics, rhythm, and multiple combination elements. No differences either in complexity and redundancy conditions or between grades in choice were found.

Results fail to support the previous research findings of Berlyne (1971, 1974), Bragg and Crozier (1974), Crozier (1973), Duke and Gullickson (1970), Overmier (1962), and Simon and Wohlwill (1968). One explanation may be that prior studies were primarily concerned with examining the pitch aspect of music. This was only one music component of concern in the present study. The present study was more comprehensive in that the music elements of form, dynamics, rhythm, and their combination were studied.

Differences in subject populations may be another explanation that could account for failure to confirm the findings of other experiments. Berlyne and colleagues have often employed volunteer populations instead of randomly selected subjects in their studies. Additionally, their research has often employed subject grade and age levels that differed from those employed in the present study, for example, university undergraduates, visitors to the Ontario Science Center in Canada, and musically trained college undergraduates.

Stimuli groupings can vary in that one may have more constituent components in it than another. The group containing more constituent components is then interpreted as being more complex. What is being responded to may not be cognitive complexity at all. Perhaps it really does not matter cognitively if a subject cannot discriminate complexity. It would appear that none of the studies has found that subjects could discriminate complexity before the experimenters conducting the studies then looked at whether or not it was complexity that was being tested.

The results of the present study indicate that the music is more reinforcing for lower grade children than the upper grade children. The latter increasingly avoided the tone row music stimuli. It may be pointed out that a possible novelty effect existed for the younger subjects regarding the music stimuli used in the present study. However, there is no evidence that tone rows are any less novel for older students. Therefore it would appear that students in upper grades become less amenable to any music other than the familiar influences. This conjecture is supported by pretest and posttest data for nursery school subjects through sixth graders (Dorow, 1977; Greer, Dorow, & Hanser, 1973; Greer, Dorow, Wachhaus, & White, 1973). While children in lower grades sampled more of the various contingencies, older grade children overwhelmingly rejected the several kinds of music offered in favor of rock music.

There is a need for continued investigation and research seeking information concerning the reinforcement value of the collative properties of complexity and redundancy in music.

Notes

(1) Music form is variously defined by music theorists and philosophers of music. In order to simulate music form, a smallest part of music form—motive—was used in the study. As few as two notes may constitute a motive (Apel, 1961). Thus, motive may embrace only an upbeat and a downbeat.

References

Apel, W. Harvard Dictionary of Music. Cambridge, Mass.: Harvard University Press, 1961.

Berlyne, D. E. Conflict, Arousal and Curiosity. New York: McGraw-Hill, 1960.

Berlyne, D. E. Aesthetics and Psychobiology. New York: Appleton-Century-Crofts, 1971.

Berlyne, D. E., ed. Studies in the New Experimental Aesthetics: Steps Toward an Objective Psychology of Aesthetic Appreciation. Washington, D.C.: Hemisphere Publishing Corporation, 1974.

Bragg, B. W. E., and Crozier, J. B. "The Development with Age of Verbal and Exploratory Responses to Sound Sequences Varying in Uncertainty Level." In D. E. Berlyne, ed., Studies in the New Experimental Aesthetics: Steps toward an Objective Psychology of Aesthetic Appreciation. Washington, D.C.: Hemisphere Publishing Corporation, 1974.

Crozier, J. B. Verbal and Exploratory Responses to Sound Sequences of Varying Complexity. Unpublished doctoral dissertation, University of Toronto, 1973.

Dember, W. N., and Earl, R. W. "Analysis of Exploratory, Manipulatory, and Curiosity Behaviors." Psychological Review, 64(2): 91-96.

Dorow, L. G. "The Effect of Teacher Approva/Disapproval Ratios on Student Music Selection Behavior and Concert Attentiveness." Journal of Research in Music Education 25 (1977): 32-40.

Duke, A. W., and Gullickson, G. R. "Children's Stimulus Selection as a Function of Auditory Stimulus Complexity." Psychonomic Science 19 (1970):119-120.

Greer, R. D.; Dorow, L.; and Hanser, S. "Music Dis-
     crimination Training and the Music Selection
     Behavior of Nursery and Primary Level Chil-
     dren." Council for Research in Music Education
     Bulletin, No. 35 (1973):30-43.

Greer, R. D.; Dorow, L.; and Randall, A. "Music
     Listening Preferences of Elementary School
     Children." Journal of Research in Music Edu-
     cation 22 (1974):284-291.

Greer, R. D.; Dorow, L.; Wachhaus, G.; and White, E.
     "Adult Approval and Students' Music Selection
     Behavior." Journal of Research in Music Edu-
     cation 27 (1973):345-354.

Hall, R. V. Managing Behavior, Behavior Modifica-
     tion: The Measurement of Behavior. Kansas
     City, Kans.: H & H Enterprises, 1971.

McMullen, P. T. Melodic Preferences of School-age
     Subjects as a Function of Melodic Redundancy
     and Number of Different Pitches. Unpublished
     doctoral dissertation, University of Iowa,
     1973.

McMullen, P. T. "The Influence of Complexity in
     Pitch Sequences on Preference Responses of
     College-age Subjects." Journal of Music
     Therapy 11 (1974):226-233. (a)

McMullen, P. T. "Influence of Number of Different
     Pitches and Melodic Redundancy on Preference
     Responses." Journal of Research in Music Edu-
     cation 22 (1974):198-204. (b)

Overmier, J. B. Auditory Pattern Preference as a
     Function of Informational Contest. Unpub-
     lished master's thesis, Bowling Green State
     University, 1962.

Randall, C. A. The Effect of Participation in School
     Music-theater Productions on the Music Selection
     Behavior of Elementary and Secondary School
     Students. Unpublished doctoral dissertation,
     Teachers College, Columbia University, 1975.

Simon, C. R., and Wohlwill, J. F. "An Experimental Study of the Role of Expectation and Variation in Music." Journal of Research in Music Education 16 (1968):227-238.

Tanner, F. D. The Effect of Disc Jockey Approval of Music and Peer Approval of Music on Music Selection. Unpublished doctoral dissertation, Columbia University, 1976.

Winer, B. J. Statistical Principles in Experimental Design, 2nd ed. New York: McGraw-Hill, 1971.

THE ROOTS OF MUSIC EDUCATION IN BALTIMORE*

James L. Fisher

Paralleling the development of musical life in Baltimore in the late eighteenth and nineteenth centuries was the development of a system of pedagogy unique to America--the singing school. The singing school along with the emerging choral society, a European institution, seemed to have an influence on the development of music as part of public education in Baltimore. Also contributing to music development of the people of Baltimore was the publication of tunebooks. In this field of publication, Baltimore was one of the nation's leaders.

Singing Schools

Originating in the New World between 1710 and 1720, singing schools were organized to improve the singing of psalms and hymns in churches. They were popular schools that generally convened in the evenings for a period of a few weeks or months for the study of the rudiments of music and the practicing of hymn tunes. Groups of youths and adults met under the direction of a singing master, who instructed them in the intricacies of note-reading and part-singing. Many singing masters had little formal training in music and were often themselves the products of short-term singing schools.

From its beginnings in New England, the singing school movement gradually spread to other parts of the country. Itinerant singing masters moved from New England into parts of Pennsylvania. From there they established schools in Virginia, North and South Carolina, Tennessee, Alabama, Georgia, and as far west as Kentucky. Some of those singing masters

---

moving south settled in Maryland. Between 1760 and
1900, singing schools were conducted in nearly every
part of Maryland. The first such schools were organized in and around Annapolis, the cultural center
of the state until after the Revolutionary War.
Shortly thereafter, a number of prominent singing
masters set up singing schools in Baltimore. Eventually, the influence of these urban centers spread
to other parts of the state.

The first singing school activities of record
in Maryland were conducted at St. Anne's Anglican
Church in Annapolis. In 1764, Phillip Williams announced his plans to organize a singing school at the
church to teach psalmody in four parts. His school
met twice a week from five until eight o'clock in
the evening and cost twenty shillings. Even though
Williams stayed in Annapolis less than one year, his
instruction must have aroused some interest; for in
1765, Hugh Maguire advertised that he would open a
singing school at St. Anne's and teach the singing of
psalms.

In all probability, the Revolutionary War inter-
fered with cultural and musical pursuits. There seem
to be no further notices in the newspapers of that
time about singing school activities until after the
war, and even then notices were somewhat sporadic.
In 1786, Alexander Gray announced that he would conduct a school for instruction in church music and
teach the divine service as far as his knowledge
extended.(1) It is possible that Gray or other
singing masters continued their work in Annapolis.
Considerably more information is needed about the
teaching of psalmody in tidewater Maryland. Probably
singing school activities had significantly diminished
during the last decade or so before 1800. Such a
decline would have coincided with the general demise
of theatrical and concert endeavors during the same
period. Annapolis seemed to remain economically
static, and by the early part of the nineteenth century it was completely overshadowed by the growing
port town to the north. Baltimore had assumed the
economic and cultural leadership of the state during
the last decade of the eighteenth century.(2)

The first singing school in Baltimore was established shortly after the Revolutionary War.
Ishmael Spicer opened a school in the Court House
during the early part of November 1789. The school

46

met four evenings a week; its sole purpose was the improvement of "church musick." Tuition was set at two dollars and a half per quarter for each student. Spicer announced that he would teach not only the most improved tunes of the different churches in Baltimore, but also the rules of music from the "newest and most approved plan in America."(3) The system of teaching to which Spicer was probably referring was one advocated by a contemporary, Andrew Adgate, who established an institute for vocal music in Philadelphia around 1785. The plan of teaching, not highly innovative, consisted of a progressive arrangement of the musical elements to enhance note reading. He used the four sol-fa syllables. It is uncertain how long Spicer conducted a singing school in Baltimore. It is known that he spent several years there and that he was successful. In fact, in one of his announcements he indicated that the public had looked favorably upon his venture and that he had met with general encouragement.(4) Perhaps the greatest tribute to his success was a reference to one of his students, who was described in a flattering biographical sketch as one who by diligent study and practice "soon grew wiser than his teachers" and became a teacher of psalmody.(5) The student was Baltimore's John Cole.

As a teacher, compiler of tunebooks, and music publisher, Cole played an important role in the development of a musical public and the improvement of musical taste in Baltimore. He protested the musical style of the early singing masters in New England, whose repertoire relied heavily on music of indigenous culture. He made every effort to bring to the public dignified humn tunes, music of the European master composers, and planned instructional materials. No one influenced music instruction in the city more during the 1800s than Cole. Born in Tewksbury, England, in 1774, Cole and his parents settled in Baltimore in 1785. As a youth he attended singing schools conducted by Spicer and others. By 1802, at the age of twenty-eight, Cole was conducting a school of sacred music. The school met twice a week in a Presbyterian church at a fee of three dollars per quarter. Cole used one of his own tunebooks, The Divine Harmonist. This was the beginning of Cole's career in Baltimore as a conductor of sacred singing schools, a profession he followed for several decades. A general decline in musical and cultural life occurred around the time of the War of

1812, and this was reflected in a diminishment of singing school activities. However, in 1817 Cole opened a singing academy with an Englishman, Samuel Dyer. They offered practice in sacred music. Although Cole and a few other masters were active during much of the first quarter of the nineteenth century, announcements about schools were infrequent after the first decade. It was not until 1834 that A. Brevoort organized a number of classes for instruction in sacred music.

The singing schools in Baltimore in the early nineteenth century, as those in Boston, were organized for the purpose of teaching sacred music or psalmody. For the most part, the schools were conducted by individuals who were associated with certain churches. Shortly after 1830, a number of basic changes occurred in Baltimore singing schools. Masters began to broaden the repertoire to include secular music, and many of the schools were no longer affiliated with specific churches. As the repertoire broadened, the schools attracted more students. As enrollments increased, singing masters began to group their students. Classes were organized for girls, boys, men, and women. Singing school masters chose to identify these more broadly conceived schools and classes by such names as singing academies, musical institutes, juvenile classes, vocal classes, and glee schools.

Among the first of these new schools to be opened in Baltimore was the Academy established in 1834 by Ruel Shaw, and the Musical Institute, opened a few years later and conducted by John Hewitt and William Stoddard. From all accounts the two schools seemed to be friendly rivals even though their organization was different at the outset. The Academy apparently did not have classes for children or juveniles until 1841. The Musical Institute offered sessions in secular music for women and men, classes in sacred music for adults, and separate classes for children or juveniles.(6) If public concerts were an indication of success, both schools were successful. The students of Ruel Shaw's Academy gave a vocal concert with instrumental accompaniment in the Saloon of the Anthenaeum in 1834, a few months after the Academy opened. A juvenile concert, the fourth of its kind, was given in 1838 by students of the Musical Institute. They presented Flora's Festival, an oratorio written by Hewitt and Stoddard.

48

About the same time two other singing masters, William Tarbutton and Alonzo Cleaveland, organized classes. Cleaveland's classes in his Glee School were especially successful. He furnished books without extra charge and gave the first lesson free. The school drew immediate interest and continued to attract students for more than a decade. By 1854, Cleaveland presented the first of a series of programs involving about fifty girls. The occasion was a floral concert during which the oratorio Flower Queen by George F. Root was performed. So many attended that the performance was repeated on the following evening. Later in 1854 and in 1855, similar programs were given by Cleaveland and his pupils. These programs of secular music clearly indicated a departure from the purpose of the early singing schools, which was to teach the rudiments of music and psalmody.

While the juvenile concerts by classes in the Academy, Institute, and Glee Schools featured secular music, classes associated with religious groups gave concerts of sacred music. Numerous juvenile concerts occurred at several churches in the area in 1850. Two singing masters, D. Kemmerer and C. Kemmerer, organized at least nine such concerts involving hundreds of children. It is uncertain how long the Kemmerers were engaged in singing schools in the Baltimore area. After their extensive series of juvenile concerts, S. Jordan, rather than the Kemmerers, taught singing classes at several of the churches. Evidently, the Kemmerers were itinerant singing masters who specialized in short-term singing schools for children.

Apparently the decade around 1850 was a period of transition for music instruction in Baltimore. At this time a basic change occurred in the organization of singing schools. The classes for children, which became popular around 1838, were no longer mentioned in newspapers after 1855. The demand for juvenile singing classes diminished after public school music instruction was introduced into the public schools in 1843. Music in the public schools was taught by specialists in nearly all grades. Shortly after the demise of classes for children, singing schools began a steady decline. The gradual success of the public school music program probably played an important part in this decline. As the children learned the rudiments of music and developed singing skills in

public school music classes, there was less need
for singing school instruction. The publishers of
tunebooks shifted emphasis; they compiled sacred,
evangelical songs intended for the rural sections of
Maryland.(7)   At the same time, music associations
increased in popularity after the Civil War. First
established at the beginning of the nineteenth century, groups such as the Liederkranz, Euterpe Musical
Association, German Singing Associations, and Haydn
Society were only a few that involved scores of
amateur and professional singers.

     The establishment of singing schools in Balti-
more in the late eighteenth century and the growth
and development of private music schools near the
middle of the nineteenth century parallels the
development of music education in other eastern
cities. In these cities singing masters and their
schools were supported by the public, and the music
they performed had popular appeal. The singing masters developed no special system of pedagogy, but
they adapted various methods to their needs. Although they did not contribute directly to public
school music, the singing schools did provide music
instruction for the masses. In so doing, they
helped establish a favorable atmosphere for music
and music instruction. A direct contribution to
public school music was made by those singing masters
who later became public school teachers. The methods
and materials they used, especially in the early
decades of public school music, evolved from singing
school methods and tunebooks.

Tunebooks

     Tunebooks, which were compiled by singing
school masters and others, were important to instruction in the singing schools of Maryland. These books
were published primarily in Baltimore, where the
Baltimore Foundry and similar facilities made the
printing of music possible. One of the first of
these books to be published was the Baltimore Collection of Sacred Music. Unfortunately, little is
known about the book except that it was published in
1792. Oblong in shape and usually seven by ten
inches in size, the tunebook generally had an introduction explaining theoretical information about the
rudiments of music, such as rhythm, melody, and
harmony. Quite often the author used this section
to describe a particular system of note-reading.

50

At times, detailed musical exercises were provided.
While the main body of the tunebook included choral
music arranged in three and four parts, the majority
of songs were simple hymn tunes grouped according to
the meter of the verses. Choral pieces other than
hymn tunes were sometimes included. Identified as
anthems, these pieces were somewhat lengthier and
more complicated and were intended for choirs or
groups of moderately trained singers. Anthems frequently were written with a short introduction to be
played on keyboard instruments. At times the anthems
included an instrumental accompaniment different from
the voice parts, a feature never displayed by hymn
tunes. Compared with hymn tunes, anthems had extreme
vocal ranges, more eighth and sixteenth notes, and
imitative scoring.

At the turn of the century, tunebooks became a
vehicle for expressing reaction to the popular style
of singing in churches throughout the Northeast. The
method of hymn singing had grown out of the musical
style of colonial singing masters and New England
composers such as William Billings and Timothy Swan.
The characteristics of this style included lively
folk-like tunes, fuguing devices (or fugues), unor-
thodox harmony (for example, parallel motion), and
the practice of placing the melody or air in the
tenor voice. Musical leaders in Baltimore, particularly John Cole, believed that excessive emphasis
on these characteristics had brought about a low
point in congregational singing. In 1804, Cole
published a tunebook that illustrated his position.
In the preface to the Beauties of Psalmody. . . ,
he deplored the "poor state of singing in public
worship." He felt that congregations were accustomed
to "trifling and doleful ditties." He was particularly opposed to the use of "fugeing" (sic) tunes.
Cole's sixty-four page collection contained a pre-
dominance of "reserved hymn tunes" exhibiting simple
harmonies and rhythms. The melodies were placed in
the soprano part and generally lacked wide skips or
chromatic tones. Imitative scoring or fuguing was
held to a minimum.(8)

Between 1800 and 1842, Cole compiled and published at least thirteen tunebooks. Many of his
collections included what he considered to be
dignified music. In 1827, in the preface of The
Seraph, he wrote that a great change had taken place
in the style of church music. His contemporary,

Samuel Dyer, referred to Cole's successful influence:

> At a very early period in his musical
> career, Mr. Cole discovered the necessity of
> a change in the then prevailing taste of the
> public, and by extraordinary and persevering
> exertions, induced a few others to join with
> him in opinion; by which means Baltimore was
> foremost in putting a stop to that species of
> psalmody which then universally prevailed in
> the schools throughout the continent.(9)

Cole did not weaken in his campaign to improve the
quality of church music. As late as 1832 he published
a compilation of hymns for the Protestant Episcopal
Church. This 119-page book contained mostly psalm
tunes of various metrical classes. European tunes,
many of English and German origin, still predominated;
indigenous folk materials were rejected. Simple
tunes were arranged from the choral works of such
masters as Haydn, Handel, Beethoven, and Mozart. No
theoretical introduction was included in the book,
indicating that it was primarily intended for congregational singing and not for use in the singing
schools.(10)

In addition to being collections of hymn tunes
and anthems, tunebooks were also used for instructional purposes in singing schools. Numerous systems
of instruction were prescribed by singing masters,
and various instructional plans were set forth in
the theoretical introductions to the books. The
musical contents often reflected the instructional
plans. In a sense, Cole's emphasis on dignified
music was considered a part of his instructional
plan. He produced at least one tunebook that dealt
entirely with the matter of instruction. In 1810,
he published a book that introduced the musical
rudiments in a progressive order.(11) After a
verbal explanation of the various rudiments, Cole
gave some directions about graceful singing. Next,
he included a series of note-reading exercises progressing from simple to difficult. Finally, there
was a "Musical Catechism" that included questions
about musical symbols.

A number of other compilers of tunebooks also
were active in Baltimore during the first quarter of
the nineteenth century. One of the earliest was
Wheeler Gillet, who opened a school for sacred music

in 1805 and published his Maryland Selection of
Sacred Music in 1809.(12) The book contained a large
variety of sacred tunes arranged according to meter,
many of them taken from European sources. Unlike
Cole, Gillet placed the melody part in the tenor
voice. He did, however, agree with Cole regarding
the choice of reserved and dignified music. Samuel
Dyer was also a compiler of tunebooks. In 1817, just
two years after arriving in Baltimore, Dyer's New
Selection of Sacred Music was published. By 1825,
the book had gone through three editions. The range
of musical styles in this collection was somewhat
broader than had been demonstrated in Cole's publications. Even "animated" and "fuging" (sic) tunes, to
which Cole objected, were included. In addition,
the tunebook contained many selections of European
derivation.(13) Before leaving Baltimore, Dyer
published a two-volume collection known as the
Selection of Anthems, which included anthems by both
American and European composers.(14)

     Other compilations of sacred music were pub-
lished in Baltimore during the first quarter of the
nineteenth century. These were apparently the work
of persons not greatly involved in singing school activities.(15) The contents of these books, like
many others published through 1835, drew heavily upon
the music of European composers. Many tunes were
written by Englishmen such as T. Clark, Thomas Tallis,
John Blow, and Samuel Chapple. The works of other
Europeans were also popular. Thus, Baltimore compilers took a decidedly different approach in
selecting music for tunebooks than that of the
pioneer singing masters of New England, who had
relied almost exclusively on indigenous materials.

     The publications of the singing masters of this
period indicated experimentation with various types
of pedagogy. In 1836, Ruel Shaw released a third
edition of The Seraph, noting that it was organized
according to the Pestalozzian system. This is the
first evidence of the influence in Baltimore of
Lowell Mason, the American interpreter of Heinrich
Pestalozzi, whose pedagogical system swept the
country before the Civil War. Shaw, who later became
a public school music teacher in Baltimore, offered
a number of suggestions for applying the Pestalozzian
system to music instruction. He advocated that
children should be taught through the use of examples
drawn on a blackboard, that they should learn each

lesson well before proceeding to the next, and that less emphasis should be placed on memory. Shaw also broke with the tradition of using the sol-fa syllable system. Like Mason, he recommended the use of seven syllables, do through ti. (16) In keeping with a general trend toward the use of secular materials, Shaw compiled a fourth edition of The Seraph in 1840. He removed the subtitle, "Baltimore Collection of Church Music," and for the first time included a number of secular works considered appropriate for singing schools or social gatherings. These songs were nothing more than nonreligious verses set to simple four-part tunes.(17)

Later compilations continued to emphasize secular music. In 1856, while employed as a public school music teacher in Baltimore, Calvin Root published a tunebook entitled Root's Choral: or The Baltimore Collection of Church Music. Although the subtitle indicated the collection was intended for churches, Sabbath schools, and seminaries, the contents consisted of hymn, folk, and national tunes arranged in three and four parts. Root's extensive introductory section included thirty-two pages of musical elements and vocal exercises. Like Ruel Shaw, Root was influenced by the Pestalozzian system. His book contained a "complete course of instruction based on the Inductive System."(18) Root arranged a series of vocal exercises from simplest to most complex. He used seven syllables and numbers as aids to music reading.

There is little doubt that the compilers of tunebooks were motivated by the rising popularity of children's classes in private as well as public schools.(19) Before 1840 few, if any, tunebooks published in the city included music considered appropriate for children. Shortly thereafter, entire collections for youth were commercially available.(20) The books were intended to be used in teaching vocal music in classes, whether in public schools, private academies, or singing schools.(21)

Instructional methods that were developed in the private school were not limited to Pestalozzianism. Sometime around 1851 a Baltimore musician and singing school master, James M. Deems, convinced the Baltimore school commissioners to use his book, Vocal Music Simplified, in the grammar schools. The book was a compilation of progressive vocal music exercises and solfeggi, using the Italian system of fixed do.(22) Although never a public school music teacher, he succeeded in having his book and presumably the Italian system adopted by the commissioners. There is evidence that use of the system caused considerable friction within the ranks of public school music teachers.(23)

Singing teachers, compilers, and publishers generally were influenced by the growing popularity of musical instruction for children. Soon methods and tunebooks were developed that could be used in privately conducted children's classes or public and private schools. In addition to Deems and Shaw, several other singing teachers apparently succeeded in having tunebooks or instructional methods adopted by the public schools. (24) Most likely, there was a considerable interchange of teaching methods and materials throughout the first several decades of music instruction in the Baltimore public schools.

Choral Societies

Choral societies, sometimes known as musical associations, began to flourish during the first part of the nineteenth century, especially as the German population increased. Involving many amateurs, these societies were a phenomenon that grew to large proportions. They were organized by groups of amateurs for the purpose of performing choral works of some length and technical difficulty, unlike singing schools, which were organized primarily for vocal music instruction. At first, singing schools and choral societies often studied and performed the same music. As the nineteenth century progressed, the choral societies performed lengthier and more technically demanding choral works. Singing school participants may have increased in musical proficiency during that time, but the schools' primary objective continued to be instruction. Baltimore choral societies undoubtedly evolved from the popular singing groups in Europe rather than from singing schools, as in New England. At first choral societies studied and performed sacred music. Undoubtedly they were first associated with churches or had a religious orientation. John Cole published several tunebooks that were dedicated to such groups. As the number of German and central European immigrants increased, the societies became secular in emphasis, often reflecting strong ethnic ties. German choral societies, for example, were active in Baltimore as early as 1837, when a group known as the Liederkranz gave its first concert.

Oratorio singing became one of the major objectives of choral societies as their size and proficiency increased. As early as 1803, performances of Messiah and The Creation were given by some of the more advanced societies. Choral proficiency continued to develop in Baltimore until, by 1821, oratorios were performed by groups numbering up to two hundred singers with orchestral accompaniment. Such works as Pergolese's Stabat Mater, Mozart's Requiem, and masses by Haydn and Beethoven were performed.

The surge of interest in choral societies began at an important moment in the musical history of Baltimore. For the first time, music was taught in the public schools. At the request of citizens, the school commissioners arranged for vocal music to be introduced into the curriculum sometime during 1843. The assumption is quite tenable that the involvement of citizens in choral singing precipitated demands for vocal music instruction in the schools. Several factors support this position. First, hundreds of people in Baltimore were members of choral societies just prior to 1843. These people were convinced of the rewards and personal values associated with vocal music. Probably they would have constituted a block of citizens likely to request the introduction of vocal music into the schools. Second, it may be significant that those making the request included ordinary citizens in addition to patrons. The distinction would suggest that not all the petitioners had children attending schools. Certainly, one of the few groups having a vested interest in vocal music instruction in the schools would have been the singing societies. In the third place, leading Baltimore musicians had noted earlier that many of the citizens involved in singing groups were not familiar with the rudiments of music. The public schools were suggested as a likely place to carry out such rudimental training. These same musicians reminded Baltimore residents that music was taught in schools conducted by the Germans and suggested the public schools follow suit. Finally, German-Americans in the city had achieved some political influence. Members of the group included representatives from local and state governments and the city school board. Any request by members of the singing societies would have in all likelihood received support from certain elected officials closely affiliated with the German community. Of course, none of the above explanations provide direct evidence of the influence of choral societies on the school curriculum in 1843.

Choral societies, especially among the German population, did not diminish after the introduction of vocal music in the public schools. Numerous groups were active during the latter half of the century, and by 1867 joint concerts became popular. A concomitant of the great interest in singing societies was the gradual improvement in the quality of repertoire. Oratorios and other large choral works became standard. Toward the last half of the century, music festivals became popular in various parts of the United States, especially among the German choral societies. Baltimore had its share of these festivals and was occasionally national host. The diminishing of ethnic ties among the Germans after 1890, however, brought a gradual decline in the societies, and only a few continued into the twentieth century.

References

(1) _Maryland Gazette_, May 4, 1786. Gray acknowledged in his advertisement that he had some limitations in knowledge about the various tunes used in singing the psalms.

(2) Matthew Page Andrews, _History of Maryland: Province and State_ (New York: Doubleday, Inc., 1929), p. 414.

(3) _Maryland Journal_ and _Baltimore Advertiser_, October 30, 1789.

(4) _Maryland Journal_.

(5) Samuel Dyer, _Anthems, Set Pieces, Odes and Choruses_, third edition (Philadelphia: J. C. Auner, 1834), p. 184.

(6) From existing records, it is not possible to determine the age of juveniles. They were probably between six and fourteen, the ages at which many children attended public schools. High school

education was not yet available to a large majority of youth, and those over fourteen were often considered a part of the adult working force.

(7) E. Heginbotham, The Peninsula Collection of Church Music (Baltimore: J. W. Bond and Co., 1863), preface; and W. D. Roedel, Carmina Ecclesiae (Baltimore: T. N. Kurtz, 1872), preface.

(8) John Cole, The Beauties of Psalmody Containing a Selection of Sacred Music in Three and Four Parts; Adapted to Dr. Watt's Psalms and Hymns (Baltimore: Sower and Cole, 1804). A copy of this book, heretofore unlocated, is in the Maryland Historical Society Collection of tunebooks.

(9) Dyer.

(10) Cole, Primitive Psalmody (Baltimore: John Cole and Son, 1836). A copy of this book, heretofore unlocated, is in the Maryland Historical Society Collection of tunebooks.

(11) Cole, The Rudiments of Music, or An Introduction to the Art of Singing Compiled for the Use of Schools (Baltimore: G. Dobbin and Murphy, c. 1810).

(12) Wheeler Gillet, The Maryland Selection of Sacred Music (Baltimore: Henry A. Keatinge, 1809).

(13) Dyer, A New Selection of Sacred Music (Baltimore: Murphy and Milless, 1817). Second edition, 1820; third edition, 1825.

(14) Dyer, Dyer's Second Edition of a Selection of Upwards of Sixty Favourite and Approved Anthems, Set Pieces, Odes and Choruses (Baltimore: Joseph Robinson, 1823). According to remarks in the preface, a first edition appeard in 1817.

(15) Arthur Clifton, An Original Collection of Psalm Tunes (Baltimore: T. Murphy, 1820); and Emanuel Kent, David's Harp (Baltimore: Armstrong and Plaskitt, 1812).

(16) Ruel Shaw, The Seraph, or Baltimore Collection of Church Music, third edition (Baltimore: John Cole and Son, 1836), preface.

(17) Shaw, _The Seraph_, fourth edition (Baltimore: John Cole and Son, 1840).

(18) Calvin Root, _Root's Choral: or The Baltimore Collection of Church Music_ (Baltimore: by the author, 1856).

(19) Music was introduced into the Baltimore public schools during the summer of 1843.

(20) A. J. Cleaveland, _The Chorister and School Harmonist_ (Philadelphia: John Ball, 1852), preface. Cleaveland was active as a teacher of private and public school music classes in Baltimore.

(21) Cleaveland.

(22) James M. Deems, _Vocal Music Simplified_, third edition (Baltimore: by the author, 1851), preface.

(23) _Forty-Third Annual Report of the Board of Commissioners of Public Schools, to the Mayor and City Council of Baltimore, for the Year Ending December 31, 1871_ (Baltimore: J. Cox, 1872), pp. 216-221.

(24) According to the _Baltimore Sun_, December 28, 1870, on that date the school commissioners adopted a system of music instruction developed by Harry Rosewald. A few years later, John Hewitt wrote in _Shadows on the Wall_ (Baltimore: Turnbull Brothers, 1877), p. 73, that a system of "vocal class teaching" he and J. T. Stoddard introduced into Baltimore had been used in the public schools.

RELATIONSHIP OF SELECTED FACTORS IN TRUMPET
PERFORMANCE ADJUDICATION RELIABILITY*

Harold E. Fiske Jr.

Abstract

This study investigated the relationship between reliability of music performance, adjudication,
judge performance ability, and judge nonperformance
music achievement. Thirty-three recent music education graduates rated a series of trumpet performances. Individual judge reliability was calculated
and applied music, music history, and music theory
academic grades were collected for each of the
subjects. In addition, a composite variable labeled
"nonperformance music grade" was obtained by averaging each subject's music theory and music history
grades. Results of statistical analyses showed:
(1) no relationship between judge performing ability
and judge reliability, (2) no relationship between
judge performing ability and judge nonperformance
music achievement, and (3) a statistically significant inverse relationship between judge reliability
and judge nonperformance music achievement.

Key Words: academic achievement, assessment, music
achievement, music contest, performance ability,
trumpet.

The evaluation of student music performance is
an essential and pervasive part of music education.
Evaluation occurs constantly, on an informal level
during lessons, classes, and rehearsals, as well as
in competitions, auditions, and placement examinations. In either case, the role of the evaluator
consists of weighing a student's performance against

the evaluator's own performance concept for the purpose of assigning grades or making suitable comments.

One question raised by this process concerns the criteria used for identifying competent evaluators. Selection of judges for formal adjudications often is based on the performing ability of the prospective judge, because it is assumed that a good judge must also be a capable and experienced performer. Performing ability alone, however, may not be enough to insure reliable judging.

An earlier study (Fiske, 1975) investigated differences between panels of judges of differing areas of expertise. The present study investigated the relationships between judge reliability, judge performance ability, and judge music knowledge.

Procedure

Thirty-three subjects, all recent graduates of a music education program, rated an audition tape of performances by twenty trumpet players. To calculate judge reliability the tape included a retest, consisting of the same performances heard over again. The judges were not aware of the test-retest construction and assumed they were hearing forty different trumpet players.

The rating sheet included five performance traits: intonation, rhythm, technique, phrasing, and overall. The trait "overall" was defined as a separate trait including all relevant aspects of performance rather than as an average of the other traits. Each performance was rated on a scale from 1 (low) to 5 (high) for each of the five traits.

One rating session was held for the subjects. At the beginning of the session each subject was given a rating sheet, a page of instructions, and a copy of the trumpet solo (The Hollow Men by Vincent Persichetti). After reading the instructions the subjects listened to a sample tape containing five examples similar to those that were to be rated. The sample tape prepared the judges for the range of performances and familiarized them with the trumpet solo. The rating session, including the instruction period and listening to the sample tape, lasted slightly less than one hour.

Data related to music knowledge and performance ability was obtained from student records. The judges' undergraduate grades in the areas of applied music, music history, and music theory were located and recorded. Most of the subjects were recent graduates from the University of Western Ontario, but a few had records from other institutions. Although course requirements differed considerably in some cases, satisfactory data was obtained for all 33 judges.

Judge stability--The test scores for all items were correlated with the retest scores for each of the judges under each of the five traits. Five reliability coefficients thus were obtained for each of the traits. These five scores then were averaged to obtain a mean reliability coefficient for each judge. The mean reliability scores served as the dependent variable in subsequent analyses.

Group reliability differences--The 33 judges possessed a variety of applied instrument skills. Although the 1975 study showed no differences in ratings by a panel of brass judges versus a panel of nonbrass judges in the adjudication of trumpet performances, it was hypothesized for this study that brass versus nonbrass judge-group reliability differences might exist. A t test was employed to compare brass and nonbrass judges' average reliability coefficients.

Trait intercorrelations--To determine the relationships between variables, a trait intercorrelation matrix was calculated. Data included the average reliability coefficients, applied music grades, music history grades, and music theory grades. This analysis was carried out for brass judges alone, for nonbrass judges alone, and for the complete judge panel.

Multiple regression analysis--The principal object of the study was to determine the extent to which the dependent variable (judge reliability) could be predicted through the independent variables (applied music grade, music history grade, and music theory grade). These relationships were tested through a stepwise multiple regression analysis.

TABLE 1
JUDGE STABILITY

	Intonation	Rhythm	Phrasing	Technique	Overall	$\overline{X}$
J1	.52*	.65*	.52*	.60*	.85*	.63
J2	.33	.27	.20	.50*	.32	.32
J3	.42	.65*	.76*	.67*	.81*	.66
J4	.61*	.45*	.63*	.70*	.78*	.63
J5	.58*	.59*	.71*	.77*	.72*	.67
J6	.00	.66*	.75*	.62*	.79*	.56
J7	.57*	.53*	.55*	.53*	.76*	.59
J8	.37	.34	.40	.46*	.72*	.46
J9	.44*	.65*	.56*	.60*	.59*	.57
J10	.47*	.41	.53*	.57*	.81*	.56
J11	.38	.48*	.43	.09	.44*	.36
J12	.65*	.67*	.75*	.71*	.69*	.69
J13	.70*	.84*	.67*	.88*	.69*	.76
J14	.71*	.49*	.64*	.77*	.73*	.67
J15	.05	.70*	.52*	.56*	.58*	.48
J16	.41	.74*	.71*	.61*	.80*	.65
J17	.08	.80*	.74*	.45*	.61*	.54
J18	.02	.56*	.73*	.64*	.71*	.53
J19	.09	.84*	.73*	.48*	.73*	.57
J20	.65*	.82*	.89*	.86*	.90*	.82
J21	.35	.54*	.55*	.59*	.66*	.54
J22	.42	.72*	.75*	.70*	.83*	.68
J23	.65*	.83*	.91*	.49*	.86*	.75
J24	.24	.34	.37	.60*	.48*	.41
J25	.62*	.79*	.66*	.60*	.72*	.68
J26	.69*	.47*	.69*	.37	.44*	.53
J27	.66*	.66*	.72*	.56*	.85*	.69
J28	.39	.88*	.59*	.64*	.75*	.65
J29	.61*	.69*	.60*	.42*	.70*	.60
J30	.57*	.63*	.64*	.53*	.73*	.62
J31	.74*	.80*	.70*	.76*	.85*	.77
J32	.64*	.47*	.58*	.59*	.56*	.57
J33	.68*	.78*	.72*	.80*	.84*	.76
$\overline{X}$	.46	.60	.63	.60	.71	.60

* Significance $<$ .05 (d.f. = 18).

Results

Judge stability--Table 1 shows the results of the judge stability analysis, including the average reliability coefficient (average of the five traits) for each of the judges. The average reliability variable was found to range from +.32 to +.82 with an average of +.60.

Differences in group reliability--When brass judge reliability coefficients were compared with those of nonbrass judges, a t value of 2.113 was found, which was significant beyond the .05 level (two-tailed test with 31 degrees of freedom). Previous studies that tested reliability of subjects who were more experienced in teaching and adjudicating showed no difference in reliability between panels of specialists. But this study's results suggest that judge reliability improves through teaching experience, particularly with instruments other than those of one's specialty.

Trait intercorrelations--Table 2A shows the correlations between applied music grades and the remaining independent variables. The correlations were not statistically significant, suggesting that performing ability is independent of academic achievement.

TABLE 2A

TRAIT INTERCORRELATIONS: APPLIED MUSIC
WITH OTHER INDEPENDENT VARIABLES

	Music History	Music Theory	Nonperformance Music Average
Applied music			
Brass judges	-.01	.07	.05
Nonbrass judges	.00	.33	.20
All judges	-.01	.20	.12

Tables 2B, 2C, and 2D present the results of the intercorrelations of the various performance trait reliability coefficients and average judge

TABLE 2B

TRAIT INTERCORRELATIONS: ALL JUDGES

	Intonation r	Rhythm r	Technique r	Phrasing r	Overall r	Average Reliability
Music history	-.27	-.48*	.09	-.29	-.22	-.34*
Music theory	-.33*	-.28	-.01	-.25	-.11	-.29
Applied music	-.11	.23	.30	.18	.20	.19

* Significance < .05 (d.f. = 31).

TABLE 2C

TRAIT INTERCORRELATIONS: BRASS JUDGES

	Intonation r	Rhythm r	Technique r	Phrasing r	Overall r	Average Reliability
Music history	-.42	-.45	-.22	.39	.71*	-.19
Music theory	-.55	-.45	-.46	-.18	.12	-.57
Applied music	-.07	.59	.31	.46	.13	.34

* Significance < .05 (d.f. = 7)

65

TABLE 2D

TRAIT INTERCORRELATIONS: NONBRASS JUDGES

	Intona-tion r	Rhythm r	Tech-nique r	Phras-ing r	Over-all r	Average Relia-bility
Music history	-.17	-.46*	.26	-.45*	-.34	-.36
Music theory	-.25	-.29	.18	-.30	-.22	-.29
Applied music	-.17	.11	.34	.07	.30	.14

* Significance < .05 (d.f. = 22)

66

reliability coefficients with music history, music theory, and applied music grades. The analysis was carried out for all judges, brass judges alone, and nonbrass judges alone. For Table 2B, the range of the correlations was -.48 to +.30; for Table 2C, -.57 to +.71; for Table 2D, -.46 to +.35. Most of the correlations were not statistically significant, suggesting no relationship between the tested variables. To accept this conclusion would mean that reliability in adjudication is related to neither academic achievement nor performing ability, a conclusion contrary to what one might expect. Perhaps other variables that may be related to reliability should be selected to further test this research question.

Closer examination of Table 2, for instance, suggests a trend in which nonperformance music variables (music history and music theory) correlates negatively with reliability while the performance variable correlates positively. The most interesting aspect of these correlations is the large number of negative coefficients for music history and theory (30 negative versus 6 positive). Although few coefficients were significant, the trend was investigated further. For each judge, music history and music theory grades were averaged together to obtain a mean nonperformance music grade. The nonperformance music grades were then correlated with the mean reliability scores. This analysis was carried out for all judges, brass judges alone, and nonbrass judges alone.

Table 3 presents the results of this analysis along with the previously obtained applied music correlations. Two of the three correlations for nonperformance were significant; the third, although moderately strong, failed to reach significance due to the relatively small sample. The trend towards an indirect relationship between nonperformance music grades and judge reliability thus seemed substantial, at least for the group of judges as a whole.

Multiple regression analysis--Two sets of multiple regression analyses were performed on the data, and, for each set, analyses were made for brass judges alone, nonbrass judges alone, and all judges. Tables 4 and 5 show the summaries for each of these analyses.

67

TABLE 3

REGROUPED VARIABLES CORRELATED WITH AVERAGE JUDGE RELIABILITY

	All Judges (d.f.=31)	Brass Judges (d.f.=7)	Nonbrass Judges (d.f.=22)
Nonperformance	-.33*	-.51	-.34*
Applied music	.19	.34	.14

* Significance <.05 (one-tailed test).

In general, the analyses confirmed a tendency in which nonperformance scores inversely predict reliability.

Conclusions and Discussion

Three conclusions can be drawn concerning the relationships between judge reliability, judge performing ability, and judge music knowledge in this sample.

First, there was no relationship between performing ability (as measured by applied music grades) and judge reliability.

Second, there was no relationship between performing ability (as measured by applied music grades) and nonperformance music achievement (as measured by music history and theory grades).

Third, there was a statistically significant inverse relationship between judge reliability and nonperformance music achievement (as measured by music history and theory grades).

One possible implication of these findings is the existence of an evaluation mediator located in the brain and employed under conditions that require subjective decisions. This mechanism may aid consistent decisions by contributing to the efficiency and stability of the comparison process. Factors affecting the mechanism might include the amount of experience with specific music stimuli and the amount of practice in making qualitative decisions

TABLE 4

MULTIPLE REGRESSION SUMMARY: ALL JUDGES

Step	Variable Entered	B	F to Enter	Signif-icance	Multiple r	r^2	r^2 Change	Simple r	Overall r	Signif-icance
1	Music history	-.75	4.07	.05	.34	.12	.12	-.34	4.07	.05
2	Applied music	-.26	1.29	.27	.39	.15	.04	.19	2.69	.08
3	Music theory	-.45	1.68	.21	.45	.20	.05	-.29	2.40	.09

TABLE 5

REGROUPED VARIABLES MULTIPLE REGRESSION SUMMARY: ALL JUDGES

Step	Variable Entered	B	F to Enter	Signif-icance	Multiple r	r^2	r^2 Change	Simple r	Overall r	Signif-icance
1	Nonperformance grade	-.89	5.06	.03	.37	.14	.14	-.37	5.06	.03
2	Applied music	.33	2.17	.15	.45	.20	.06	.19	3.71	.04

about stimuli that lie on a continuum. Decisions based solely on stored facts and knowledge would be less dependent upon the mechanism than decisions that require relative comparisons, weightings, and categorizations.

Disciplines that require absolute responses, such as music history and music theory, ordinarily would provide little practice for such a mechanism and, at worst, would tend to extinguish its use altogether. Conversely, teaching experience in performance would tend to strengthen the mechanism since student progress in performance depends upon ongoing evaluation.

This speculation should not imply that academic courses are not suitable for music training. Rather, it supports the contention that students need opportunities to evaluate performance, either their own or others. A complete music background may well demand the inclusion of evaluation ability training; educators may not be justified in assuming such ability is a gift or is developed naturally with other skills.

Reference

Fiske, Harold E., Jr. "Judge-Group Differences in the Rating of Secondary School Trumpet Performances." Journal of Research in Music Education, Vol. 23 (1975), pp. 186-196.

THEORIES OF AFFECTIVE RESPONSE TO MUSIC*

Mary Friedmann**

Perception and Response: General Concerns

Music education today is concerned with helping
people develop aesthetic sensitivity.   Gerard
Kneiter defines this sensitivity as "man's capacity
to respond to the emotional values and cognitive
meanings of art."(1)   Those who hold this view believe that the capacity to respond is developed as
one becomes increasingly perceptive of the elements
of music that embody the emotional content, namely,
melody rhythm, harmony, tone color, dynamics, and
form.

Two of the principal behaviors associated with
this conception of aesthetic sensitivity, and therefore two of the principal concerns of those involved
in aesthetic education are perception of and response
to music and the other arts.   Interests in these two
areas can be seen in more recently developed materials for practical use in the classroom as well as in
articles and books that deal with the philosophy of
education in the arts.

Much research in music education has focused on
the relationship between perception and response.
Some investigators have explored subjectively reported
mood response to music, others have examined physiological reactions, while still others have attempted
to show relationships among affective responses,
musical stimuli, and traits of the listener.

---

* Reprinted by permission of Mary Friedmann and
Contributions to Music Education, No. 4 (Winter,
1976), pp. 1-18.

** The second part of this article dealing with
the homeostatic model is taken from background material presented in the author's doctoral dissertation, "Affective Response to Distorted Melodies"
(Case Western Reserve University, 1975).

While experimental research has dealt mainly
with stimulus and response, the reason why relationships exist between them has been largely a matter of
theory and speculation. The purpose of the present
paper is to discuss theories that might be considered
by future researchers exploring responses to music.

Meyer's Theory and Information Theory

That music evokes some kind of feeling is
fairly well agreed. Volumes of empirical evidence
are available to support the notion; scientific data
can also be found, though not in the same quantity.
Philosophers have tried to analyze the components of
an "aesthetic experience," physiologists have carried
out experiments in an attempt to pinpoint physiological functions that are operative in affective experience, and psychologists have formulated theories
that might explain feelings.

One of the most respected explanations for
affective response to music has come from music
theorist Leonard B. Meyer. His approach to the
problem appeared in 1956 in Emotion and Meaning in
Music wherein he explored the relationship between an
established psychological theory of emotion and affective and intellectual meaning in music.(2)

Meyer later determined that some of the concepts
he had explored were equivalent to those developed
under information theory, a theory that deals with
the content of messages transmitted by twentieth-
century communications media such as radio, television, and computors. Similarities between the two
theories are treated in Music, the Arts, and
Ideas.(3)

The first section herein is intended as a digest
of Meyer's original theory and its relationship to
information theory. If the thoughts appear sketchy
at times, the reader is urged to go directly to the
source given in the footnotes. The sequence presented below follows Meyer's in most instances.
Additional examples have been included, and references
to the writings of other authors have been made for
purposes of clarification.

Psychological Theory of Emotion

Meyer builds his thesis on a psychological theory of emotion which asserts that "emotion or affect is aroused when a tendency to respond is arrested or inhibited."(4) It is a theory enunciated in the writings of many psychologists whom Meyer cites in Emotion and Meaning, and one that can be easily grasped since it applies to situations encountered daily. For example, a man who is ready to leave for work reaches into his pocket for the keys to his car. They are not there. He looks in the pockets of other suits and does not find them. His tendency to respond has been inhibited, and he experiences some emotion. Let us assume that he finally finds the keys and starts out for work. He stops for a red light. Minutes pass and the light does not turn green. He looks at his watch and sees that five minutes have gone by. Again his tendency to respond has been halted, and the man may experience emotional arousal.

In these examples, no distinction was made between the affect evoked on the two occasions. The feelings aroused were treated in a general way as if there were no difference between them. According to Meyer, the affect evoked in any stimulus situation is more or less the same whether misplaced keys, a delayed red light, or anything else was the cause. The underlying affect is the same in all--an undifferentiated feeling.(5)

This idea is difficult to accept when we compare the way we feel as an old friend approaches with the way we feel when a tornado is sighted. How can it be said that the affect is the same? Meyer explains that the differences we ascribe to emotional states, feelings of joy, love, fear, and so on, are due to our awareness of the stimulus. He calls these "affective experiences," and says that they are differentiated.(6) Thus, we have joyful experiences, loving experiences, and fearful experiences, all of which are differentiated because of the association we make with the stimulus; but the affect underlying all of them is more or less the same and is, therefore, undifferentiated.

The distinction between differentiated and undifferentiated feeling is critical in the development of Meyer's rationale. He wishes to apply a psychological theory of emotion which is used to

explain responses to everyday situations to an experience that is generally considered unique, namely,
the musical experience. He can do this only if he
can demonstrate that feelings produced in all situations are the same.

His argument for undifferentiated feeling is
summarized in the following passage:
    a) The more intense emotional behavior is, and
    presumably therefore the more intense the
    affective stimulation, the less the control
    exerted by the ego over behavior and the
    greater the probability that the behavior is
    automatic and natural.
    b) The more intense affective behavior is, the
    less differentiated such behavior tends to be.
    In general, the total inhibition of powerful
    tendencies produces diffuse and characterless
    activity. For example, extreme conflict may
    result in either complete immobility or in
    frenzied activity, while weeping may accompany
    deepest grief, tremendous joy, or probably any
    particularly intense emotion.
    c) Thus the more automatic affective behavior
    is, the less differentiated it tends to be.(7)

Meyer's case for undifferentiated feeling appears to rest on the assumption that automatic behavior offers evidence of sameness in affect. Behavior
is likely to be automatic when emotions are strong,
and during these times it can be impossible to dis-
tinguish the emotional state by observing overt
actions. Since these actions are the same for different affective experiences, then the underlying
affect must be the same.

The Tendency to Respond and Expectation

Having explained in a general way a psychological theory of emotion, and having shown that it
can be applied to all stimulus situations, Meyer
proceeds to examine more closely what is involved in
a "tendency to respond." A tendency to respond consists of a series of responses that once set in
motion continue in a particular order and in a particular time sequence.(8) One response gives rise to
the next, and so on through the series. Each response occurs at a particular place in the series, and
each occurs at a particular time.

There may be a disturbance in the order, the timing, or in both. If, for instance, the second response occurs after the third instead of after the first, the order is disturbed. If a response comes too soon or is delayed, the timing is disturbed. The response pattern in making a phone call might be (1) pick up the phone, (2) put the phone to the ear, (3) listen for the dial tone, (4) dial the number, (5) hear the phone ring, (6) and finally, either hear or not hear a voice at the other end. The order and timing of this series is disturbed if the person at the other end picks up his phone before it rings. The order was disturbed since the fifth response was omitted; the timing was disturbed since the last response occurred too soon.

Many response patterns do not consume as much time as the one just described. Indeed, not all of the automatic responses involved in the phone call were included in the example, for without doubt there are many responses required in dialing the number. Most patterns run their course very rapidly, and the individual is not aware of them.

Unless there is a disturbance in the order, the timing, or in both, tendencies usually remain unconscious. For instance, how often are we consciously aware of the dial tone? It usually comes on, the responses run their course, and we are unconscious of our tendencies. Should the dial tone not be heard, the tendency to respond to it rises to consciousness. Therefore, it can be stated that tendencies may be either conscious or unconscious, and they become conscious when a response pattern is inhibited or delayed.

A tendency to respond is also known as an expectation. It follows then that what has been said regarding tendencies also holds for expectations; they may be inhibited or delayed, and they may be conscious or unconscious. At first it may seem unusual to think of an expectation as unconscious. In ordinary parlance, the word is used to indicate the condition of "looking forward to" which implies conscious awareness. However, Meyer says that in the sequence of responses involved in an expectation one response "expects" the next.(9) We expect to see when we open our eyes; we expect our legs to carry us when we decide to walk; we expect morning to follow night, and so on. In this sense unconscious tendencies are expectations.

Expectation and Music

In the preceding pages, Meyer's ideas regarding the following have been treated: (1) the arousal and inhibition of tendencies to respond (expectations); (2) the differentiation of affect; and (3) conscious and unconscious tendencies. With this background, it is possible to demonstrate how music evokes affect.

If one were to hear the first seven pitches of the C major scale beginning with small c, with each note receiving one beat, he would probably expect to hear c^1 on the eighth beat. It is certainly the note he would expect if he were studying for a degree in music at a college in the United States. If instead of hearing C^1 he hears $C\#^1$, his expectation would be inhibited since he was prepared to respond to another pitch. On the other hand, the expectation would be delayed if the pitches following small b were g - b - g - a - b - c^1. In both examples the conditions for arousal are present.

Two assumptions were made in the examples: (1) that the respondent had previously been exposed to the series of notes, and (2) that the psychological laws of mental behavior were functioning.(10)   Habit responses or expectations are the result of both. Whether or not one is able to estimate what will occur next depends on the learning that may take place through formal training or through extended exposure. The listener in the above example was familiar with the major scale and therefore envisaged a particular musical consequent. An individual from another culture, such as India, probably would not have expected c^1 on the eighth beat; conversely, most Americans could not anticipate the final pitch of an Indian raga.

The music of various cultures, historical periods, composers, and even periods within a composer's creative career have unique characteristics. The listener who is well acquainted with the music of a given style develops habit responses or expectations relative to the style. Therefore, learning is a significant factor in the development of expectations.

The second assumption made in the examples given earlier was that certain psychological laws of mental life were functioning. The specific manner in which each person perceives, selects, and organizes stimuli is determined to some extent by his past experience. However, there are certain modes of mental life that appear to be common to most people. These include, among others, the following: the desire for continuation, with minimal resistance, a mental process that has been set in motion; the desire for completeness, stability, and rest; the belief that an activity will not continue in exactly the same pattern, but will eventually change and grow; the desire for a return to that which was stated at the beginning; and the need for a shape that the mind can perceive.(11)

A discussion of the relationship of each of these "laws" to music requires separate treatment which will not be presented here. It should be pointed out, however, that violations of these laws produce inhibition or delay and are therefore conditions for affective arousal.

The mental activity involved in the operation of these laws does not necessarily imply conscious awareness. If we are thinking through a problem and peripheral matters enter our minds, we do not usually stop and consciously note that we are now thinking about a matter that is not central to the point. Such mental activity frequently remains unconscious, even though a tendency to respond has been inhibited or delayed.(12) Whether or not the event rises to consciousness depends on the individual respondent.

Some people, because of training or natural disposition, are given to reflection, and in such a person an inhibited expectation will likely rise to consciousness. However, in those not so inclined, the tendency may remain unconscious. Regarding the effect of the two types of behavior, Meyer writes: "If intellectual activity is allowed to remain unconscious, then the mental tensions and the deliberations involved when a tendency is inhibited are experienced as feeling or affect rather than as conscious cognition."(13) Here we see the distinction between an affective and an intellectual response; whereas the individual who experiences affect has allowed the tendency to remain unconscious, the one who intellectualizes the experience has objectified it by making it the object of reflection. Both responses are activated when the tendency to respond is inhibited or delayed.

Meyer does not make a value judgment regarding the superiority of one response over the other. On the contrary, he states that mental activity need not become conscious in musical experiences.(14)

Expectation and Musical Meaning

Until now the topic of meaning in music has not been discussed, and it might be avoided except that Meyer applies concepts found in information theory not so much to affective or intellectual experiences per se as he does to musical meaning. It is therefore desirable to understand the relationship between meaning and affect in order to better understand the relationship between information theory and affect.

According to Meyer, there are two kinds of meaning: designative and embodied. The term "designative" is applied to the meaning of a stimulus which is different in kind from that which it signifies.(15) For example, "rose" is a word, a symbol, which is used to indicate a plant that has soft petals, a stem with leaves, and so on. The word and the plant itself are different in kind. Therefore, the word "rose" has designative meaning; it designates something that is different in kind, something that is not a word. The term "embodied" is applied to the meaning of a stimulus that is related in kind to that which it points. The sound of thunder, a phenomenon of nature, points to other natural phenomenon, i.e., a disturbance in the sky, overcast skies, and possibly rain. The meaning of thunder is embodied in the sound itself.

Meyer reasons that musical meaning is embodied since one musical event points to another event which is like in kind, namely, more music. He defines the conditions for musical meaning in this way: "If, on the basis of past experience, a present stimulus leads us to expect a more or less definite consequent musical event, then that stimulus has meaning."(16)

When we hear the progression I-VI-II-V^7, we expect a musical consequent that is most likely I, the tonic chord. One musical event points to another. According to the definition given above, this progression has meaning.

If the antecedent does not lead us to expect one or more consequents, the musical event is meaningless. For this reason some music, for instance music of the avant-garde, is meaningless to many people. They have not learned the idioms of the style, or they have not learned to organize sound. If no expectations are aroused, no consequents can be envisaged, and so the event is meaningless.

From what has been said the following concepts emerge: (1) the same conditions that give rise to expectations also provide meaning; (2) past experience is a determining factor in developing expectations and also in perceiving meaning; and (3) the mental processes that are operative when expectations are inhibited--perception, cognition, envisaging, and so on--are the same as those that function when meaning is sensed. If there are not expectations, there is no meaning, or in Meyer's words: "Embodied meaning is, in short, a product of expectation."(17)

The traditional dichotomy between reason and emotion might make it difficult to accept the idea that both affect and meaning are dependent on the same conditions and processes. Meyer asserts that this is no problem: "Once it is recognized that affective experience is just as dependent upon intelligent cognition as conscious intellection . . . then thinking and feeling need not be viewed as polar opposites but as different manifestations of a single psychological process."(18)

With an understanding of the basic concepts of Meyer's theory that have been presented, we can proceed to explore the relationship between his theory and information theory.

Information, Choice, and Probability

In <u>Music, the Arts, and Ideas</u>, Meyer proposes the following hypothesis: "The stylistic conditions which give rise to musical meaning, whether affective or intellectual, are the same as those which communicate information."(19)

The word "information," as used in the theory
of communication, is not to be confused with its
usual meaning. Warren Weaver defines information as
"a measure of one's freedom of choice when one selects a message."(20) If one has many choices, the
information is greater than if he has only a few
choices. Thus, if a person has only one choice, the
amount of information provided by the stimulus is
zero.

From the viewpoint of communication systems,
choices are governed by probabilities, and by probabilities which depend on the preceding choices.(21)
To elaborate on only the first part of this passage,
the fewer the number of choices, the more probable
the outcome. Keeping in mind the relationship
between choices and information, it can now be
stated that the more probable the outcome of a
situation, the less information generated; and the
less probable the outcome, the greater the information. A musical illustration may serve to clarify
these relationships, and also explain the second
portion of the opening statement.

Let us say that a person who is thoroughly
familiar with the tonal tendencies of the major scale
hears for the first time a melody written in a major
key. Each time he hears an antecedent phrase he
correctly anticipates the consequent which always
follows tonal tendencies. After his expectations
have been met several times, the probability that he
will correctly predict the following consequents
increases. The number of possible consequents de-
creases as the music continues, and so the probability of predicting correctly increases. Had he
anticipated five possible consequents when he heard
the first phrase, and had there been only five
choices, the probability that he would correctly
anticipate the next phrase would be 5:1. When he
hears the final antecedent his chances of correctly
predicting the consequent might increase to 1:1.

The information in the opening measures of
the music was greater than the information in the
closing measures since the choices available to the
listener at the beginning were greater than the
choices at the end.

In this example, the probability that the
listener's expectation would be met was determined

by the number of choices known to him. He was
familiar with certain tonal relationships. It has
already been pointed out that any given piece of
music has certain stylistic characteristics which are
due to the more or less frequent occurrence of particular temporal-tonal successions. These successions are more or less probable. From this Meyer
reasons that "once a musical style has become part
of the habit responses of composers, performers,
and practices listeners, it may be regarded as a
complex system of probabilities."(22)

From what has been said, the reader might conclude that probabilities and expectations are identical. This is not the case. The probability that
a particular musical event will occur is determined
by the actual number of times it appears, i.e., the
actual probabilities. Expectencies, on the other
hand, are determined by the listener's estimate of
how often it will occur, i.e., the known probabilities.(23) Thus it is the known choices, the
expectations, that limit the information.

Markoff Process, Redundancy, and Noise

In the above example, the known probabilities
increased as the music continued. The tendency for
this to occur is an example of what is known as a
Markoff process, a process in which the increase in
probability of future events depends on previous
events.(24) Most music is, to some extent, an
example of a Markoff process since the notes at any
given point are determined to a degree by the previous ones.

A Markoff process is the result of redundancy.
Abraham Moles defines redundancy as "a measure of the
relative 'wastage' of symbols in transmitting a message."(25) In music certain pitch relationships
and rhythmic relationships are reiterated as the
music moves forward. If the music is tonal, for
instance, relationships between pitches within the
key will recur; with each recurrence, there is increased redundancy.

By means of mathematical laws developed under
information theory, it is possible to determine the
redundancy of some messages. It is also possible to
ascertain how much can be omitted from a message
without affecting communication.(26) Meyer

suggests that the aspect of omitting explains why a person is able to understand incomplete music events. He gives the example of solo sonatas for string and wind instruments in which only the melodic line is heard but in which harmonies are filled in by the listener.(27)

Meyer suggests further that the concept of redundancy explains how a listener is able to combat what information theorists refer to as <u>noise</u>.(28) Some noise is caused by physical conditions such as echoes, dead spots, talking, and street sounds. Meyer terms these "acoustical noise." A second kind of noise called "cultural noise," is defined by Meyer as "disparities which may exist between habit responses required by the musical style and those which a given individual actually possesses."(29) Judging from the explanation and examples given by Meyer, it appears that cultural noise is any style characteristic that has not been learned, and background that an individual lacks becuase of his cultural and/or historical background. For example, difficulties experienced in listening to the music of the far East are due to cultural noise, as are the difficulties encountered in understanding the music of historical periods other than our own.

Since cultural noise provides uncertainty, and therefore arouse expectations, it can be desirable. It becomes undesirable when too many uncertainties are created, when there is not enough redundancy to combat it, and when the listener is unable to project probable consequents. There can be little doubt that the music of John Cage contains much cultural noise for many people of the twentieth century despite the fact that he is the product of the same historical period and the same culture as those from whom his music receives a negative response. Since his music contains no redundancy, and since there are no stylistic idioms from composition to composition or within compositions--other than randomness--a listener cannot estimate specific temporal or tonal alternatives.

From this we can understand that a degree of redundancy is necessary. However, excessive redundancy is also undesirable and leads to monotony. In order to avoid this extreme, a composer will introduce into his music deviations from the predictable course. According to Meyer, three types of deviations may be distinguished:

(1) The normal, or probable, consequent event may be delayed

(2) The antecedent situation may be ambiguous and several equally probable consequents may be envisaged

(3) The consequent event may be unexpected.(30)

The psychological effect of the first two types is similar insofar as there is uncertainty regarding the consequent. When either occurs, the mind sets up alternatives for modes of continuation.

Meaning, Information, and Feedback

Since Meyer has shown that meaning and expectation arise from the same conditions and the same mental processes, and that expectations are known probabilities, he revises the definition of meaning to reflect the relationship between meaning and probabilities: "Musical meaning arises when an antecedent situation, requiring an estimate of probable modes of continuation, produces uncertainty about the temporal-tonal nature of the expected consequent."(31)

This definition explains how meaning is provided when there is a delayed consequent and when there is an ambiguous antecedent. Both types of deviation require an estimate of probable modes of continuation. The definition does not make clear how meaning is provided by an unexpected consequent, the third type of deviation.

The manner in which an unexpected consequent indicates further probabilities becomes apparent when one considers various stages of meaning. (1) Hypothetical meaning is the meaning given the antecedent when it is heard. At this stage, probable alternatives are selected. (2) Evident meaning is the meaning attributed the antecedent in light of the consequent. The meaning originally given the antecedent is re-valuated and in view of this further probable events are envisaged. (3) Determinate meanings are those seen after the composition has ended. They are meanings that arise from all antecedent-consequent relationships on all hierarchic levels, i.e., relationships within phrases, between phrases, between and among phrases, periods, sections, and so forth.(32)

When one hears an unexpected consequent, the
meaning originally attributed the antecedent is
revaluated. The probable consequents envisaged at
first were incorrect, there is uncertainty, and so
the number of probable consequents for future
events increases.

This situation brings to mind the last movement
of the Haydn Quartet, Opus 33, No. 2, "The Joke,"
in which there is increasing uncertainty with each
succeeding unexpected delay. The story goes that
Haydn deliberately set out to make it difficult to
predict when the composition would end.

The well known "surprise" chord in the first
movement of Symphony No. 94 is another example of
the unexpected in music. The famous chord causes
the listener to revaluate the meaning of the earlier
portion of the music and set up new expectations for
future events.

The process involved in revaluation is comparable to feedback in automatic control and information theory. Meyer writes that "both feedback and
revaluation are processes whereby future behavior,
whether of automatic systems, motor reflexes, or
expectations, is conditioned and controlled by the
results of past events."(33)

Feedback, then, serves in decision making for
future events not only in cases of the unexpected,
described above in the Haydn examples, but also
serves in cases wherein the consequent was more or
less expected. As long as there is any uncertainty
regarding the consequent, feedback is useful. By
means of feedback the meaning of the antecedent is
either confirmed or changed, and in the latter case
a new set of alternatives for the future are projected. If the antecedent arouses no uncertainty
and the consequent occurs as anticipated, feedback
serves no purpose, the musical event is neutral
with regard to meaning, and since no probabilities
are involved no information is generated.(34)

Information and Affect

The uncertainty created in antecedent-consequent relationships provide both meaning and
information. But uncertainty is a mental state
that exists when a tendency to respond is inhibited

84

or delayed, conditions which are said to give rise
to affect. Therefore, all antecedent-consequent
relationships described above which provide meaning
and information may also arouse emotions.

The relationship between information and
affect is further clarified if we consider that the
uncertainty arising when habit response have been
arrested or delayed is caused by a disturbance in
the order and/or timing of a sequences of responses.
Information is the measure of uncertainty, and
uncertainty may arouse emotions. A situation in
which there is no uncertainty, one in which the
tendency to respond runs its course without disturbance, provides no information and no cause for
arousal.

Summary

The fundamental concept on which Meyer builds
his theory is that emotions are aroused when tendencies to respond, or expectations, are inhibited
or delayed. Music, as well as other stimulus situations, is capable of activating such tendencies and
does so when alternative modes of continuation in
music present themselves to a listener. However,
not all listeners will experience affect when habit
responses are disturbed. Affect is likely to be
aroused when the mental activity involved in the
situation does not rise to consciousness. Listeners given to self-conscious reflection will not
experience affect. Thus responses may be either
emotional or intellectual.

Information theory deals with uncertainty,
choices, and probabilities. Since expectations are
known probabilities relationships appear to exist
between Meyer's theory and information theory.
While mathematical formulas developed under information theory can be used to measure information,
they cannot be used to measure affect. Neither can
musical meaning, which arises from the same conditions that evoke affect, be measured.

In <u>Music, the Arts, and Ideas</u>, Meyer outlines
some of the problems associated with statistical
investigations of musical meaning, but he nevertheless encourages research in this area: "such
experiments, carried on by students who understand
the mechanism of musical communication, might

reveal much not only about music but also about some
of the constants in human perception."(35)

The Homeostatic Model

Before proceeding to a discussion of the
homeostatic model, which is based on physiological
responses to the arts, it might be well to describe
briefly the currently used measure of affective
arousal, i.e., "activation," or in layman's terms,
"tension." Activation is the total energy mobili-
zation of all physiological functions involved in
arousal under any stimulus situation. The activation
continuum is represented at one end by the person
who does not respond to stimuli, and at the other end
by the person experiencing strong emotion. According
to Woodworth and Schlosberg, the organism is, at any
one moment, in balance at a particular activation
level.(36) Some tasks require lower levels than do
others. However, if the activation level is below
that required, the performance will lack energy and
persistence; but if the activation level is above
that required, the performance will lack precision.

When activation is in balance with a task,
behavior is more efficient since it is organized by
"learned patterns of the cortex." But if activation
is too low or too high, behavior is less efficient
since it is "organized in terms of inherent neural
patterns of lower centers."(37) Ideally, then, a
balance or "homeostatic" condition is desirable, a
condition in which the activation, or tension level,
is in balance with the "energy" required for the
situation.

The homeostatic model proposed by Hans
Kreitler and Shulamith Kreitler incorporates tension and relief as basic responses. It is based on
the assumption that an organism, in order to exist,
requires a balance between internal and external
processes as well as a balance among internal
physiological processes.(38) Since a homeostatic
condition is necessary for the survival of an
organism, there is a constant effort to maintain it.
An imbalance results in activation, i.e., arousal
or tension.

According to Kreitler and Kreitler, pleasure
causes a rise or tension followed by reduction in
tension. Displeasure results in high degrees of

tension except under certain conditions. Higher
degrees of tension do not follow upon displeasure if
(1) satisfaction is certain, (2) meaning is perceived,
(3) the situation is under the control of the perceiver, or (4) the stimulus is within the perceiver's
set of expectations. A delay in gratification, if
the delay is too long, causes a rise in tension provided the discomfort is not unbearable, since anticipated pleasure is itself a source of
pleasure.(39)

Since works of art cause tension, the question
arises, Why does one seek that which provokes homeostatic imbalance? The answer, according to Kreitler
and Kreitler, involves some critical notions regarding two types of tensions--diffuse and specific.

When there is a disruption of homeostasis, it
is not always possible to perform immediately an
activity that would reinstate balance. Indeed, the
cause of arousal is not always identifiable and
therefore the person is not aware of the specific
activity that would reduce tension. The general
feeling of tension thus experienced is said to be
diffuse. In order to reinstate a homeostatic condition, the person experiencing this state seeks a
specific activity that will channel the energy thus
created. Works of art serve the dual purpose of
giving direction to diffuse tension and providing
further arousal. The arousal produced by works of
art is accompanied by specific tension that the
perceiver believes will be followed by adequate
relief. The displeasure that may accompany the
experience is thus mitigated by anticipated
pleasure.(40)

Kreitler and Kretler pose a further question:
How does the art work act as a cue that specifies
tension? The answer lies in a related theory, the
theory of cognitive orientation.

When confronted with a stimulus of a magnitude
to be noticed, a series of physiological activities
begin, the purpose of which is to answer the question, What is it? The process is the orienting
response and the answer to the question constitutes
the meaning of the stimulus. It is by means of the
answer that tension is specified. "The whole set
of meanings involved in the elicitation and

directing of any action is designated by the term 'cognitive orientation.'"(41)

Recently published works by Juan Roederer provide evidence from physiology that support Kreitler and Kreitler's theories.(42) Two aspects of Roederer's experiments must be considered in order to understand the relationship between the works of these authors—the time scale and the effect of meaning on arousal.

Roederer explains that there are three distinct time scales on which psychoacoustic reactions occur, each requiring successively longer periods of time. Within the first time scale, covering the initial 50-70 milliseconds of contact with the stimulus, pitch, loudness, and timbre are perceived; in the second time scale, requiring about one-tenth of a second, additional information regarding timbre and discrimination is received; during the third time scale, which occurs in a few seconds or less, "analysis, synthesis, memory storage, and retrieval operations involved in conscient music perception" take place.(43) It would seem, from what Roederer says, that actual perception does not take place during the third stage unless what is sensed is meaningful, that is, related to previously stored messages.

These findings provide a physiological explanation of why an untrained listener does not perceive what a trained listener does. The trained listener can relate what he hears to a previous message whereas the untrained listener cannot.

He states further that the "nervous system tries to use whatever information is available from previous experiences to <u>anticipate</u> the identification process of new incoming information," and when this fails because of an unexpected sound "the extra work required for re-identification gives "a particular sensation of 'musical tension.'"(44)

Roederer's work provides scientific support for the Kreitler theory that tension is produced when a listener is not able to answer the question "What is it?" This is the question that the Kreitlers say must be answered in order to specify and so reduce diffuse tension. The broader the background from which the listener is able to draw associations, the less likely is he to not be able to answer the question.

Despite the emphasis in the preceding pages on the desirability of a homeostatic condition, tensions arising from imbalance are not necessarily unpleasant. The theory presented here is based on the idea that the musical experience provides tension, and it is tension which is followed by relief that makes music appealing.

Summary

Homeostasis is a condition in which certain physiological functions are in balance. When there is a disruption of the balance, arousal or tension is evoked. Music as well as other stimulus situations cause tension; however, music is capable of channelizing or specifying tension.

Pleasure causes a rise in tension followed by a reduction in tension. Displeasure results in even higher degrees of tension except under certain conditions: (1) if satisfaction is certain, (2) if meaning is perceived, (3) if the situation is under the control of the perceiver, or (4) if the stimulus is within the perceiver's set of expectations.

These conditions are met in musical experiences. Thus, although music may cause a disruption of the homeostatic condition, the experience may cause pleasure.

Conclusion

In the digests which have been presented, many concepts found in Meyer's theory, information theory, and the homeostatic model were either omitted or not fully developed. However, there has been an attempt to include the basic issues involved in each.

In Emotion and Meaning in Music, Meyer devotes an entire chapter to the relationships between expectation and learning, and three chapters are given over to the operation of psychological laws of mental life in musical experiences. In the present article, these topics received only a passing nod.

Whereas music is the focus of attention in Meyer's works, the visual arts, dance, and literature as well as music, are the concerns of Kreitler and Kreitler. The development of the homeostatic theory presented in the first chapter of Kreitler and Kreitler's book is quite convincing. However, the chapter dealing with music is somewhat disappointing, since it presents nothing new regarding the psychological effect of music. It does bring together several theories on the development of music, and a great number of the better studies in the area of perception and response.

The researcher seriously considering an investigation of reasons for relationships that exist between musical stimuli and listeners' responses will also be interested in the further exploration of Meyer's theory found in Emotion and Meaning and in his 1973 volume, Explaining Music.(45)

Other works that may be of value are the experimental studies carried out by Paul Vitz, who investigated relationships among quantified information of aural stimuli, affective responses of listeners, and musical background, and the research of this writer in which listener responses to deviations from hypothesized melodic expectancies were related to theories treated in this article.(46)

The way people respond to music is a central concern of those attempting to help others perceive the expressiveness of music, and while there is a need to study relationships between particular musical stimuli and particular responses, a more basic need might be an understanding of the reason(s) for the relationship. If the reason is based on expectancies, then researchers might do well to pursue investigations in this area. Studies of expectancies within persons with various backgrounds, of different age levels, and with different musical experiences might provide data that would enable educators to broaden perceptive listening in an organized fashion.

It is strongly recommended that psychological theories concerning affective responses to music be tested in any studies of perception and response that are undertaken.

Footnotes

(1) Gerard Kneiter, "The Nature of Aesthetic Education," in _Toward an Aesthetic Education_, ed. Bennett Reimer (Washington, D.C.: Music Educators National Conference, 1971), p. 3.

(2) Leonard B. Meyer, _Emotion and Meaning in Music_ (Chicago: University of Chicago Press, 1956; Phoenix Books, 1956).

(3) Meyer, _Music, the Arts, and Ideas_ (Chicago: University of Chicago Press, 1967; Phoenix Books, 1969).

(4) Meyer, _Emotion and Meaning_, p. 14.

(5) _Ibid._, p. 16.

(6) _Ibid._

(7) _Ibid._, p. 18.

(8) _Ibid._, p. 24.

(9) _Ibid._, p. 25.

(10) _Ibid._, p. 30.

(11) _Ibid._, chapters 3-5.

(12) _Ibid._, pp. 30-31.

(13) _Ibid._, p. 31.

(14) _Ibid._, p. 30.

(15) _Ibid._, p. 35.

(16) _Ibid._

(17) _Ibid._

(18) _Ibid._, p. 39.

(19) Meyer, _Music, the Arts_, p. 5.

(20) Claude E. Shannon and Warren Weaver, <u>The Mathematical Theory of Communication</u> (Urbana: The University of Illinois Press, 1949; Illini Books, 1972), p. 9.

(21) <u>Ibid.</u>, pp. 10-11.

(22) Meyer, <u>Music, the Arts</u>, p. 8.

(23) <u>Ibid.</u>

(24) <u>Ibid.</u>, p. 15.

(25) Abraham A. Moles, <u>Information Theory and Esthetic Perception</u>, trans. Joel E. Cohen (Urbana: The University of Illinois Press, 1966), p. 42.

(26) <u>Ibid.</u>, pp. 44-49.

(27) Meyer, <u>Music, the Arts</u>, p. 16.

(28) <u>Ibid.</u>

(29) <u>Ibid.</u>

(30) <u>Ibid.</u>, p. 10.

(31) <u>Ibid.</u>, p. 11.

(32) <u>Ibid.</u>, pp. 12-14.

(33) <u>Ibid.</u>, p. 13.

(34) <u>Ibid.</u>

(35) <u>Ibid.</u>, p. 21.

(36) Robert S. Woodworth and Harold Scholsberg, <u>Experimental Psychology</u> (New York: Henry Holt, 1954), p. 136.

(37) <u>Ibid.</u>, p. 110.

(38) Hans Kretler and Shulamith Kreitler, <u>Psychology of the Arts</u> (Durham, N.C.: Duke University Press, 1973), p. 13.

(39) <u>Ibid.</u>, pp. 13-15.

(40) <u>Ibid.</u>, pp. 17-20.

(41) Ibid., p. 23.

(42) Juan C. Roederer, "The Psychophysics of Musical Perception," Music Educators Journal 60 (February 1974): 20-30; and Introduction to the Physics and Psychophysics of Music (New York: Springer-Verlag, 1973).

(43) Roederer, "The Psychophysics," p. 25.

(44) Ibid., p. 20.

(45) Leonard B. Meyer, Explaining Music (Berkeley: University of California Press, 1973).

(46) Paul C. Vitz, "Preference for Rates of Information Presented by Sequence of Tones," Journal of Experimental Psychology 68, No. 2 (1964): 176-183; "Affect as a Function of Stimulus Variation," Journal of Experimental Psychology 71, No. 1 (1966): 74-79; and Mary F. Trolio, "Affective Response to Distorted Melodies" (Ph.D. dissertation, Case Western Reserve University, 1975).

FRAY PEDRO DE GANTE
PIONEER AMERICAN MUSIC EDUCATOR*

George Heller

Abstract

Fray Pedro de Gante was an important figure in
the history of American music education. His life
and work in Mexico City predate similar activities
in the United States by at least a century. He
worked in a radically changing ethnic and sociocultural environment and was a principal agent in
the acculturation process. In teaching music he
also became involved in the arts in general education, multicultural education, and student teaching.
He was the first European to teach music in the
Western hemisphere and taught thousands of students
during his 45-year tenure. His school served as a
model for later Franciscan schools in the south-
western United States. The documents show that he
was not only successful by European standards, but
that he was also highly respected and admired by
the Indians he taught.

Key Words: cultural background, geographical environment, historical period, historical research,
music teacher, socioeconomic status, teaching
ability.

In Foundations and Principles of Music Education, Charles Leonhard and Robert House (1959, p. 39)
note the need for music teachers to know the history
of music education. They point out the need to
understand continuity, growth and developments,
antecedents and consequences, and the context in
which music has developed in American schools.

---

* Copyright (c) 1979 by the Music Educators National Conference. Reprinted by permission of
George Heller and the Journal of Research in Music
Education, Vol. 27, No. 1 (Spring, 1979), pp. 21-
28.

94

Their argument is contained in the statement, "Without doubt, the issues in music education today have been met in other forms by our predecessors."

Four centuries ago, Fray Pedro de Gante faced challenges that still confront today's serious-minded music educators. That he handled them successfully makes it worthwhile to know more about him; that he did things in music education for the first time in the Western hemisphere makes the study of his life and work even more important.

Many of the current ideas in music education—career education, the arts in general education, and multicultural education—are not new. These ideas and others are part of the introduction of European music in the schools of the Western hemisphere. The story may not be well known not only because the time of its occurence is remote and the place somewhat distant, but also because the primary sources are not yet readily available in English.

The introduction of European music, and with it European language, religion, politics, economics, and culture, is a pivotal point in the history of American music and music education. Though it is difficult to ascertain in the literature, music education held a vital role in pre-Columbian America. What occurred in Mexico City during the sixteenth century was not so much an initiation as it was a transformation. As with many other signal events in the history of music education, a single personality was the dynamic force behind the event. Fray Pedro de Gante's work in Mexico City from 1523 to 1572 succeeded in transplanting the achievements of Renaissance Europe in the New World. It demonstrates an interesting contrast with the failure of similar efforts by missionaries to merge the European and indigenous cultures in the United States a century later.

De Gante's success was probably the result of his background of education and experience, his energetic attitude toward his mission, and his skill in human relations. Though he faced many problems, he was also blessed with some fortuitous circumstances. He worked in an area that was formerly an imperial capital, and the people with whom he worked had a heritage that included music education in a context not unlike that which de Gante sought

95

to develop.

The primary sources for de Gante are his five
extant letters, reports from his contemporaries, and
a short biography written by a colleague in the
Convent of San Francisco in Mexico City. The first
letter was written on July 27, 1529, from Mexico
City and was addressed to his brothers and sisters
in Flanders. The second, third, and fourth letters
were written in Mexico City and were all to the
Spanish King (and Holy Roman Emperor) Charles V;
they were dated October 31, 1532; July 20, 1548;
and February 15, 1552. The fifth letter was to
Philip II and was written shortly after the death
of his father, Charles V. It was sent from Mexico
City and dated June 23, 1558 (Heller, 1973, pp.
155-185). The short biography by Mendieta was
part of a four-volume study on the work of the
Franciscans among the Indians of Mexico, first published in 1596 (Mendieta, 1945, pp. 53-57).

Pedro de Gante lived the first 40 years of his
life in Flanders, in what is now Belgium. Both his
letters and Mendieta's biography state that he was
born in Ygüen, a town that is probably the equivalent
of the modern Ayghem-St. Pierre on the outskirts of
Ghent. The date of his birth is not known, but a
report to the inspector-general of the Council of
the Indies, written in late 1569 or early 1570,
gives his age as 90 years (García Icazbalceta,
1941, p. 7). This would make his birth date either
1479 or 1480.

His early years saw the twilight of an era of
opulence for Flanders and its Burgundian rulers.
Situated in the delicate balance between France,
Germany, and England, Flanders reached a cultural
zenith in the fifteenth century. Life in the
great cities of Bruges, Ghent, Liege, Louvain,
Brussels, and Dijon was the most cosmopolitan in
Europe from 1420 to 1460. It was even rated as
superior to life in Florence, then under the spell
of the great Cosimo de' Medici (Durant, 1957,
p. 127).

Following this grand climax, the road downhill
began with the merger of Burgundy and Austria.
Flanders became part of the dowry of the daughter
of a Burgundian prince, thus being attached to the
Hapsburg Empire. Ultimately, the area became a

part of the Holy Roman Empire when Charles V began his reign in 1515.

This homeland of de Gante was in the midst of another turmoil that was greater than the political machinations of kings and emperors--the Reformation. Martin Luther was but four years younger than de Gante and was also a cleric with a pioneering mission. Savonarola in Florence, Erasmus in Flanders and England, and Henry VIII in England were beginning to influence events. The printing presses of Venice, Germany, and Paris were initiating popular, vernacular, and secular currents that would continue through modern times. In music, de Gante could hardly have avoided the achievements of Franco-Flemish polyphony. His youth and early adulthood were the years in which Ockeghem, Tinctoris, Obrecht, Isaac, Josquin, Glareanus, Pierre de la Rue, and many others were reaching maturity.

De Gante's music education was probably taken at the University of Louvain in Flanders (González Vera, 1868, p. 383). According to Carpenter, Louvain was modeled after the University of Cologne (Carpenter, 1959, p. 240) where music held a traditional place in the mathematical quadrivium along with arithmetic, geometry, and astronomy. Texts were by such classic authors as Aristotle, Isidorus, and Boethius. The _Musica_ of Jean de Muris was required reading. Rudolf Agricola probably was on the Louvain faculty at the time of de Gante's study. Louvain also followed the English practice of providing scholarships for boys who provided the music for the cathedral, an example de Gante followed later in Mexico City.

In the midst of this atmosphere of music achievement, political change, social and religious turmoil, and incipient decline from greatness, Charles V came to Ghent in 1522 bringing news of Cortés's discovery and conquest of Mexico. That year de Gante was living in the Franciscan convent of Ghent under the command of Fray Juan de Tecto. He and another Franciscan priest, Fray Juan de Ayora, petitioned the King to be allowed to go to the New World to evangelize the Indians. Permission was granted.

The three Franciscans departed Ghent on April 27, 1522, and went in the retinue of the King of Spain to visit Charles V's sister, Catherine of Aragon. The royal entourage arrived in Spain at the port of Santander on July 22, 1522. Thus, de Gante and his two companions became part of the great Flemish emigration that saw Josquin, Isaac, and many others achieve fame in other lands. According to de Gante's first letter, they departed Seville on May 1, 1523, and arrived in Mexico at the port of Villa Rica on August 13, then traveled inland to Mexico City (Heller, 1973, pp. 155-159).

The conquest of Mexico City by Cortés in 1519 left most of the former Aztec capital in ruins, and the rebuilding was not completed when the three Franciscans arrived in Autumn of 1523. They therefore went to the city of Texcoco, the capital city of a tribe that had been allied with Cortés, which was across the lake from Mexico City. The missionaries were cordially welcomed by Cortés and the Texcocoan chieftain, Ixtlilxochitl, whose grandson of the same wrote an account of the occasion. In that account, he noted that the three friars were given rooms for a school in the palaces of a former chieftain, Nezahualcoyotzin (Ixtlilxochitl, 1952, p. 398).

The friars had to learn the language before evangelizing the Indians. De Gante described the task as being so difficult that it was accomplished not by him, but by God. He complained of the lack of letters and writing that might have served him as aides to learning the idiom. Whatever the difficulties may have been, sources agree that he not only learned the language better than either of his two companions, but was also more proficient than any of the later arrivals. Bishop Zumárraga testified to de Gante's excellence in the language of the Aztecs, as well as his diligence in caring for 600 youths or more, in a letter to Franciscans in France, dated June 12, 1532 (Oroz, Mendieta, and Suárez, 1947, p. 55). De Gante was not always easily understood by his Spanish-speaking colleagues, but Mendieta wrote that the Indians had no difficulty in understanding him when he spoke Nahuatl (Mendieta, 1945, pp. 53-54).

De Gante's first school for the sons of leaders of the Indian tribes was opened in Texcoco sometime prior to the arrival of Fray Martín de Valencia and his group of 12 Franciscans in 1524. During the day at Texcoco he taught his students to read, write, and sing; at night he preached and taught Christian doctrine. In the Spring of 1527 he moved the school to Mexico City. By 1529, eighteen months after moving the school, he wrote that he was teaching reading, writing, singing, and religion to 500 sons of the leading Indian families. Since he had so many students and only two assistants, he developed a system of training the most able students to become his assistants.

De Gante ran more than a school for the Indian boys. His building served as chapel, school, and community gathering place for the entire Indian community in Mexico City. He supervised the work of educating the young and spreading the Spanish and Catholic heritage throughout the area. He spread his influence to the surrounding countryside, erecting churches and schools, and staffing them with his graduates. According to one source, he built as many as 100 churches in the Valley of Mexico during his years there (Mendieta, 1945, pp. 54-55).

Comprehensive arts education or "the arts in general education" were not familiar terms in de Gante's time, but he was an outstanding practitioner of these "new" ideas. He had studios built adjacent to his school for his children to learn painting. He taught arts and crafts, stone masonry, carpentry, sewing, and embroidery, as well as music and the academic subjects. He organized groups (cofraídas) of singers and instrumentalists to provide music for the churches, and he organized groups of craftsmen and artists to decorate them. These groups were probably modeled after the guilds that abounded in Flanders in his youth and were similar to those known to have been in existence at the University of Louvain and other schools that followed the English system of allowing boys to work their way through school.

The number of students who attended his school attest to de Gante's popularity and success. His letters follow the growth of the school until it reached 1,000 students in 1539. Judging from the sorrow that swept the country when he died, he remained popular and his school continued to flourish.

99

De Gante's sensitivity in working with the Indians was best demonstrated in an event reported to Philip II in the letter of 1558. In that letter, he tells of how he discovered the importance of music in religious celebrations in pre-conquest times. Noting the importance of dance and vocal and instrumental music to the Aztecs, he provided the students with dance costumes on which religious motifs had been painted. Then he set verses written in Nahuatl to Indian tunes. The verses were from the Catechism that he translated and adapted so the Indians could sing them to familiar tunes.

The fifth letter also describes in some detail the daily routine of the students under de Gante's supervision. The report reveals that the character of the school was similar to that of a monastery. The students observed canonical hours, reciting and singing the divine offices. This regimen was probably a case of de Gante teaching as he had been taught rather than an attempt to prepare the Indian boys to take ecclesiastical orders.

In his later letters, de Gante's concern seems to be more with the social problems of his students than with the academic. He writes less about how well they are doing in learning music and other subjects and more about how they are being mistreated by the Spaniards. He exposed at great length the injustices and abuses the Indians were forced to endure, and he was not afraid to invoke the king's favor to help win support for his proposals for reform. The problems for the Indians seemed to increase with the rise of Spanish immigration and the decline of Spain's wealth and political power in Europe.

De Gante also suffered some difficulties in his relations with his contemporaries as a result of his outspoken defense of the Indians. Rumors were a nagging problem for him to contend with. One of these concerned a widely circulated notion that he was the illegitimate son of Charles V. This idea is clearly refuted by the fact that he was twenty years old when Charles V was born. Other writers have speculated that he was the son of Philip the Handsome (Duke of Burgundy), but this is hardly likely since the two were about the same age. A close personal relationship did exist between the friar and Charles V, but probably because they were both from Flanders rather than from any blood relationship.

Regardless of his relations with his peers, there can be no question about the feelings of the hundreds of thousands of Indians he served. Mendieta (1945, pp. 54-55) quoted the Archbishop of Mexico, Alonso de Montúfar, who commented on the strength of de Gante's following among the Indians, "I am not the Archbishop of Mexico, but rather, Fray Pedro de Gante, a lay brother of San Francisco." Montúfar was not only describing the high regard the Indians held for their teacher, but he was also aware that de Gante was the first choice of Charles V to be archbishop. De Gante refused this position and he also turned down opportunities for ordination as a priest. The first such offer was made by Pope Paul II, the second was by the provincial=general of the Franciscan order, and the third was by the papal nuncio to the Spanish court in connection with the king's offer to make de Gante the archbishop of New Spain. He apparently felt he could better accomplish his goals in a teaching position that kept him in direct contact with the Indian community.

Among the many incidents reported by his contemporaries is one that underlines the affection of the Indians for de Gante. At one time he was exiled for a short period to a nearby town on the order of the provincial-general. The exile was the result of false testimony that led to a reprimand (Torquemada, 1969, p. 431). Mendieta (1945, p. 55) describes his return to Mexico City:

> The natives also loved this servant of God
> very much, especially the natives of Mexico
> City, as they showed on his return from
> Tlaxcalla, where he had been exiled for a
> short time. They received him with a beautiful
> flotilla of canoes, and made a solemn ceremony
> in the style of a naval combat on the great
> lake of Texcoco, and they carried him to his
> quarters with much rejoicing.

Fray Pedro de Gante died in mid-April, 1572. The exact date is not known, but a portrait by a contemporary artist, Aubin, notes that he was buried on Sunday, April 21, 1572. All sources agree on the year, though some speculate that he died on June 29, the day of his patron saint (García Icazbalceta, 1896, pp. 35-36). His death caused great outbreaks of sympathy and mourning among the Indians (Mendieta, 1945, p. 56):

> The natives felt much sadness and pain, and they showed it in public. At his burial many of them shed copious tears, and many of them wore signs of mourning which are normally worn when one's father dies.

Following the official burial rites, each of the cofraídas he founded held separate ceremonies in the various towns and villages in the Valley of Mexico. The offerings given at these various services were much larger than normal, even in the poorest parishes. For many years following his death, services were held and offerings were given in his name for the benefit of the needy. The convent of San Francisco in Mexico City received provisions for the entire year from the memorial services held for de Gante.

The Indians asked and received permission for de Gante to be buried in the chapel of San José where he had spent most of his life teaching. His remains were lost in 1862 when the convent and its chapel were razed to make room for a street that still bears his name, Calle de Gante (García Icazbalceta, 1896, pp. 35-56).

In 1572, the provincial of the Franciscans in New Spain wrote to Philip II to report de Gante's death (Gonzalez Vera, 1868, p. 386):

> We have lost one of our greatest workers in Fray Pedro de Gante. God took him to his reward as He takes all who serve Him well. It would be a great burden to Your Majesty if I told of all the work he accomplished here, because the country is full of his fame. He was a tireless shepherd, working fifty years and dying among the sheep. . . . The Indians owe him a great debt of gratitude, and we friars are also in his debt for the many favors the very Christian father of Your Majesty granted us because of the close relationship between him and Fray Pedro.

Fray Pedro de Gante's impact on music education in the Western hemisphere was enormous. Almost single-handedly he taught 1,000 students each year. Fully 100 years before any sizeable colonization efforts were noticeable in North America, his students in Mexico City were singing European music, copying Franco-Flemish polyphony, playing and building violins and organs, and composing and teaching music in the European style. His teaching and his school served as models for other Franciscans and their missions throughout Central America and as far north as San Francisco, Arizona, New Mexico, Texas, and Colorado. He may have had a direct influence on Fray Juan de Padilla, also a Franciscan, who was probably the first teacher of European music in what is now the United States.

The problem of cultural change is a pervasive one in music education. It occurs in communities that are experiencing changing socioeconomic characteristics; it happens when new graduates of music schools take their first jobs in small, rural communities, and it happens when adult teachers work with members of the youth culture. The process of cultural change is affected by the degree of change, the intensity of the contact, and the contact agents. The results may be merger, incorporation, or extinction. Pedro de Gante faced a cultural change of immense degree and intense contact. His actions as a contact agent helped control the circumstances of the contact in such a way as to result in merger of the indigenous Indian culture with the immigrant Spanish culture. His success is unparalleled in the history of music education.

References

Carpenter, Nan Cooke. Music in the Medieval and Renaissance Universities. Norman, Oklahoma: University of Oklahoma Press, 1959.

Durant, Will. The Reformation. The Story of Civilization, vol. 6. New York: Simon and Schuster, Inc., 1957.

García Icazbalceta, Joaquín. Obras, vol. 3. Mexico City: V. Agüeros, 1896.

García Icazbalceta, Joaquín, ed. <u>Códice Francis-cano</u>. Mexico City: Salvador Chávez Hayhoe, 1941.

González Vera, Francisco de. <u>Revista de España</u>, vol. 3. 1868.

Heller, G. N. <u>Music Education in the Valley of Mexico during the Sixteenth Century</u>. Unpublished doctoral dissertation, University of Michigan, 1973.

Ixtlilxochitl, Fernando de Alva. <u>Obras históricas</u>, vol. 1. Edited by Alfredo Chavero. Mexico City: Editoria Nacional, 1952.

Leonhard, C., and House, R. <u>Foundations and Principles of Music Education</u>. New York: McGraw-Hill Book Company, Inc., 1959.

Mendieta, Fray Gerónimo de. <u>Historia Eclesiástica Indiana</u>, vol. 4. Edited by Joaquín García Icazbalceta. Mexico City: Editorial Chávez Hayhoe, 1945.

Oroz, Pedro; Mendieta, Gerónimo de; and Suárez, Francisco. <u>Relación de la Descripción de la Provincia del Santo Evangelio que es en las Indias Occidentales que Llaman la Nueva España</u>. Edited by Fidel de J. Chavet. Mexico City: Aguilar Reyes, 1947.

Torquemada, Fray Juan de. <u>Monarquía Indiana</u>, vol. 3. Mexico City: Editorial Porrua, 1969.

CONFORMITY BEHAVIOR REFLECTED IN THE
MUSICAL PREFERENCE OF ADOLESCENTS*

Howard G. Inglefield**

The research in adolescent musical preferences
has been mostly descriptive in nature. Such studies
by Baumann(1), Erneston(2), Nash(3), Rogers(4),
and Rubin(5) have described the stated musical preferences of particular age or socio-economic levels
in group settings. Many social and psychological
determinants of the stated musical preference of an
individual cannot be studied in group settings using
only questionnaire data. The social nature of musical preferences, especially in the adolescent sub-
culture, suggests that they are the end result of
a complex set of social interactions between the
individual and his environment. These interactions
must be isolated and studied separately, along with
the individual's relevant personality variables,
before the socio-psychological nature of his musical
preferences can be described.

The peer group is often identified as one of
the most influential factors in the adolescent sub-
culture. According to Parsons and Bales:(6)

> The family offers a wide range of role par-
> ticipations only for the young child. He must
> learn by actual participation, progressively
> more roles than his family of orientation can
> offer him. It is at this point that peer

---

* Reprinted by permission of Howard G. Inglefield and <u>Contributions to Music Education</u>, No. 1
(Fall, 1972), pp. 56-65.

** This article is based on the author's doctoral dissertation, <u>The Relationship of Selected
Personality Variables to Conformity Behavior Reflected in the Musical Preferences of Adolescents
when Exposed to Peer Group Influences</u> (Columbus,
Ohio: The Ohio State University, 1968).

group and school assume paramount importance.

In a discussion of teenage musical preferences,
Riesman(7) describes the social structures of the
teenager:

> When he listens to music, even if no one else
> is around, he listens in a context of
> imaginary "others"--his listening is indeed
> often an effort to establish connection with
> them. In general what he perceives in the
> mass media is framed by his perception of the
> peer groups to which he belongs. These groups
> not only rate the tunes but select for their
> members in more subtle ways what is to be
> "heard" in each tune. It is the pressure of
> conformity with the group that invites and
> compels the individual to have recourse to
> the media both in order to learn from them
> what the group expects and to identify with
> the group by sharing a common focus for atten-
> tion and talk.

The apparent strength of peer group influences
upon the adolescent sub-group suggests that the
stated musical preferences of the individual adolescent may be the result of conformity behavior induced
by peer group pressure. Considering this hypothesis,
the following questions are relevant:

1. Do the stated musical preferences of individual adolescents tend to conform to the stated
musical preferences of the adolescent's peer group?
2. Are selected personality variables of the
adolescent related to his conformity behavior as
reflected in stated musical preferences?
3. What conformity behavior differences in
musical preferences occur when the adolescent is
influenced by various types of peer groups?
4. What conformity behavior differences in
musical preferences occur between various types of
musical stimuli?

This study was an investigation of conformity
behavior as a factor in the formation and fluctua-
tion of adolescent musical preferences. Musical
preference conformity was studied in relation to
(1) influence pressure exerted by various types of

peer leaders, (2) selected personality variables of the subjects, and (3) various types of musical stimuli.

Method

Selection of Personnel

The Sample.--The personnel for this study were selected from the entire population of the grade 9B students in a junior high school in Milwaukee, Wisconsin. From this population of 378, 18 experimental subjects, 6 control subjects, and 67 peer group leaders were selected.

The Subjects.--Eighteen experimental subjects were chosen for the following logistical reason: each experimental subject underwent two periods of experimentation, or a total of thirty-six periods for all experimental subjects. The addition of a pretest period for all subjects and the posttest for the control subjects raised the total periods of testing to thirty-eight. The school administration preferred that the experimentation time-span be limited to approximately one week, or thirty-five school periods.

A group of potential subjects was chosen first on the basis of personality variables. Representative of the many personality variables operating in the conformity behavior literature, the following three were selected as variables in this study: (1) inner-otherdirectedness, (2) need for social approval, and (3) independence.

Several studies have shown significant relationships between inner-otherdirectedness and conformity behavior. Studies of interest in this area are by Centers(8), Back and Davis(9), and Gross(10). Kassarjian(11), conversely, found no relationship between her I-O scale and conformity behavior in a social pressure experiment. The Kassarjian Inner-otherdirectedness Scale(12) was modified for use in this study to identify innerdirected and otherdirected subjects.

Strickland and Crowne(13) identified need for social approval as a significant factor in conformity behavior. Their scale, the Crowne-Marlowe Social Desirability Scale(14), was modified for use in this study to identify subjects with high need for social approval and subjects with low need for social approval.

Bradbard(15) and Barron(16) identified significant relationships between independence and conformity behavior. Their scale, the Barron Independence Scale(17), was modified for use in this study to identify independent subjects and dependent subjects.

The group of potential subjects included those scoring extremely high or extremely low on each of the above scales. The cut-off points were approximately the second standard deviation above and below the mean of each scale, thus eliminating about ninety-five percent of the population.

The final twenty-four experimental and control subjects (eighteen experimental, six control) were selected using the following criteria:

1. All potential subjects with intelligence quotients beyond the "normal" range of 88 to 112 were eliminated. The data were obtained from school records of Lorge-Thorndike tests or interpolated from Differential Aptitude Test scores.
2. A Musical Background questionnaire was administered by the school counselor. An attempt was made to equalize the musical background of the final group of subjects.
3. The socio-economic status of the subjects was assumed to be relatively homogeneous because only one school constituted the sample. A review of parent occupation ratings based on Clarke's revision of the North-Hatt Occupational Prestige Scale(18) determined that no extreme socio-economic levels existed in the final group of subjects.

The Control Group.--One subject from each personality variable extreme was selected at random to form the control group of six subjects.

The Peer Group Leaders.--A Leadership Questionnaire was developed in which the experimental subjects were asked to choose from a list of peer group leader types those types that were most and least important to them. This Leadership Questionnaire was administered by the school counselor. To insure as much difference in influence pressure as

possible, the most important and least important
were chosen as peer influence groups for this study.
These were "social leaders" (most important) and
"rebel leaders" (least important). It was necessary
to learn from the experimental subjects themselves
which individuals they considered as leaders in
these two categories. In another questionnaire,
the subjects were asked to list names of leaders in
each category. These peer leaders were used to
furnish influence pressure in the experiments.

Materials

The Personality Scale Modifications.--The
personality scales used in this study were all
originally constructed using college-age populations.
The scales were modified to be relevant to the ninth
grade level in the following ways:

1. The vocabulary level was revised to the
ninth grade level.
2. The revised scales were pretested in an
independent, random sample of ninth grade students
in a nearby school. The clarity of the vocabulary
was established.
3. A Pearson correlation using the split-half
method established the internal reliability of each
scale. The results are shown in Table 1. In each
case, except the Barron scale, the revised reliability compared favorably with the original scale.

TABLE 1

PERSONALITY SCALES: ORIGINAL AND
REVISED FORM RELIABILITY

Scale	Orig. Form Reliability	Rev. Form Reliability
Kassarjian I-O Scale	.85	.74
Crowne-Marlowe S.D. Scale	.89	.71
Barron Independence Scale	.88	.55

The Musical Preference Inventory.--The important responses in this study were not the level
of preference for the musical examples as the end
result; the important data were the changes in
preference level induced by peer leader influence.

The Musical Preference Inventory did not attempt to test the entire range of musical experience but rather contained four distinct and well-established categories of music representative of a wide range of musical experience.

The categories of music presented were "classical" music(19), jazz music, folk music, and rock music. Eight examples from each category were recorded in random order on magnetic tape. The performers were selected from well-known performers at that time. To insure the validity of the categories of music to the ninth grade level, the M.P.I. was played for a sample of sixty ninth grade students in a nearby school. The students identified the musical category of the examples with ninety-nine percent accuracy.

The Electric Response Units.--As an experimental control, it was necessary to eliminate extraneous visual and aural influences. This was accomplished by (1) separating the participants with screens, (2) instructing them to make no sounds, and (3) providing a non-verbal response system. This system had the following features:

1. It allowed the experimenter to furnish predetermined influence responses to the subject. The subject assumed that the responses were supplied by the peer leaders.
2. It allowed the experimenter to know and record the subject's response.
3. It allowed the peer leaders to know each other's responses as well as a spurious response of the subject which was actually supplied by the experimenter.

It was determined that interconnected light and switch panels would meet these requirements and the Electric Response Units were constructed.

The Experiment

The Pretest.--The validity of the experiment depended, in part, on the success of obtaining true musical preference responses to the M.P.I. from all subjects in the pretest. It was conducted in a setting of relative isolation, the subjects being seated approximately twenty-five feet apart in the school cafeteria. All subjects, after listening to an example, marked an appropriate blank indicating his preference according to the following five point scale:

1. I like it very much.
2. I like it.
3. I neither like nor dislike it.
4. I dislike it.
5. I dislike it very much.

The Experimental Posttests.--Each experimental subject participated in two additional hearings of the M.P.I.; each was in the presence of three peer leaders. The first was in the presence of social leaders; the second in the presence of rebel leaders. Following each musical example, the participants were asked--one at a time--to indicate their preference by activating the appropriate switch on their Electric Response Unit. The subject was asked to respond last in all but four instances. Whenever a peer leader responded, a predetermined light showed on the subject's Electric Response Unit which was activated by the experimenter. In this way, an attempt was made to influence the subject to the extent that he would change his pretest response to a conforming response. When the subject responded, the experimenter activated an appropriate response light on the peer leaders' response units. The participants accepted the procedures at face value without question.

The Control Posttest.--Following the experimental posttests, the M.P.I. was played for the control subjects under the same conditions as the pretest.

Scoring of Response Variations.--The data obtained in this study concerned musical preference response changes. The data were quantified as the relationship of the amount of musical preference change to the amount of peer leader influence exerted. The former factor was designated the Conformity Difference Score (C.D.S.); the latter, the Influence Difference Score (I.D.S.).

The C.D.S., if scored positively, was the difference in points, on the five point scale, between the pretest and experimental posttest scores occuring toward the influence response for a single M.P.I. item. The positive C.D.S. described a conforming response change.

The I.D.S. was the difference in points between the experimental subjects' pretest response and the mean of the three influence responses for that item.

The relation of the C.D.S. to the I.D.S. was quantified as the Conformity Score (C.S.), using the following formula:

$$C.S. = \frac{C.D.S.}{I.D.S.} \times (100)$$

The following example illustrates the calculation of the C.S. for one musical example:

On the five point scale, the experimental subject made a "2" response (I like it) in the pretest (represented by "P"). In the experimental posttest, he made a "4" response (I dislike it) as indicated by E. The subject had been influenced by two "5" and one "4" responses as indicated by "X". The I.D.S. was 2.6; the C.D.S. was 2.0; the C.S. was 77.

	(like very)	(like)	(neither)	(dislike)	(disl. very)
Response Scale:	1	2	3	4	5

Subject Responses:

P ← — — — — — → E
  C.D.S. = 2.0

X⟩ ← XX
I.D.S. = 2.6

Mean = 4.6

$$C.S. = \frac{2.0}{2.6} = .77 \times (100) = 77$$

Results

The data in all tests were in the form of Conformity Scores (C.S.). The tests for determining the significant difference between the mean C.S. of each hypothesized data group was the t test. In each case, the samples were tested for difference, a basic assumption of the t test. The results of the four primary hypotheses areas follow:

1. It was hypothesized that there would be no significant difference in the amount of conformity behavior between the experimental subjects and the control subjects. The rejection of the null hypothesis required a t of 3.55 with P = .001. The data are summarized in Table 2.

TABLE 2

TEST FOR DIFFERENCE BETWEEN THE MEANS:
EXPERIMENTAL AND CONTROL SUBJECTS

Source	N	X	SDX	DF	t	P
Experimental	36	29.3				
			3.6	40	5.56	.001
Control	6	9.3				

The t was significant at the .001 level: the null hypothesis was rejected. The mean conformity score of the experimental subjects was significantly higher than that of the control subjects.

2. It was hypothesized that there would be no significant difference in the amount of conformity between the extremes of each personality type. The rejection of the null hypothesis required a t of 2.57 with P = .05. The data are summarized in Table 3. The dependent-independent t was significant at the .05 level. The only significant difference in conformity behavior between personality extremes was between dependent and independent subjects where dependent subjects conformed significantly more than independent subjects.

3. It was hypothesized that there would be no significant difference between subjects responding in the presence of rebel leaders. The rejection of the null hypothesis required a t of 2.11 with P = .05. The data are summarized in Table 4.

The t was significant at the .05 level; the null hypothesis was rejected. Experimental subjects responding in the presence of social leaders

113

TABLE 3

TEST FOR DIFFERENCE BETWEEN THE MEANS:
PERSONALITY EXTREMES

Source	N	X	SDX	DF	t	P
Otherdirected	6	69.8	7.55	5	1.26	N.S.
Innerdirected	6	60.2				
High Social Approval Need	6	62.5	5.3	5	.79	N.S.
Low Social Approval Need	6	58.3				
Dependent	6	88.7	11.9	5	2.86	.05
Independent	6	54.7				

TABLE 4

TEST FOR DIFFERENCE BETWEEN THE MEANS:
SOCIAL AND REBEL LEADER DATA

Source	N	X	SDX	DF	t	P
Social Leaders	18	67.4	1.73	17	2.31	.05
Rebel Leaders	18	63.4				

conformed significantly more than experimental subjects responding in the presence of rebel leaders.

4. It was hypothesized that there would be no
significant difference in conformity behavior between subjects responding to classical music, jazz
music, rock music, and folk music. The rejection of
the null hypothesis required a t of 2.03 with P = .05,
a t of 3.6 with P = .001. The data are summarized
in Table 5.

TABLE 5

TEST FOR DIFFERENCE BETWEEN THE MEANS:
CATEGORIES OF MUSIC

Source	N	X	SDX	DF	t	P
Classical Music	36	42.3	1.41	35	10.0	.001
Jazz Music	36	56.4				
Jazz Music	36	56.4	2.06	35	4.1	.001
Rock Music	36	47.9				
Classical Music	36	42.3	1.5	35	3.78	.001
Rock Music	36	47.9				
Classical Music	36	42.3	1.72	35	4.84	.001
Folk Music	36	50.6				
Jazz Music	36	56.4	2.3	35	2.5	.05
Folk Music	36	50.6				
Folk Music	36	50.6	1.0	36	2.67	.05
Rock Music	36	47.9				

All t scores were significant at the .001 or
.05 level; the null hypothesis was rejected. There
were significant differences in the amount of conformity behavior when responding to different types
of music.

Principal Findings and Conclusions

It was found at the .001 level of significance
that all experimental subjects exhibited overall
conformity behavior in their musical preferences when
exposed to peer leader influence. This finding is a
very significant factor in the understanding of the
social nature of teenage musical preferences.

It was found at the .05 level of significance that dependent subjects conformed more than independent subjects. This suggests that the <u>Barron Independence Scale</u> is a valid predictor of musical preference conformity behavior. Also, the differences in conformity behavior between personality types, although not always statistically significant, always occurred in the empirically logical direction; the otherdirected subjects conformed more than innerdirected, the high social approval need subjects more than the low need, the dependent more than the independent. This confirms the contention that the variables of inner-otherdirection, need for social approval, and relative independence are all operating variables in musical preference conformity behavior.

It was found at the .05 level of significance that subjects conformed more in the presence of social leaders than in the presence of rebel leaders. This confirms the fact that the ninth grade subjects in this study could accurately predict the relative amounts of influence of various types of peer leaders in their school environment.

It was found at either the .001 level or the .05 level of significance that the subjects conformed most when responding to jazz music, next to folk music, thirdly to rock music, and least to classical music. This finding may be interpreted as an indication of the relative stability of the subject's musical preferences.

The subjects in this study were very susceptible to conforming pressure when responding to jazz music; their preferences for jazz music are very unstable. This may be explained by the fact that the jazz idiom is not generally a part of the adolescent musical environment; it is more an adult medium. At the other extreme, the subjects' responses to classical music were relatively stable. Most classical music responses were well established negative responses and not likely to change under peer group pressure.

Footnotes

(1) V. H. Baumann, _Socioeconomic Status and the Musical Preferences of Teenagers_ (doctoral dissertation, University of Southern California, 1958).

(2) N. Erneston, _A Study to Determine the Effect of Musical Experience and Mental Ability on the Formation of Musical Taste_ (doctoral dissertation, Florida State University, 1961).

(3) L. P. Nash, _The Enjoyment of Music by Junior High School Students: Their Responses to Five Methods of Presenting Recorded Music_ (doctoral dissertation, University of California, 1962).

(4) V. R. Rogers, _Children's Expressed Musical Preferences at Selected Grade Levels_ (doctoral dissertation, Syracuse University, 1956).

(5) L. Rubin, _The Effects of Musical Experience on Musical Discrimination and Musical Preferences_ (doctoral dissertation, University of California, 1952).

(6) T. Parsons and R. F. Bales, _Family, Socialization and Interaction Process_ (London: Routledge and Kegan Paul, 1956), p. 38.

(7) D. Riesman, _Individualism Reconsidered_ (Glencoe, Ill.: The Free Press, 1954), p. 189.

(8) R. Centers, "Social Character and Conformity: A Differential in Susceptibility to Social Influence," _Journal of Social Psychology_, LX (1964): 343-349.

(9) K. W. Back and K. E. Davis, "Some Personal and Situational Factors Relevant to the Consistency and Prediction of Conforming Behavior," _Sociometry_, XXVIII (1965): 227-240.

(10) H. W. Gross, _The Relationship between Insecurity, Self-acceptance, Otherdirection, and Conformity under Conditions of Differential Social Pressure_ (doctoral dissertation, University of Buffalo, 1959).

(11) W. M. Kassarjian, A Study of Riesman's Theory of Social Character (doctoral dissertation, University of California, Los Angeles, 1960).

(12) Kassarjian, 1960. A discussion of the scale modifications is presented under Materials.

(13) B. R. Strickland and D. P. Crown, "Conformity under Conditions of Simulated Group Pressure as a Function of Need for Social Approval," Journal of Social Psychology, LVIII (1962): 171-181.

(14) Strickland and Crowne, 1962.

(15) Bradbard, Dependence, Denial of Dependence, and Group Conformity (doctoral dissertation, Boston University, 1964).

(16) F. Barron, "Some Personality Concepts of Independence of Judgment," Journal of Personality, XXI (1953): 287-297.

(17) Barron, 1953.

(18) A. C. Clarke, The Use of Leisure and Its Relation to Social Stratification (doctoral dissertation, The Ohio State University, 1955), p. 301.

(19) A convenient and popular synonym for serious art music.

A CASE STUDY OF A CHROMESTHETIC*

Paul A. Haack
Rudolf E. Radocy

Abstract

D, a middle-aged female art educator, exem-
plifies the phenomenon of chromesthesia or "color
hearing," a form of synesthesia in whîch a tone
elicits a visual color experience as well as an
auditory sensation. Extensive interviews and tests
with music stimuli over a five-year period revealed
a remarkable range and consistency of tone-color
linkages. Absolute pitch, which D possesses independently of her chromesthesia, showed less stability than the chromesthesia. Synesthesia, while
not unnatural, rarely is demonstrated because of
societal constraints in childhood. Potential
learning problems are revealed that should be considered in the development of instructional programs. Also, individual perceptual differences
may significantly influence learning style.

In synesthesia a person responds to one
stimulus in more than one sensory mode simultaneously (Radocy and Boyle, 1979, pp. 323-324).
Chromesthesia, in the form of "color hearing," is a
type of synesthesia in which tone elicits a color
as well as an auditory sensation.

Synesthetic phenomena may seem bizarre or
incredulous to those who never have experienced
them, but synesthesia may not be rare. Wilentz
(1968, p. 316) noted one authority's estimate that
14% of men and 31% of women experienced some sort of

---

* Copyright (c) 1981 by The Music Educators
National Conference. Reprinted by permission of Paul
A. Haack and Rudolf E. Radocy and the Journal of Research in Music Education, Vol. 29, No. 2 (Summer,
1981), pp. 85-90.

synesthetic sensation. Marks (1975) was able to document vowel-color chromesthetic linkages from over 400 people. Synesthesia may be a more normal than abnormal phenomenon in the sense of "natural" sensory processing, which dissipates in many people because of a lack of reinforcement and sociocultural expectancies. After all, one is "supposed" to hear a tone, not see it.

Studies of synesthetic experiences may be confounded by studies of verbal association between sound and color. In one study (Omwake, 1940), 555 school children matched red, blue, black, or yellow to eight tones and four compositions. While there was variability, the dominant color associations for the eight tones were G_1 and C_2-black, $F\#_3$ and G_3-blue, $C\#_5$-yellow, D_5-blue, E_5-red, and A_5-yellow. A melancholy melody elicited a dominant association of black; a lullaby was blue; a march was red, and ballet music was yellow.

In another association study, Simpson, Quinn and Ausubel (1956) had 995 elementary school children indicate whether violet, blue, green, yellow, orange, or red went with tones of 125; 250; 1,000; 4,000; 8,000; and 12,000 Hz at 40 and 50 db SPL (Sound Pressure Level). The higher tones tended to elicit associations with yellow and green. Red and orange were linked with 1,000 Hz; blue and violet generally were suggested by the low tones. No color elicited a majority of associations for any particular tone.

Karwoski and Odbert (1938) identified 34 subjects from an initial subject group of 274 who, upon intensive individual study, revealed three levels of synesthesia experienced in listening to popular music excerpts. Thirteen people tended to see vague patterns of colors. Twelve saw relatively concrete images based on past experiences. Nine saw highly detailed color abstractions. Five of those nine maintained a high degree of similarity (as indicated by drawings) between listening sessions eight months apart. Such occurrences certainly are more than verbal associations.

According to Marks (1975), simultaneous tone-color sensations are idiosyncratic, although chromesthetic effects are consistent for each individual. Curiously, vowel-color sensations appear

consistent across individual respondents: low
frequency sounds are accompanied by dark colors;
bright colors accompany high frequency sounds. Consistent observed linkages include red and yellow for
"ah," white for "ay," red and black for a long "o,"
and blue, brown, and black for "oo" (as in "boot").

Individual case studies include a thirty-one
year old woman and her sister who were reported to
experience colors with all sounds (Ostwald, 1964).
Similarly, two pianists, each having absolute pitch,
discovered that they had simultaneous tone-color
perceptions (Carroll and Greenberg, 1961). In
another case, McCluskey (1975) discussed the difficulty of trying to convey through words, photographs,
and drawings the way his synesthetic wife "sees"
the pronunciation of her name or nonlinguistic
sounds because of the lack of depth, perspective,
and a characteristic shimmering.

How many teachers are able to identify and
understand chromesthetic individuals in their
classes and help such students cope with their
synesthetic tendencies? Unique modes of perception
present unique problems of instruction. In today's
multimedia world there is a growing realization
that varying levels of synesthetic experiences may
not be rare. Considering the elusive nature of the
synesthetic phenomenon, intensive clinical study of
documented cases is required to enhance understanding.

The Case

The following study of a chromesthetic individual is based on information obtained from four
interviews and testing sessions conducted during
the period 1974-79. Consistency of response to
identical stimuli throughout the period was sought
and documented as a means of internal validity.
This was accomplished by means of structured interviews and testing sessions wherein responses were
recorded via audio tape and data assessment forms
for comparative analyses over time. The format is
unique among studies of chromesthesia in its longitudinal approach, which among other things lent
assurance that the multisensory sensations the
subject reported are not merely verbal associations.

121

The Subject

D, a middle-aged woman, was born and raised in the central United States and continues to reside in that region. She grew up in, and continues to live in a middle-class environment.

When she was approximately five years old, D began to show interest in singing, piano, and art. She was provided with many years of piano lessons and continued this instruction during her first two years of college. At this time she also elected two music fundamentals courses and one music history course. Her college degrees, however, were in art and art education, and her professional work has been in the field of art education. D recalls becoming conscious of her chromesthesia during grade school while doing art work and listening to music. She cannot specify the exact year. She regarded the chromesthetic phenomenon as an ordinary condition, similar to wearing glasses or having a dark complexion. To her knowledge, no ancestors or other relatives are chromesthetic or synesthetic in any way.

D also has absolute pitch and believes that there may be some connection between this phenomenon and chromesthesia: "I knew that an A was an A and could see lavender with it. I think this happened to me as a child at one and the same time. I don't remember one without the other." She says that she names tones directly from their sound and not via their color references, but a tone triggers both a name and a color sensation.

For D, the chromesthetic effect occurs regardless of whether her eyes are open or closed. Her color sensations are "not something seen outside, like spots on a wall, but more internal."

Pitch Related Phenomena

D reported that the following pitch-color relationships are experienced consistently: A, lavender; B, orange; C, red; D, blue; E, green; F, brown; and G, black. She noted that the primary color yellow is absent: "I never see yellow much. I don't paint with yellow either, but it is my favorite color."

D's pitch-color associations do not vary in basic hue from octave to octave; however, high octaves of a tone tend to evoke a lighter color value, and lower octaves a darker value. In general the colors were said to be "strongest" or most saturated in the range from two octaves below middle C to one octave above.

"Black key" pitches were reported to elicit a greater color intensity. For example, D# tended to be blue-green, but a more intense color than either D (blue) or E (green). This phenomenon was constant regardless of the key signature in which the pitches were located; that is, B♭ in the tonally established and announced key of F major evoked greater color intensity, just as the D# in B major did.

Atonal Pitch Phenomena

D was asked to indicate her color hearing responses to excerpts from tonal folk melodies and to investigator-contrived atonal sequences. Atonal sequences resulted in the same pitch-color relationships as did sounds in the tonal context.

D was asked also to respond to a "siren scale" sequence (C → G ⤳ A ⤳ C), which was produced on the variable pitch keyboard of a Johnson Intonation Trainer. She reported that the appropriate colors were experienced when the siren tone was proximate to established (Western tuning, keyboard) pitches; however, these colors tended to be encroached upon by white "interference" at the approximate quarter-tone points, after which the next appropriate color would emerge. In other words, a bright white interference was reported as the siren tone deviated from the standard keyboard pitches. This may be a form of categorical perception (Siegel and Siegel, 1977).

Arpeggios and Harmonic Phenomena

Rapidly arpeggiated, major chord tone sequences (sixteenth notes at 130 beats per minute) were played for D, and her chromesthetic response involved rapid flashes of colors, "somewhat like fireworks exploding." For many of the arpeggios, one color tended to predominate, with the others flashing around it. The predominant color tended

to be either that related to the root of the arpeggiated chord or the first (accented) tone of the
arpeggio.

Color sensations resulting from hearing harmony are consistent with the foregoing information.
When a number of pitches were sounding simultaneously, D reported seeing pointilistic dots of
color. Each pitch tended to be represented, and
the colors did not fuse but maintained their
identity.

Loudness, Timbre, Tempo, and Envelope Phenomena

Increases in loudness resulted in the related
color or colors becoming more saturated or
"stronger," and vice versa. This was true whether
changes were sudden or gradual.

Based on her recollection of a variety of
recent music experiences, D did not feel that differing timbres resulted in appreciably stronger or
weaker color effects. She reported that tones from
a piano do not elicit different effects regarding
color strength than do other types or combinations
of timbres.

On the other hand, when D heard the same
fundamental pitch played with different timbre
contexts, as produced by gross spectral differences, she reported that differing visual sensations
resulted from concentration on the tone, although
the basic hue remained the same. A fairly pure
middle C brought about a rather dull red. When the
timbre was altered to include some octave content,
the red tended to "lighten and brighten" a bit:
two red stripes varying in value were reported to
run parallel to and merge with one another. When a
still more complex timbre, one with third partial
content in addition to the octave, was presented,
an added line of dark blue to light black was reported. The Johnson Intonation Trainer again was
used as the tone generator for this aspect of the
inquiry, and while most listeners would not be
able to analyze the harmonic content of the tones
presented, D did so in a qualitative way, in terms
of her color sensations, though probably not as a
direct result of conscious aural acuity.

D's color responses remained essentially the same regardless of tempi and tonal envelopes. However, these variables, along with timbre and combinations of timbres, tended to influence the shapes of the color phenomena being experienced. Under varying circumstances "patches," "puffs," "fingers," rectangles, lines, and "pointilistic sparkles" were experienced.

Conflictual Phenomena

When hearing choral music, including excerpts wherein the name of a color not conforming to the synesthetically perceived color was sung, D encountered no problem. She reported simply that she never has attended to the words in music, only the tones and colors.

Attendance at a light show or similar production, wherein colors programmed to the music conflicted with her own associations, could cause her distress. "It bothers me intensely . . . . I feel it in my chest mostly. It's like a reverberation." D reported the same unpleasant chest reverberation sensation when she was exposed to a unison mistuned by 15 to 20 cents.

Another problem concerned painting to music. D reported that as part of an undergraduate art course she had created a series of paintings while listening to various kinds of music. This was done at the urging of her instructor, with the intent that her chromesthesia would influence the paintings. "I didn't feel good about it; I felt pressured. The paintings were abstracts; I was not pleased with them."

D reported one other problem relating to chromesthesia: "It is a handicap when I listed to music because I constantly listen for the individual tones themselves. Rather than listening to the overall thing, I dissect it . . . into notes and colors." It is clear to the investigators that D enjoys attending concerts and other music events, but she reports being exhausted afterward.

Finally, when D was asked to listen to a musical passage and to try with as much effort as possible to block or otherwise eliminate the color experience, she could not.

Conclusions

Five years after first noting D's specific pitch-color perceptions, she was retested with sound stimuli. Her color responses to each of the given pitches were 100% consistent with her earlier responses.

She had lost some of her certainty about the names of the pitches she was hearing, at least temporarily. She felt that some recent illnesses and being away from music making for a while may have caused some deterioration in her absolute pitch abilities; however, even when she was not as certain of the names of the pitches she was hearing, she responded absolutely with regard to the evoked color perceptions.

For D, the little known or understood chromesthetic phenomenon is a very real, consistent, and enduring one. Perhaps this information and that from related studies can enhance music educators' awareness regarding one aspect of the many individual differences found among their students. Unique and personal modes of perception may significantly influence learning style, and those concerned with instruction and theories thereof must accommodate such variations. Possible learning advantages and particularly some of the problems described above need to be considered in the ongoing development of instructional systems and strategies.

References

Carroll, J. B., and Greenberg, J. H. "Two Cases of Synesthesia for Color and Musical Tonality Associated with Absolute Pitch Ability." Perceptual and Motor Skills 13 (1961): 48.

Karwoski, T. F., and Odbert, H. S. "Color-music." Psychological Monographs 50, 2 (1938) (Whole No. 222).

Marks, L. E. "Synesthesia: The Lucky People with Mixed-up Senses." Psychology Today 9 (1): 48-52.

McCluskey, K. W.   "Diary of a Synesthetic: Chris-
    tina's Color-drenched World."   <u>Psychology</u>
    <u>Today</u> <u>9</u>(1): 50-51.

Omwake, L.   "Visual Responses to Auditory Stimuli."
    <u>Journal of Applied Psychology</u> <u>24</u> (1940):
    468-481.

Ostwald, R. F. "Color Hearing." <u>Archives of</u>
    <u>General Psychiatry</u> <u>11</u> (1964): 40-47.

Radocy, R. E., and Boyle, J. D. <u>Psychological</u>
    <u>Foundations of Musical Behavior.</u> Springfield,
    Illinois: Charles C. Thomas, 1979.

Siegel, J. A., and Siegel, W.   "Categorical Per-
    ception of Tonal Intervals: Musicians Can't
    Tell Sharp from Flat." <u>Perception & Psycho-</u>
    <u>physics</u> <u>21</u> (1977): 399-407.

Simpson, R. H., Quinn, M., and Ausubel, D. P.
    "Synesthesia in Children: Association of
    Colors with Pure Tone Frequencies." <u>Journal</u>
    <u>of Genetic Psychology</u> <u>89</u> (1956): 95-103.

Wilentz, J. S.   <u>The Senses of Man</u>.   New York:
    Thomas Y. Crowell, 1968.

SELECTED INDEXES OF THE ACADEMIC AND PROFESSIONAL PREPARATION OF MUSIC SUPERVISORS IN CANADA*

Estelle R. Jorgensen

Abstract

The purpose of this baseline study was to describe indexes of the academic and professional preparation of music supervisors in Canada, with particular emphasis given to the effects of geographic region in Canada, music supervisor type, and jurisdiction size type on these indexes. The study constitutes a first step toward the generation of a theoretical model and subsequently, of a competency-based model of the academic and professional preparation of music supervisors. The study is based on descriptive data derived from a national questionnaire survey of music supervisors in Canada.

Administration is a basic element in the process of music education and an essential component in any theoretical formulation of music instruction. School music instruction does not proceed in isolation but takes place within a macroorganizational framework. The administration and supervision of school music forms a part of what Sidnell (1972) identifies as "the environment of instruction"; a "central variable" in music education research.

There have been relatively few research studies on school music supervision. Studies published in the Journal of Research in Music

Education include those by Banse (1956), Blakely (1960), Dawson (1972), Heller and Quatraro (1977), McQuerrey (1972), and Molnar (1955). Most research in the supervision and administration of school music consists of doctoral dissertations, which fall into several principle categories:

1. Descriptions and analyses of music supervision in selected jurisdictions in the United States (Cohen, 1963; Landon, 1959; Marsh, 1969; Maynard, 1958; Mills, 1975; Robinson, 1964; Thomas, 1957; Wheeler, 1967; Ziegler, 1970).
2. Descriptions and analyses of state music supervision in the United States (Gabriel, 1962; Kennard, 1974; Martin, 1960).
3. Comparative assessments of supervisory-administrative processes or analyses of supervisor roles in the United States (Foster, 1959; Henderson, 1959; Tuttle, 1971).

The literature is oriented toward the supervisor role, and specific supervisor tasks, such as building music curriculums and fiscal management. Bessom (1969), House (1973), Klotman (1973), and Weyland (1968) have illustrated such practically oriented studies. There is also a particular need for theoretical research, specifically, the development of theoretical models relating to aspects of music supervision. The question of the utility and feasibility of theoretical modeling in music education research has already been discussed by the author (Jorgensen, 1977a, 1977b, 1978).

Few national studies of school music in Canada have been conducted. Brown's (1960) landmark study of teacher certification in Canada is one example. But statistical information from the Canadian government relating specifically to school music supervision is sparse (Jorgensen, 1974), necessitating a baseline descriptive study of school music supervision in Canada.

With respect to the academic and professional preparation of music supervisors, five theoretical principles were formulated by the author in the light of extant educational administrative theory (Wiles, 1967; Zentner, 1973), music supervision in Berrien County, Michigan (Jorgensen, 1970). The following principles formed the basis of the instrument in the study.

1. A music supervisor should be well prepared academically and musically;
2. There is a distinctly different role for
music supervision and administration than for music
teaching, and this difference should be reflected
in professional preparation, specifically for the
music supervisor role;
3. Music supervisor credibility with music
teachers is influenced, in part, by evidence of
successful teaching experience by the music supervisor, both in terms of length of teaching experience and breadth of that experience;
4. Some degree of mobility among music
supervisors is useful in providing a variety of
perspectives from which music education may be
viewed and in avoiding a narrow provincialism and
an "in bred" music education system;
5. Ongoing professional musical and pedagogical activity by music supervisors is essential.

Procedures

A questionnaire survey of all music supervisors in Canada listed by Laughton (1974) was
conducted in January 1977. The base year for which
data was reported was 1976. The findings reported
are based on a sample of 79 returned questionnaires,
which represented a response rate of 43.2% from all
provinces in Canada.

The instrument was a 12-page questionnaire that
was refined over a six-year period (1970-1976),
following its use in a pilot study of music supervision in Berrien County, Michigan (Jorgensen, 1970).
A final questionnaire was prepared in November 1976
and mailed in January 1977. Follow-up letters were
mailed in February 1977 to respondents whose completed questionnaires had not been received. The
cut-off date for receipt of completed questionnaires
for inclusion in the study sample was May 31, 1977.

The questionnaire consisted of four sections.
Section I elicited information concerning the academic and professional preparation of music supervisors; Section II included statistical and historical information with respect to the jurisdictions
administered by music supervisors; Section III took
information about music supervisor functions,
attitudes about the supervisor role, and problems
faced in the supervision of jurisdictions; and

Section IV asked about joint planning of activities with other music supervisors. Pivotal questions ensured the development of a variety of profiles for the sample.

Based on the five theoretical principles of academic and professional preparation of music supervisors, the following indexes were selected.

1. Academic qualifications: The variations across Canada in length of preuniversity schooling, together with the various types of degrees, teaching certificates, and music diplomas acquired necessitated the use of a simple categorization in terms of highest academic qualification held.

2. Preparation in administrative theory: The index chosen was the number of full-year university courses in administration or supervision taken.

3. Teaching experience: The two indexes chosen were the number of years of teaching experience (excluding supervisory experience), and the number of categories of teaching experience, indicating the breadth of the supervisor's teaching experience. Eight categories were identified: elementary, junior high school choral, junior high school instrumental, junior high school general music, senior high school choral, senior high school instrumental, senior high school academic music (history, theory), and other teaching experience.

4. Mobility: The criterion for this index was the number of jurisdictions in which the music supervisor had gained teaching or supervisory experience.

5. Professional activity: Two indexes were chosen--the number of memberships held in music-oriented professional associations and the number of memberships held in education-oriented professional associations. Music-oriented associations were defined as associations that specifically mentioned music or one aspect of music in their titles. Similarly, education-oriented associations were defined as associations (excluding music associations) that specifically mentioned education or one aspect of education in their titles.

Responses were categorized as follows.

1. Music supervisor--Type I: The chief administrative officer responsible for school music

in a given jurisdiction, and whose function includes both the hiring and dismissal of music teachers.

2. Music supervisor--Type II: The chief administrative officer responsible for school music in a given jurisdiction, who is responsible for either the hiring or dismissal of music teachers.

3. Music supervisor--Type III (music consultant): The chief administrative officer responsible for school music in a given jurisdiction, who has no function with respect to hiring or dismissal of music teachers.

4. Jurisdiction: The school board or province (state) over which the supervisor administers the school music program.

5. Jurisdiction--Size type I: A jurisdiction having a minimum of 29 music specialists (a minimum of 11 secondary school specialists); a minimum of 1,900 students in secondary school music programs; and music specialists at both the elementary and secondary levels.

6. Jurisdiction--Size type II: A jurisdiction having five and less than 11 music specialists at the secondary level; and a minimum of 500 students in secondary school music programs.

7. Jurisdiction--Size type III: A jurisdiction having less than five secondary school music specialists and less than 500 students in secondary school music programs.

8. Geographic region: A tract of country with more-or-less definitely marked boundaries or characteristics defined by politico-geographic criteria. Five regions in Canada were identified in this study as follows: British Columbia, the Prairie Provinces, Ontario, Quebec, and the Maritime Provinces. The Northwest Territories and the Yukon were not included in the present study.

In terms of condition of appraisal, a preliminary descriptive statistical analysis constituting an overview of the findings was conducted and has been reported by the author (Jorgensen, 1978). Subsequently, a more systematic statistical analysis of the data was undertaken and the present report constitutes a part of this follow-up research.

132

Results

Table 1 profiles selected indexes of the academic and professional preparation of music supervisors in Canada. The preparation in administrative theory appeared to be low ($\overline{X}$ = 1.65 courses) and quite variable (SD = 2.11). Teaching experience appeared to be substantial ($\overline{X}$ = 14.53 years), although variable (SD = 8.37). Breadth of teaching experience appeared quite considerable ($\overline{X}$ = 5.25 of a possible eight categories). A low degree of mobility was indicated ($\overline{X}$ = 2.51 jurisdictions), although it varied significantly by geographic region in Canada. There also appeared to be a significantly lower participation in education-oriented associations than in music-oriented associations ($\overline{X}$ = 0.70 for education-oriented associations; $\overline{X}$ = 3.37 for music-oriented associations).

TABLE 1

INDEXES OF THE ACADEMIC AND PROFESSIONAL
PREPARATION OF MUSIC SUPERVISORS
IN CANADA

Indexes	Mean	SD
Highest academic qualification held[a]	1.85	0.86
No. of full-year administrative courses taken	1.65	2.11
Years of teaching experience	14.53	8.37
No. of categories of teaching experience	5.25	2.10
No. of jurisdictions in which teaching and supervisory experience gained	2.51	1.58
No. of memberships held in music-oriented professional associations	3.37	1.65
No. of memberships held in education-oriented professional associations	0.70	0.98

[a] Categories of academic qualifications were converted to numerical scores where:
1. Master's degree
2. Bachelor's degree
3. Teaching certificate
4. Music diploma

Table 2 shows selected indexes of academic and professional preparation of music supervisors by geographic region in Canada. A statistically significant difference by geographic region was found for number of years of teaching experience. Music supervisors in the Prairie Provinces had the lowest mean years of teaching experience ($\overline{X}$ = 10.1 years) followed by those in British Columbia ($\overline{X}$ = 13.7 years), Ontario ($\overline{X}$ = 16.2), Quebec ($\overline{X}$ = 18.8), and the Maritime Provinces ($\overline{X}$ = 19.7).

TABLE 2

CHI-SQUARE STATISTICS FOR SELECTED INDEXES OF
ACADEMIC AND PROFESSIONAL PREPARATION OF
MUSIC SUPERVISORS BY GEOGRAPHIC REGION

Indexes	χ^2	df	p
Highest academic qualification held[a]	17.30	12	
No. of full-year administrative courses taken	17.39	16	
Years of teaching experience	28.30	16	p < .05
No. of categories of teaching experience	34.98	28	
No. of jurisdictions in which teaching and supervisory experience gained	10.13	16	
No. of memberships in music-oriented professional associations	20.58	12	
No. of memberships in education-oriented professional associations	14.91	16	

Note.   Six comparisons were not significant (p > .05).
* Categories of academic qualifications were converted to numerical scores where:
1.   Master's degree
2.   Bachelor's degree
3.   Teaching certificate
4.   Music diploma

Table 3 lists selected indexes of academic and professional preparation of music supervisors by music supervisor type. A statistically significant difference by music supervisor type was found for number of memberships in music-oriented professional associations than was found for Type III music supervisors.

TABLE 3

CHI-SQUARE STATISTICS FOR SELECTED INDEXES OF
ACADEMIC AND PROFESSIONAL PREPARATION OF
MUSIC SUPERVISORS BY SUPERVISOR TYPE

Indexes	χ^2	df	p
Highest academic qualification held[a]	4.30	6	
No. of full-year administrative courses taken	7.71	8	
Years of teaching experience	5.93	8	
No. of categories of teaching experience	14.99	14	
No. of jurisdictions in which teaching and supervisory experience gained	10.27	8	
No. of memberships in music-oriented professional associations	16.38	6	p < .05
No. of memberships in education-oriented professional associations	13.10	8	

Note. Six comparisons were not significant (p > .05).
[a] Categories of academic qualifications were converted to numerical scores where:
1. Master's degree
2. Bachelor's degree
3. Teaching certificate
4. Music diploma

Table 4 shows selected indexes of academic and professional preparation of music supervisors by jurisdiction size type. Five out of the seven indexes did not reveal statistically significant differences by jurisdiction size type. A statistically significant difference by jurisdiction size type was found for highest academic qualification held and number of memberships in music-oriented professional associations. Table 5 shows the breakdown of the highest academic qualification held by music supervisors by jurisdiction size type. Academic qualifications of music supervisors were high in

135

size type I jurisdictions than in size type III jurisdictions. The range was narrower in numbers of memberships held in music-oriented associations by supervisors in size type I jurisdictions than in size type III jurisdictions.

TABLE 4

CHI-SQUARE STATISTICS FOR SELECTED INDEXES OF
ACADEMIC AND PROFESSIONAL PREPARATION OF
MUSIC SUPERVISORS BY JURISDICTION
SIZE TYPE

Indexes	χ^2	df	p
Highest academic qualification held[a]	12.83	12	$p < .05$
No. of full-year administrative courses taken	9.28	8	
Years of teaching experience	11.04	8	
No. of categories of teaching experience	13.72	14	
No. of jurisdictions in which teaching and supervisory experience gained	10.20	8	
No. of memberships in music-oriented professional associations	12.55	6	$p < .05$
No. of memberships in education-oriented professional associations	13.52	8	

Note. Five comparisons were not significant ($p > .05$).
[a] Categories of academic qualifications were converted to numerical scores where:
1. Master's degree
2. Bachelor's degree
3. Teaching certificate
4. Music diploma

Based on the results of this study, the following conclusions were reached:

1. The profile of academic and professional preparation of the typical music supervisor in Canada varies significantly in practice from the theoretical principles that characterize the

136

TABLE 5

BREAKDOWN OF HIGHEST ACADEMIC QUALIFICATIONS HELD BY MUSIC
SUPERVISORS BY JURISDICTION SIZE TYPE

Highest Academic Qualification Held	Jurisdiction Size Type							
	Type I		Type II		Type III		Total	
	f	%	f	%	f	%	f	%
Master's degree	8	53.3	8	33.3	9	23.7	25	32.5
Bachelor's degree	6	40.0	13	54.2	21	55.3	40	51.9
Teaching certificate					7	18.4	7	9.1
Music diploma	1	6.7	3	12.5	1	2.6	5	6.5
Total	15		24		38		77	

Note: Two missing scores.

137

academic and professional preparation of music supervisors. The differences occur in preparation in administrative theory, mobility, and the direction of professional activity (educational compared to music orientation).

2. Six out of the seven indexes in the profile of academic and professional preparation of music supervisors do not differ significantly by geographic region in Canada. The number of years teaching experience does vary significantly by geographic region in Canada.

3. Music supervisors in the Prairie Provinces have the lowest mean years of teaching experience, followed by British Columbia, Ontario, Quebec, and the Maritime Provinces, in order of increasing mean years of teaching experience.

4. Six out of the seven indexes in the profile of academic and professional preparation of music supervisors in Canada do not differ significantly by music supervisor type. The number of memberships in music-oriented professional associations does vary significantly by music supervisor type.

5. Type I and II music supervisors hold more memberships in music-oriented professional associations than do type III music supervisors.

6. Although five of the indexes of academic and professional preparation of music supervisors in Canada do not differ significantly by jurisdiction size type, two indexes do vary significantly--highest academic qualification held and number of memberships in music-oriented professional associations.

7. There is less spread in academic qualifications and music supervisors are better qualified academically in size type I jurisdictions than in size type II jurisdictions.

8. There is less spread in numbers of memberships held in music-oriented associations by supervisors in size type I jurisdictions than in size type III jurisdictions.

Discussion

A discrepancy between theory and practice in the profile of academic and professional preparation of the typical music supervisor in Canada was indicated from the findings of this study. Two elements that may be particularly important are the low degree of preparation for the role of supervisor and the low degree of orientation toward education associations as compared with the attitude toward music associations, which reflects a possible isolation from other related education or pedagogic concerns. Both factors can conceivably reduce the effectiveness of music supervision.

The findings also implied a considerable degree of homogeneity in the indexes of academic and professional preparation of music supervisors in Canada, despite the wide variation in geography, supervisor function and authority, and size of music programs administered across the country. The reasons for this homogeneity warrant further investigation. The use of refined indexes and more powerful statistical procedures in future investigations may reveal a greater degree of variation than that demonstrated in the present study.

Further, the study raises a number of issues that have far-reaching implications. First, there is potential for examining the variables of academic and professional preparation of music supervisors in a systematic way. In order to do this, however, the elements must be clearly conceptualized and formulated, and the indexes must reflect the dimensions of these elements. It should then be possible to develop "norms" for each of these indexes.

The next step in the study is to investigate the "mix" of elements of academic and professional preparation of music supervisors that will optimize supervisor effectiveness under specified conditions. This step involves two procedures. First, it is necessary to determine the supervisor role (operationalized in terms of a profile of specific tasks) that will ensure quality music instruction and the resultant student music achievement under specified conditions. Having determined the optimum combination of supervisor tasks, an evaluation of the relationship between the supervisor performance of these tasks and indexes of academic and professional

preparation is essential. Presumably, these findings will have direct relevance to a competency-
based approach to music supervision and to the
selection and preparation of music supervisors.

The politico-organizational environment in
which the supervisor works constitutes one important
condition that must be specified in determining the
optimal "mix" of elements of academic and professional preparation. To this end, it is essential
that data for subsequent studies by representative
of a wide variety of international jurisdictions.
Politico-organizational environments have been
classified into three types by the author on the
basis of executive responsibility for school music:
Type A--in which the federal or central government
has executive responsibility, for example, Hungary;
Type B--in which the state or provincial government
have executive responsibility, for example,
Australia; and Type C--in which local governments
have executive responsibility, as in the United
States and Canada. (Education in both countries
is a state or provincial power, but the executive
responsibility for education lies with the local
school boards.)

We might expect to find variation in the
academic and professional preparation of music
supervisors and in supervisor roles due to the differences in the nature and complexity of the three
politico-organizational environments. The extent
of this variation, however, requires further investigation.

The present study suggested four significant
areas for further research.

1. The refinement of a theoretical model of
academic and professional preparation of music
supervisors that is formulated at a high level of
generality and that provides a framework for subsequent investigations.
2. The experimental validation of a theoretical model of academic and professional preparation of music supervisors together with "norms" or
standards for model indexes and the development of
"metrics" to test these indexes.
3. The investigation of the relationship
between the academic and professional preparation

of music supervisors and their performance in the
field as music supervisors.

4. The development of a competency-based
model for the academic and professional preparation
of music supervisors (AERA, 1952; Aston and Lee,
1966; Biddle and Ellena, 1964; Burkhart, 1969; ERS,
1968, Klahn, 1965).

References

American Educational Research Association, Committee
on the Criteria of Teacher Effectiveness.
"Report of the Committee of Teacher Effectiveness." Review of Educational Research 22
(1952): 238-263.

Aston, A. W., and Lee, C. B. T. "Current Practises
in the Evaluation and Training of College
Teachers." The Educational Record 47 (1966):
361-371.

Banse, A. M. "Music Supervision in the Elementary
Schools of New York State." Journal of Research in Music Education 4 (1956): 26-32.

Biddle, B. J., and Ellena, W. J., eds. Contemporary
Research on Teacher Effectiveness. New York:
Holt, Rinehart and Winston, Inc., 1964.

Bessom, M. E. Supervising the Successful School
Music Program. West Nyack, N.Y.: Parker
Publishing Co., 1969.

Blakely, L. G. "The State Supervision of Music."
Journal of Research in Music Education 8 (1960):
99-109.

Brown, M. A. A Study of Teacher Education and
Certification in Teaching of Music in Canadian
Public Schools. Unpublished doctoral disser-
tation, Florida State University, 1960.

Burkhart, T. C., ed. The Assessment Revolution: New
Viewpoints for Teacher Evaluation. Albany,
N.Y.: Division of Teacher Education and
Certification, New York State Education De-
partment, 1969.

Cohen, S. G. "Supervision of Elementary School
    Music in Selected Districts of New York City."
    Unpublished doctoral dissertation, Ball State
    Teacher's College, 1964.

Dawson, N. E. "Roles of Music Supervisors in
    Selected School Districts." Journal of Re-
    search in Music Education 20 (1972): 397-402.

Educational Research Service. Evaluating Adminis-
    trative Performance, Educational Research
    Service Circular Number Seven. Washington,
    D.C.: American Association of School Adminis-
    trators and National Education Association,
    1968.

Foster, L. E. C. "Perceived Competencies of School
    Supervisors." Unpublished doctoral disserta-
    tion, Stanford University, 1959.

Gabriel, R. "Music Education and State Supervisory
    Services for Tennessee Public Schools."
    Unpublished doctoral dissertation, Florida
    State University, 1962.

Heller, R. W., and Quatraro, J. A. "Perceptions of
    Role Expectations and Performance of the
    Music Coordinator." Journal of Research in
    Music Education 25 (1977): 41-58.

Henderson, S. L. "Factors, Differences, Trends and
    Relationships in the Administration and Super-
    vision of Music in Fourteen Selected School
    Systems." Unpublished doctoral dissertation,
    State University of Iowa, 1959.

House, R. W. Administration in Music Education.
    Englewood Cliffs, N.J.: Prentice-Hall, Inc.,
    1973.

Jorgensen, E. R. "Report on a Pilot Study of Music
    Supervision in Berrien County, Michigan."
    Unpublished report available from the author,
    Faculty of Music, McGill University, 1974.

Jorgensen, E. R. "A Preliminary Statistical Analysis
    of Music Supervision in Canada." Unpublished
    paper available from the author, Faculty of
    Music, McGill University, 1974.

Jorgensen, E. R. A Critical Analysis of Selected
Aspects of Music Education. Calgary, Alberta,
Canada: Department of Educational Administra-
tion, Calgary, 1977.(a)

Jorgensen, E. R. "Some Observations on Research in
Music Education." Unpublished paper presented
to the Canadian Music Educators Association
Convention, Memorial University of Newfoundland, St. Johns, Newfoundland, May 1977.(b)

Jorgensen, E. R. "School Music Supervision in
Canada: A Questionnaire Survey." Unpublished
paper presented to the International Society
for Music Education, University of Western
Ontario, London, Ontario, August 1978.

Kennard, R. F. "The Role of State Music Supervision." Unpublished doctoral dissertation,
Brigham Young University, 1974.

Klahn, R. P., ed. Evaluation of Teacher Competency.
Milwaukee: Franklin, 1965.

Klotman, R. H. The School Music Administrator and
Supervisor: Catalysts for Change in Music
Education. Englewood Cliffs, N.J.: Prentice-
Hall, Inc., 1973.

Landon, J. W. "Music Supervision in California
City Schools." Unpublished doctoral dissertation, University of Southern California, 1959.

Laughton, W. A List of Music Consultants, Directors
and Music Supervisors. St. Catherines,
Ontario: Canadian Music Educators Association
Resource Centre, 1974.

Marsh, W. C. "The Role of the County Music Consultant in California." Unpublished doctoral
dissertation, University of Southern California, 1969.

Martin, J. H. "The Function and Responsibilities of
a State Music Supervisor for the State of
Arizona." Unpublished doctoral dissertation,
University of Arizona, 1960.

Maynard, C. "Music Supervision in Wilmington, Delaware: The Story of Ten Year Enterprise." Unpublished doctoral dissertation, Columbia University, 1958.

McQuerrey, L. "Duties and Activities of Music Supervisory Personnel in California." Journal of Research in Music Education 20 (1972): 379-384.

Mills, E. W. "The Role of Music Supervisors in the Public School Systems of Georgia." Unpublished doctoral dissertation, Florida State University, 1975.

Molnar, J. W. "The Establishment of the Music Supervisors National Conference, 1907-1910." Journal of Research in Music Education 3 (1955): 40-50.

Robinson, H. K. "Supervision and Administration of Music in the Public Elementary Schools of Indiana." Unpublished doctoral dissertation, Ball State Teachers' College, 1964.

Sidnell, R. "The Dimensions of Research in Music Education." Bulletin of the Council for Research in Music Education 29 (1972): 17-27.

Thomas, R. E. "A Report on Music Supervision in the Elementary Schools of Champaign, Illinois, 1954-1957." Unpublished doctoral dissertation, University of Illinois, 1957.

Tuttle, T. T. "An Analysis and Comparison of Two Modes of Music Supervision in the County School of Maryland." Unpublished doctoral dissertation, University of Maryland, 1971.

Weyland, R. H. A Guide to Effective Music Supervision. 2nd ed. Dubuque, Iowa: W. C. Brown Publishing Co., 1968.

Wheeler, J. F. "The Administration and Supervision of Music in Selected School Districts in the State of Washington." Unpublished doctoral dissertation, Colorado State College, 1967.

Wiles, K. <u>Supervision for Better Schools</u>. 3rd ed.
    Englewood Cliffs, N.J.: Prentice-Hall, Inc.,
    1967.

Zentner, H. <u>Prelude to Administrative Theory</u>.
    Calgary, Alberta, Canada: Strayer, 1973.

Ziegler, R. O. "A Study of Music Supervision in the
    Elementary and Secondary Schools of Alabama."
    Unpublished doctoral dissertation, University
    of Alabama, 1970.

EXPRESSIVE QUALITIES IN MUSIC PERCEPTION AND MUSIC EDUCATION*

David S. Levi

Abstract

This paper seeks to extend the significance of musical expressiveness in music education through the consideration of Gestalt perceptual concepts. The concept of expressive quality is discussed and two defining characteristics identified. First, the presence of expressive qualities, as phenomenal attributes, is indicated when emotional terms are applied to perceptions. Second, expressive qualities are determined by the structure of the percept to which they belong and are thus products of perceptual organization. The theoretical implications of the concept for music are explored and the classic objections of Hanslick reconsidered. The empirical support for extending the concept to music draws on studies showing listener agreement on emotional attributions to music and work on melodic perception that shows that music does have the kind of perceptual structure required by the concept. An expressive method, based on the relation of expressive qualities to music structure, is suggested as an educational device. An illustration of the method is given and its advantages for the student are summarized.

Key Words: auditory perception, aural discrimination, descriptive research, expressive devices, music education, psychological processes.

Discussions of music education typically include a role for musical expressiveness (see Leonhard and

---

House, 1959, pp. 81-86; Reimer, 1971, Ch. 9). However, this role is mainly a peripheral one. Expressiveness is considered with the aim of doing justice to aesthetic considerations. Perceptual investigations relevant to the phenomenon have not been organized around a set of explanatory concepts. This has prevented perceptual concepts and processes from receiving full consideration in determining the educational role of musical expressiveness. This paper attempts to remedy the situation by extending the explanatory framework of Gestalt theory to the phenomenon of musical expressiveness. When viewed in this context, musical expressiveness acquires new importance for understanding music.

Expressive Qualities

The problem of musical expressiveness arises when emotional terms are used by listeners to describe music. As a development of Gestalt theory, the application of emotional terms to perceptual material has come to indicate the physiognomic perception of that material. In such cases, the particular emotional terms refer to specific expressive qualities in this perception. It is consistent to hypothesize that cases of emotional attributions to music refer to musical expressive qualities. The first step in exploring this hypothesis is to elucidate the concept of expressive quality.

Expressive qualities have two defining characteristics in Gestalt theory. Generally, emotional or dynamic terms indicate expressive qualities when they are used to depict perception. For example, a country lane is described as appearing friendly, a scarecrow looks bedraggled, weeping willows seem forlorn or sad, a tone of voice can sound hostile, while a steady rain sounds soothing. Gestalt theorists, noting the spontaneity and ubiquity of such attributions, maintain that they must be accepted as designating actual perceptual phenomena. This requires accepting the terms "friendly," "forlorn," "soothing," and so on, as assigning attributes to the phenomenal objects or events being described. If emotional terms used in this way are taken as designative (rather than metaphoric), then the problem of term selection is raised.

The particularity of an expressive quality is determined by the structure of the percept (or phenomenal event) to which it belongs. The term structure refers to the given facts of organization present in the percept. Thus, term selection reflects those factors that determine the expressive quality itself.

Gestalt theorists have formulated the principles whereby perceptual organization takes place (Wertheimer, 1923, 1938; Koffka, 1935, pp. 106-176; Kohler, 1947, pp. 136-172). Empirical investigations have explored the relation of particular structures to perceived expressiveness in diverse materials, for example, Lundholm (1921) studied the features of visual line patterns that determine their expressiveness; the characteristics of human facial expressions have been investigated by Ekman (1971); both Heider and Simmel (1944) and Michotte (1950) have reported on expressive qualities in patterns of perceived motion; Dershowitz (1973) explored the expressiveness of tactual forms; Cort (1960) compared the expressive qualities of several melodic phrases.

Music Perception

In relating music to Gestalt theory, the use of emotional terms to describe music is taken as designating phenomenal properties of the music. The selection of particular emotional terms is understood by examination of the perceived music structure. This conception of music experience places expressiveness as a major phenomenal content of music. In addition to the empirical reasons, there are several theoretical advantages to this conception. First, it was noted earlier that extending the Gestalt conception of expressive qualities to music was theoretically consistent. This consistency can now be seen to rest on the assumption of a basic organizational similarity between music experience and other perceptual experiences. Second, viewing music in this light is in keeping with the application expressive qualities have found in the visual arts. Both Arnheim (1949; 1974, pp. 444-461) and Koffka (1940) have discussed the significance of expressive qualities, not only in understanding the visual appeal exerted by an art object, but also in understanding the selective process whereby the artist shapes the artistic composition.

Third, a particular conceptual economy is achieved by this view of music expressivenes. Since expressive qualities depend on perceptual structure, no special or additional processes need be hypothesized to account for the applicability of emotional terms to music. Those organizational processes establishing perceptual structure are also responsible for its expressiveness. Arnheim (1949) has stated this situation as follows:

> Such a theory would make expression an integral part of the elementary processes of perception. Expression, then, could be defined as the psychological counterpart of the dynamical processes which result in the organization of perceptual stimuli.

If the attribution of emotional terms to music is understood from the standpoint of expressive qualities, then nothing extra-musical or nonauditory is asserted.

The Gestalt concept allows the controversial nature of emotional attribution in the history of music aesthetics to be reconsidered. Hanslick (1957, 1854) has formulated the classic objection to emotional terms in music descriptions. This attack asserts that music, as an artistic medium, presents its own intrinsic beauty. The core of Hanslick's position is that whatever artistic significance music has, it is strictly musical, in effect, auditory in nature.

Hanslick attacks expressiveness as attaching a nonauditory significance to music. He formulates two basic conceptions of expressiveness that he exposes as relying on musically extraneous factors. Hanslick summarizes them as follows:

> On the one hand it is said that the aim and object of music is to excite emotions, in effect, pleasurable emotions; on the other hand the emotions are said to be the subject matter which musical works are intended to illustrate. (p. 9)

This latter position has two variants: (1) music can be seen as representing an emotion in the abstract, or (2) it can be interpreted as conveying the composer's own emotions.

To the position that musical significance rests on the emotional situation of the listener, Hanslick simply notes the unreliability of this criterion. For example, we can recognize musical beauty despite the fact that our emotional state goes unaffected or despite its being affected differently on separate listenings.

The contention that music represents emotion is challenged first by Hanslick's definition of representation. "The 'representation' of something always involves the conception of two separate and distinct objects which by a special act are purposely brought into relation with each other" (p. 5). A set of musical characteristics is never consistently used to indicate a particular emotion, in fact, the same musical characteristics can be used to achieve quite different effects. Hanslick views this as a lack of definiteness on the part of music, which renders representation impossible.

Given the previous exposition on expressive qualities, one point should be clear--the use of emotional vocabulary in describing music need not presuppose the involvement of any nonauditory factors (either those discussed by Hanslick or others) in establishing the aesthetic significance of music. Rather, by subsuming this vocabulary under the concept of expressive qualities, it becomes an indicator of features in the tonal experience. One can allow emotional descriptions of music, while accepting the criticisms offered by Hanslick. What Hanslick could not realize was that the occurrence of an emotion is not a necessary precondition of expressiveness. In everyday life, however, correlation of human expression with an emotion seems to be the rule.

The usual theoretical disputes, occasioned by the application of emotional terms to music, are mollified through reference to expressive qualities. The question becomes an empirical one. What evidence suggests the appropriateness of expressive qualities for music perception?

There are two kinds of evidence, one more complete than the other. First, there is the finding that listeners can agree in their application of emotional terms to music experience. This finding has been widely replicated and spans a considerable amount of investigative effort. The body of this work can be found in the following studies: Biller (1973); Brown, et al. (1957); Campbell (1942); Cort (1960); Downey (1897); Gatewood (1927); Gundlach (1935); Hampton (1945); Heinlein (1928); Hevner (1935, 1936); Odbert, et al. (1942); Rigg (1937, 1940); Sherman (1928); Shimp (1940); Watson (1942); Weld (1912). Some of the older studies rely on free report. However, the general procedure is to have listeners select terms from a checklist of emotional adjectives in describing the music presented. The checklist seems to improve agreement (Rigg, 1937). Investigations differ as to the kind of music presented (vocal or instrumental, popular or classical), length of selection (varying from a phrase to a movement), and the manner of selection presentation (whether recorded or performed live). Nonetheless, the percentage of agreement tends to be high, usually between 40 and 90 percent of the listeners.

It was noted above that the question of expressive qualities arises whenever emotional terms are used to depict perceptual experience. The consistency of these findings suggests that properties of music perception are indicated by these emotional attributions. The findings of Hampton (1945) corroborate this conclusion. He had listeners make adjective selections both to describe the music presented and to describe their own emotional state during presentation. When the music was described, he found the usual range of agreement in subjects' attributions. However, in describing their own emotional states, the average agreement was less than 10 percent (except for the widespread report of "pleasantness" as a reaction). Clearly, qualities in the perceived music were responsible for the original agreement.

This second kind of evidence contains the most gaps and is in need of the most experimental work. A number of the studies reviewed attempted to identify music features responsible for emotional attributions. Rigg (1964) reviews and summarizes the evidence. The music features discussed are: rhythm (regular and irregular), tempo, register, melodic direction, harmony (simple or complex), and dynamics. The basic findings consist of identifying the set of values these features assume in music receiving a particular emotional

151

characterization. For example, calm or dreamy music tends to be slow, soft, and consonant; graceful or playful music is likely to be high-pitched and fast. The problem here has been anticipated by Hanslick. These features are rather broad and fail to give a definite characterization of the music structure perceived. From the present viewpoint, such features as slowness and softness do not determine music expressiveness. Rather, these features are conditions favorable for the perceptual organization of various kinds of music structures.

Although these data give an insufficient account of structural determinants, the general nature of these determinants can be inferred from other studies. An important preliminary to this, however, is in taking a word of caution from the extant studies of expressive determinants. Rather than perceptual considerations, investigators have followed trends in the history of music criticism in selecting musical characteristics for study. In Gurney's classic treatise (1880, pp. 312-348), such elements as harmony, pace, and dynamics are discussed as they seem to be the expressive determinants in several music examples. The point is that the technical vocabulary of music scholarship cannot necessarily be embraced as a direct guide to perceived music structure.

A further empirical consideration underscores this point. A fugue, for example, is a polyphonic work wherein independent lines unfold simultaneously and in varying relationships, but Frances, as reported by Jacobs (1960), gives evidence that fugal design is not necessarily perceived as independent, simultaneous lines. In his study, only those listeners who had music training were able to apply the concept of the fugue correctly to their perception of music.

Actually, it seems that the relation between perceived music structure and conceived design is an empirical question, and one in need of further investigation. The nature of music structure seems better sought in the perceptual literature. The Gestalt writers consistently included melody in their discussion of sensory organization (see Wertheimer, 1938; Kohler, 1947, pp. 188; Koffka, 1935, p. 434). From their standpoint, melody is an auditory instance of perceptual figure. As such, it has the same kind of perceptual properties as figures occurring in other modalities. These include perceptual unity, relative segregation from a background, and shape or internal articulation. This conception of melody, as auditory figure, draws empirical support from studies exploring the functional bases of these properties.

Briefly, this evidence shows that melodic unity refers to the fact that independent, successive tones are not perceived as independent, but as more or less belonging together. Early work approached this phenomenon through the special case of melodic finality. Bingham (1910) and Farnsworth (1926) have shown that the perception of concluding notes as final sounding is largely dependent on the direction and size of the interval separating the notes from the remainder of the melody. Humphrey (1927) showed that tones that can be identified in isolation are seldom recognized when presented in non-isolated tonal contexts as part of a chord or melody. Guilford and Nelson (1937) provided a more systematic assessment of particular intramelodic relationships as they affect the perception of tones. Melodic unity is also apparent in the effects that a single tone can have on the perception of a whole melody. Guilford and Hilton (1933) found that alteration of tones in crucial melodic positions can have perceptual effects across the entire melody.

Organizational processes are implicated not only in producing a coherent melodic figure, but also in segregating it from the auditory environment. Miller and Heise (1950) have explored one of the simpler cases of segregation. They investigated transforming the perception of a single tone into a tonal pair. They presented listeners with a continuous sequence comprised of two alternating frequencies. With slight frequency differences between alternating notes, perception is of a single tone, continuously oscillating in pitch. If the frequency difference is enlarged, then eventually perception becomes that of two unrelated, but intermittent, tones.

Subsequent work has seen this as a special case of auditory stream segregation. Bergman and Campbell (1971) have shown that when the tonal sequence has a more varied frequency composition, then segregation occurs not between tones, but between streams of tones. Stream formation seems to proceed on the basis of relative frequency similarity across the entire frequency distribution. Bergman and Dannenbring (1973) and Dannenbring (1976) present evidence to show that segregation does not occur on the basis of absolute features in the frequency distribution. Rather, segregation seems to occur only when the distribution does not favor the operation of good continuation or closure.

Researchers of stream segregation have discussed their findings as instances of an auditory figure-ground phenomenon. This conclusion is reinforced by Dowling (1973), who presents evidence of ambiguous auditory figures, with reversal occurring between figure and ground.

Organization occurs not only in segregating a unified figure from auditory ground, but also when subgroupings are formed within a melody. These internal groups give a melody its distinctive contour or shape. Garner and Gottwald (1968) and Royer and Garner (1970) have studied the role of frequency differences in the formation of an internal melodic pattern. Handel (1974) has shown that other stimulus relations are also sufficient for such organization to occur. Thus, differences in tonal intensity, duration, and spacing can affect melodic pattern perception, although frequency relations tend to dominate.

Earlier studies have shown the impact of melodic shape for individual tone perception (Guilford and Hilton, 1933; Heise and Miller, 1951). Later work emphasizes the perceptual durability of melodic shape. Melodic figures, like figures in other modalities, tend to withstand various kinds of operations performed upon them. Cuddy and Cohen (1976) investigated the effects of transposition upon melodic recognition. Other investigators have explored an array of different operations in their effects on melodic perception. Werner (1940) has examined shrunken melodies; other manipulations of interval size, as well as diminuation and augmentation, were studied by White (1960); Dowling (1971, 1972) compares the effects of inversion, retrograde, and retrograde inversion on melodic

recognition. Generally, melodic recognition is at
its best when an operation leaves the relative
interval sizes and the direction of successive
melodic intervals intact.

The Gestalt conception of melody unifies a
considerable body of evidence. To some extent, the
perceptual structure of music resembles that found
in other perceptual materials. Thus, there is
reason to expect the structural determinants of
music expressiveness to resemble those in other
media. With line patterns, movement patterns, and
tactual forms, the particularities of shape determine expressiveness. This suggests that the particularities of melodic shape are structural
features determining melodic expressiveness. If
more complex music experiences are viewed as
melodically compounded forms, then the study of
melodic expressive qualities opens on a general
understanding of music expressiveness (see Reichenbach, 1940).

Music Education

Expressive qualities, together with melodic
figures, are the primary contents of music perception. Music education that minimizes expressiveness
is passing over an intrinsic property of music and
giving up a meaningful approach to the question of
music form. Of course, any student of music would
perforce become acquainted with musical expressiveness, but a brief consideration of a concrete usage
of expressiveness will reveal advantages to including it as an explicit focus in music education.

A schema that Arnheim (1974) formulated for the
visual arts can be generalized as a starting point.
He proposes:

> If one wishes to be admitted to the presence
> of a work of art, one must, first of all,
> face it as a whole. What comes across?
> What is the mood of the colors, the dynamics
> of the shapes? Before we identify any one
> element, the total composition makes a state-
> ment that we must not lose. We look for a
> theme, a key to which everything else relates
> . . . . Safely guided by the structure of
> the whole, we then try to recognize the

155

principal features and explore their dominion over dependent details. (p. 8)

Expressive qualities are the kind of holistic features that Arnheim suggests as points of departure in approaching a work of art. When applied to a music work, this suggests that surveying its general expressive outlay is an important first step in aesthetic understanding. To prepare for such an expressive reconnaissance, the student should be sensitized to expressive qualities by discussing common instances in everyday experience and expressiveness in familiar or popular music. The reconnaissance requires repeated listenings as expressive changes, and their determining structures, are identified.

Johann Pachelbel's Canon in D Major (as recorded by the J. P. Paillard Chamber Orchestra) can provide an example of how such a reconnaissance might proceed. As the Canon opens, there are two melodic streams. The lower, bass stream sounds calm or tranquil, while the upper stream sounds elated, this reflects structural differences. The lower stream is formed by the repetition of a single, broad figure. It is comprised of four tonal pairs. The first three pairs descend in staggered fashion and the final one ascends. The repetition on this figure creates a gently undulating curve. The higher stream is a continuous series of ascending three-tone figures. Although they differ structurally and expressively, the two streams seem to belong together. This reflects a certain structural coordination; there is one figure in the upper stream for each tone in the lower.

These two streams are soon overlaid by a third. Initially, this stream presents the same repeating figure as the lowest stream, only in a higher pitch register. This unites all three streams in a bright serenity, which gradually moves to a higher, more ecstatic quality. This is accomplished by the following transformation: The pattern that the top stream adopted from the lowest alters so that each tone of the tonal pairs becomes a pair of melodic figures, one descending and one ascending. They succeed each other so rapidly that a sense of circular motion is created. This motion appears as crowning the ascending figures of the middle stream and hence is aligned with the curve

156

of the lowest stream. Thus, broad expressive currents lead to an examination of structure, which in turn provides an experience of expressive nuance, coordinated with a more detailed structural accounting of the music.

As a tool, the expressive reconnaissance seems best supplemented by the use of guided comparisons. That is, once a work has been perceptually studied in this way, it can be further clarified by juxtaposition with other compositions. The most useful comparison would be with works having nearly opposite expressive qualities and with those of a similar expressiveness.

Reconnaissance and guided comparison, together, offer an expressive method having several advantages for the student. A major advantage is motivational. Expressiveness attracts our attention wherever it is encountered. An introduction to music that relies on its expressiveness begins with a quality that is intrinsically interesting. At the same time, a negative possibility is avoided. Students need not be confronted with technical vocabulary at the outset. Rather they are challenged to muster their own descriptive resources for operation in a new terrain.

Having explored a music domain in this fashion, the student tends to be ready for the more technical considerations of music scholarship. For example, the question of how expressive structures are compositionally manipulated is increasingly likely to arise, opening the way for both micro and macro considerations. On the microlevel, the complexity of relationships in the system of tonal stimuli can be considered; while on the macrolevel, extended designs can be compared.

Regardless of any further technical training in music, the expressive method can provide the student with an important tool. It is both openended and yet orderly. In principle, any music work can be approached in this way.

Leonhard and House (1959, p. 99) have noted that one general contribution of music education is to provide insight into life-values that are timeless. Enlarging the educational role of music expressiveness also seems a step toward this larger goal.

References

Arnheim, R. "The Gestalt Theory of Expression."
Psychological Review 56 (1949): 156-171.

Arnheim, R. Art and Visual Perception; A Psychology
of the Creative Eye; The New Version. Berkeley
and Los Angeles: University of California
Press, 1974.

Bergman, A. S., and Campbell, J. "Primary Auditory
Stream Segregation and Perception of Order in
Rapid Sequences of Tones." Journal of Experi-
mental Psychology 89 (1971): 244-249.

Bergman, A. S., and Dannenbring, G. L. "The Effect
of Continuity on Auditory Stream Segregation."
Perception & Psychophysics 13 (1973): 308-
312.

Biller, O. A. "Communication of Emotions through
Instrumental Music and the Music Selection
Preferences of Patients and Non-Patients experiencing Various Emotional Moods." Ph.D.
dissertation, University of Arkansas, 1973.
Dissertation Abstracts International 34
(1973): 3050A.

Bingham, W. van D. "Studies in Melody." Psychological Monographs 17, no. 3 (1910).

Brown, R.; Leiter, R. A.; and Hildu, D. E. "Meta-
phors from Music Criticism." Journal of
Abnormal and Social Psychology 54 (1957):
347-352.

Campbell, I. G. "Basal Emotional Patterns Expres-
sible in Music." American Journal of Psychology 55 (1942): 1-17.

Cort, H. R., Jr. "Tempo and Expressive Properties
of Auditory Figures: A Psychological Study."
Ph.D. dissertation, Cornell University, 1960.
Dissertation Abstracts International 21
(1961): 2011.

Cuddy, L. L., and Cohen, A. J. "Recognition of Transposed Melodic Sequences." _Quarterly Journal of Experimental Psychology_ 28 (1976): 255-270.

Dannenbring, G. L. "Perceived Auditory Continuity with Alternating Rising and Falling Frequency Transitions." _Canadian Journal of Psychology_ 30 (1976): 99-114.

Dershowitz, N. K. "On Tactual Perception of Physiognomic Properties." _Perceptual and Motor Skills_ 36 (1973): 343-355.

Dowling, W. J. "Recognition of Inversions and of Melodies and Melodic Contours." _Perception & Psychophysics_ 9 (1971): 348-349.

Dowling, W. J. "Recognition of Melodic Transformations: Inversion, Retrograde, and Retrograde Inversion." _Perception & Psychophysics_ 12 (1972): 417-421.

Dowling, W. J. "The Perception of Interleaved Melodies." _Cognitive Psychology_ 5 (1973): 322-337.

Downey, J. E. "A Musical Experiment." _American Journal of Psychology_ 9 (1897): 62-69.

Ekman, P. "Universals and Cultural Differences in Facial Expressions of Emotion." In _Nebraska Symposium on Motivation_. Edited by J. K. Cole. Lincoln: University of Nebraska Press, 1971.

Farnsworth, P. R. "A Modification of the Lipps-Meyer Law." _Journal of Experimental Psychology_ 9 (1926): 253-258.

Garner, W. R., and Gottwald, R. L. "The Perception and Learning of Temporal Patterns." _Journal of Experimental Psychology_ 20 (1968): 97-109.

Gatewood, E. "A Study in the Similes for Describing Music and Its Effects." In _The Effects of Music_. Edited by M. Schoen. London: Kegan, Trench, Trubner & Co., 1927.

Guilford, J. P., and Hilton, R. "Some Configura-
    tional Properties of Short Musical Melodies."
    Journal of Experimental Psychology 16 (1933):
    32-54.

Guilford, J. P., and Nelson, H. M. "The Pitch of
    Tones in Melodies as Compared with Single
    Tones." Journal of Experimental Psychology
    20 (1937): 309-335.

Gundlach, R. H. "Factors Determining the Charac-
    terization of Musical Phrases." American
    Journal of Psychology 47 (1935): 624-643.

Gurney, E. The Power of Sound. London: Elder &
    Co., 1880.

Hampton, P. J. "The Emotional Element in Music."
    Journal of General Psychology 66 (1945):
    237-250.

Handel, S. S. "Perceiving Melodic and Rhythmic
    Auditory Patterns." Journal of Experimental
    Psychology 103 (1974): 922-933.

Hanslick, E. The Beautiful in Music. Translated by
    G. Cohen. New York: Liberal Arts Press,
    1957 (originally published, 1854).

Heider, F., and Simmel, M. "An Experimental Study of
    Apparent Behavior." American Journal of Psy-
    chology 57 (1944): 243-259.

Heinlein, C. P. "The Affective Character of the
    Major and Minor Modes in Music." Journal of
    Comparative Psychology 8 (1928): 101-142.

Heise, G. A., and Miller, G. A. "An Experimental
    Study of Auditory Patterns." American Journal
    of Psychology 64 (1951): 68-77.

Hevner, K. "Experimental Studies of the Elements of
    Expression in Music." American Journal of
    Psychology 48 (1936): 246-268.

Hevner, K. "The Affective Character of the Major
    and Minor Modes in Music." American Journal
    of Psychology 47 (1935): 103-118.

Humphrey, J. "The Effect of Sequences of Indifferent Stimuli on a Reaction of the Conditioned Response Type." Journal of Abnormal and Social Psychology 22 (1927): 194-212.

Jacobs, C. "Psychology of Music: Some European Studies." Acta Psychologica 17 (1960): 273-297.

Kohler, W. Gestalt Psychology. New York: Liveright, 1947.

Koffka, K. Principles of Gestalt Psychology. New York: Harcourt, Brace & World, 1935.

Koffka, K. "Problems in the Psychology of Art." In R. Bernheimer; R. Carpenter; K. Koffka; and M. Nahm, Art: A Bryn Mawr Symposium. Lancaster, Pa.: Lancaster Press, 1940.

Leonhard, C., and House, R. W. Foundations and Principles of Music Education. New York: McGraw-Hill, 1959.

Lundholm, H. "The Affective Tone of Lines: Experimental Researches." Psychological Review 25 (1921): 43-60.

Michotte, A. E. "The Emotional Significance of Movement." In Feelings and Emotions. Edited by M. L. Reymert. New York: McGraw-Hill, 1950.

Miller, G. A., and Heise, G. A. "The Trill Threshold." Journal of the Acoustical Society of America 22 (1950): 637-638.

Odbert, H. S.; Karwoski, T. F.; and Eckerson, A. B. "Studies in Synesthetic Thinking: I. Musical and Verbal Associations of Color and Mood." Journal of General Psychology 26 (1942): 153-173.

Reichenbach, H. "Gestalt Psychology and Form in Music." Journal of Musicology 2, no. 2 (1940: 62-71.

161

Reimer, B. A Philosophy of Music Education. Engle-
    wood Cliffs, N.J.: Prentice-Hall, 1970.

Rigg, M. "Musical Expression: An Investigation of
    the Theories of Eric Sorantin." Journal of
    Experimental Psychology 21 (1937): 442-455.

Rigg, M. "Speed as a Determiner of Musical Mood."
    Journal of Experimental Psychology 27 (1940):
    566-571.

Rigg, M. "The Mood Effects of Music: A Comparison
    of Data from Four Investigators." Journal of
    Psychology 58 (1964): 427-438.

Royer, F. L., and Garner, W. R. "Perceptual Organi-
    zation of Nine-Element Auditory Temporal
    Patterns." Perception & Psychophysics 7
    (1970): 115-120.

Sherman, M. "Emotional Character of the Singing
    Voice." Journal of Experimental Psychology 11
    (1928): 495-497.

Shimp, B. "Reliability of Associations of Known and
    Unknown Melodic Phrases with Words Denoting
    States of Feeling." Journal of Musicology 1
    (1940): 22-35.

Watson, K. B. "The Nature and Measurement of Musical
    Meanings." Psychological Monographs 54, no. 2
    (1942).

Weld, H. P. "An Experimental Study of Musical Enjoy-
    ment." American Journal of Psychology 23
    (1912): 245-308.

Werner, H. "Musical 'Micro-Scales' and 'Micro-
    Melodies.'" Journal of Psychology 10 (1940):
    149-156.

Wertheimer, M. "Laws of Organization in Perceptual
    Forms." In A Source Book of Gestalt Psychology.
    Edited and translated by W. D. Ellis. London:
    Routledge & Kegan Paul, 1938.

White, B. W. "Recognition of Distorted Melodies."
    American Journal of Psychology 73 (1960):
    100-106.

AN EXPERIMENTAL STUDY OF A KEYBOARD SIGHTREADING TEST ADMINISTERED TO FRESHMAN SECONDARY PIANO STUDENTS AT THE OHIO STATE UNIVERSITY*

Jerry Lowder

Most colleges and universities in the United States today require their music students who are instrumental and vocal majors to study piano as a secondary instrument. Because of the large number of music students who are required to learn basic keyboard skills, many institutions hire teachers whose primary duty consists of teaching secondary piano in groups.

Although teachers of piano group instruction differ about teaching objectives, most of them do agree that the ability to sight-read simple music accurately and fluently is one of the most vital skills to be included in the group piano curriculum.

Many American universities offer courses in piano group instruction for non-music majors, including elementary education majors. Most courses in piano group instruction, however, are designed for music education majors who proficiently read music in at least one clef but are unable to sight-read music fluently at the keyboard. Because these students have been accustomed to reading single melodic lines while performing on their primary instruments, they usually lack the ability to recognize chordal shapes from melodic patterns. They tend to be inconsistent in their choice of fingering patterns and selection of hand positions while performing at the keyboard.

This inconsistency can be explained in part by the lack of keyboard performance experience and a tactile knowledge of the keyboard that usually accompanies such experience. Because of these

---

* Reprinted by permission of Jerry Lowder and Contributions to Music Education, No. 3 (Autumn, 1974), pp. 97-105.

weaknesses, several assumptions can be made concerning the teaching of sight-reading techniques in piano classes:

1. One of the primary objectives of the instructional program should be emphasis on the development of sight-reading skills.

2. The functional piano skills of harmonization, transposition, improvisation, and sight-reading involve tertian harmonies, and it is essential that the keyboard performer perceive chord patterns inferable from melodic outlines. Such inferences might also suggest specific fingerings and hand positions.

3. The problem of playing hymnlike textures might be facilitated by permitting the "secondary" pianist to perform initially such four-voice textures with three notes by the right hand the bass note by the left hand. This arrangement of voices will be referred to hereafter as "close position."

Most group piano texts include hymns and patriotic songs in the more traditional "open position," that is, arrangements requiring two voices to be performed by each hand. There are several advantages, however, that are peculiar to the use of the close position, namely, harmonization of melodies, performance of "popular" music arrangements, and performance of cadences, chord progressions, and figured bass exercises.

Although the functional skills of sight-reading, harmonization, transposition, and improvisation comprise sufficient goals for a first-quarter or first-semester class of secondary pianists, the writer believes that precise and habitual fingerings for certain chord shapes and scale patterns should be introduced during this initial period of instruction through close position, in order to prevent the formation of inaccurate motor responses and careless reading habits.

The writer conducted an early study at Indiana University during the autumn semester of 1969.(1) A single posttest was administered to twenty-three subjects after completion of their initial semester of piano group instruction. The posttest consisted of a fifteen-item sight-reading test, which included intervals; two-, three-, and

164

four-voice textures; and two melodies requiring harmonization by the subject.

The period of instruction lasted thirteen weeks, and the subjects received instruction during two forty-five minute periods each week. Four classes of freshman secondary piano students comprised the test population. Two classes were designated as the experimental group, and the remaining two classes were designated as the control group. In addition to basic instruction received by both groups, the experimental group received the writer's method of instruction which stressed reading and performance skills according to principles of harmonic intervals and figured bass.

Mean test scores of both groups were compared through the use of the t test, resulting in a t value that was not significant at the .05 level. The writer therefore accepted the null hypothesis of no significant difference in the achievement of the two groups.

The writer replicated the study at The Ohio State University for several reasons:

1. The Indiana study used only twenty-three subjects, and a larger number of subjects might produce different results.

2. Whereas the previous study had utilized a single posttest design, another study incorporating the pretest-posttest design might provide a better comparison between the performance of both groups.

3. The writer wanted to compare the sight-reading achievement of students enrolled in the quarter system with that of students enrolled in the semester system. Secondary piano students at The Ohio State University attend classes on the quarter system, meeting Monday through Thursday each week for forty-eight minute periods of instruction, contrasted to Indiana University students who attended class only two hours each week during the semester system.

Purpose of the Study

The purpose of the study was to determine whether the teaching of vertical intervallic relationships according to figured bass principles would improve the ability of college secondary pianists to sight-read piano music based on tertian harmony.

The investigation was based on the evaluation of a sight-reading test designed by the writer, and administered to two experimental classes and two control classes at The Ohio State University in a pretest-posttest design during the Autumn quarter of 1972.

The Sightreading Test

During the earlier study at Indiana University, the writer constructed a sight-reading test comprised of fifteen items. The test used in the present study was a revised form of the test utilized in the earlier study, that is, it was reduced from fifteen to ten items. The items were composed by the writer to represent typical materials presented to college piano classes.

The test purported to measure the ability of the students to sight-read pitches correctly, to interpret accurately and perform the rhythmic values of the notation, and to maintain the same general tempo throughout the item.

The two criteria of sight-reading proficiency chosen by the writer for the test were (1) performance of correct pitches and (2) maintenance of a steady tempo and accuracy of note values.

Control and Experimental Groups

The study was conducted at The Ohio State University during the Autumn Quarter of 1972. The subjects were thirty-six freshman students enrolled in four different sections of the first-quarter level of piano group instruction. The majority of the students were music education majors; the remainder were instrumental performance and theory-composition majors.

Because all students were assigned to classes by computer, no attempt was made by the investigator to randomize further the test population. Each class was taught by a different instructor. One section was taught by the writer. The remaining sections were taught by experienced teaching assistants who were given their assignments according to their own graduate course schedule.

The instructional period extended over a period of eight weeks. Each of the classes met in the same sixteen-unit Wurlitzer piano laboratory, scheduled at either 8:00, 9:00, 11:00, or 12:00 A.M., Monday through Thursday, for forty-eight minute periods of instruction. The investigator taught the 11:00 A.M. class.

Prior to the beginning of the quarter, the writer selected the 8:00 and 9:00 A.M. classes for the experimental group and the 11:00 and 12:00 A.M. classes for the control group. This particular selection of experimental and control groups and instructor assignments was made by the writer in order to provide a similar time of day for each group and to avoid any possible bias by the investigator in the presentation of the experimental treatment.

Although the original enrollment for the four classes was fifty-eight students, only thirty-six were included in the test groups. Attrition was due to students' non-completion of the course, absence during the pretest or posttest, and mechanical failure during the audio tape recording of the pretest or posttest.

The Experimental Treatment

All four classes received the same basic instruction in the development of the following skills: sight-reading, five-finger positions in all major and minor keys, transposition, cadences and chord progressions, basic music theory, harmonization of melodies, and improvisation.

In addition to the above-mentioned basic instruction, the experimental group received supplementary pages of the writer's textbook.(2) This section of the text deals with the development of consistent fingering patterns by the right hand, according to the recognition of "chord shapes," synonymous with chordal inversions and based upon an adaptation of figured bass. For example, the soprano pitch F with $^6_3$ written below indicates

167

that the intervals of a sixth and third are formed
below F, found by counting down a sixth to A, then
up a third to C.

When the student initially attempts to perform
such three-note chords with the right hand, it is
necessary for him to count vertical intervals.
During subsequent drills, however, the student learns
to perform specific fingering patterns for certain
chord shapes: $\frac{5}{3}$ (root position) is performed by the
right-hand fingering 1-3-5, $\frac{6}{3}$ (first inversion) by
1-2-5, and $\frac{6}{4}$ (second inversion) by 1-3-5.

The Testing Procedure

The Sight-reading Test was administered as a
pretest during the first full week of instruction and
as a posttest during the final week of instruction.
The Test was announced to all four classes one day
prior to its administration in the same piano laboratory where the subjects received daily instruction.
One class period at each of the four scheduled hours
was used for both the pretest and the posttest.

The writer read the following instructions to
each class before administering the Test:

1. This is a brief sight-reading test which
is designed to evaluate your improvement in
sight-reading ability.

2. Your performance on the test will be recorded on audio tape for later evaluation and
will have no bearing on your class grade.

3. The test consists of ten items, ranging
from melodic and harmonic intervals to four-
voice examples.

4. The first eight test items are to be
performed by one hand alone. Use the right
hand for items written in the treble clef and
the left hand for items written in the bass
clef. The last two test items require performance by both hands simultaneously.

5. Only accuracy of pitch and rhythm will be
evaluated. Therefore, choose a comfortable

tempo which will permit accuracy of pitches and steady rhythm.

6. The test should be performed without interruption. Scan the entire test and ask any necessary questions before beginning to play.

7. If you believe that one or more test items will be impossible for you to play, tell the examiner which items you wish to omit before beginning to record.

8. Signal the examiner when you are ready to have your performance recorded.

After reading the instructions to each class, the writer reminded the subjects to work on their individual assignments until one of the test pianos was available for the next subject to record.

Four of the laboratory pianos were used as test pianos. Each piano had a cassette tape recorder connected to it; the four recorders were identical in make.

A copy of the Piano-Sight-reading Test Roster was placed on each of the test pianos, and the subjects were asked by the writer to print their names on the roster at their piano before beginning the test. A copy of the Sight-reading Test also was placed on the music rack of each of the test pianos. Each subject was permitted to try the action of the piano prior to the test and to scan each page of the test before beginning.

The subjects were asked to indicate which test item or items they wished to omit. They were allowed to indicate such omissions verbally before beginning the test or after having completed the test. The numbers of the omitted item(s) were then written in the right-hand margin of the Roster by the instructor of the class.

The class instructor activated the "Record" and "Stop" buttons on the tape recorders when each subject signaled his readiness by raising his hand.

Evaluation of the Taped Performances

The taped performances of the Sight-reading Test were evaluated by the investigator alone, due to the difficulty in finding qualified auditors who could spend the many hours necessary for the task.

During the evaluation of the tapes, the writer was aided by his sense of relative pitch and familiarity with the test items. He listened to the performance of each test item twice, placing marks on a tally sheet for pitch errors during the first hearing and marking similarly during the second hearing for rhythm errors.

Errors were recorded on the tally sheet as negative scores. During the subsequent tabulation of the data, the number of errors was subtracted from the number of possible points for the test examples, resulting in a positive score.

Test Scoring Method

The two variables evaluated on the Sight-reading Test were pitch and rhythm. Pitch errors were entered as tally marks in the "P" column of the Scoring Sheet, and rhythm errors were indicated as tally marks in the "R" column.

The numbers in parentheses on the Scoring Sheet represented the total number of possible points for each test item, the first number indicating pitch (P) and the second number indicating rhythm (R).

Pitch. When a note or chord was played more than once by the subject, only the first version was evaluated.

Single pitches performed an octave above or below the correct pitch were considered incorrect. However, successive melodic pitches played an octave from the original pitch were counted correct, marking only the first note of the melody as a pitch error.

Repeated notes or chords were considered incorrect when held as tied note values rather than being restruck.

170

Rhythm. Rhythm was scored only on test items three through ten. A rhythmic error was considered to be a pause between consecutive pitches lasting as long or longer than the basic pulse within the test item. An error was also marked if the subject performed any note value that differed significantly from the notation of the test items.

Analysis of the Data

One of the main purposes of the study was to determine whether any significant difference might be found between the posttest mean scores of the experimental and control groups.

Table 1 presents a comparison of the experimental and control group mean scores obtained from the evaluation of the posttest.

TABLE 1

COMPARISON OF EXPERIMENTAL AND CONTROL
GROUP POSTTEST MEAN SCORES

Group	Total Score	Mean Score	t	Sig
Experimental (N = 21)	4662	222.00		
Control (N = 15)	3430	228.67	3.54	N.S.

The experimental group achieved a total score of 4662 points on the posttest, resulting in a mean score of 222.00, while the control group attained a total score of 3430 points for a mean score of 228.67.

The t test was utilized to compare the difference between the two independent means, and the value of t was found to be .354. Based on the .05 level of significance for a two-tailed test, the t value is 2.03. Therefore, the t value of .354 was not significant, and the writer accepted the null hypothesis of no significant difference in the achievement of the two groups.

Conclusions

Based upon the problems and data of the study, the writer drew the following conclusions.

1. Emphasis upon harmonic intervals and chord shapes during the instructional period of the experimental group appeared to produce no significant difference in sight-reading achievement. Although such drill may have improved the subjects' ability to perceive chordal configurations, it apparently did not improve their ability to perform them within a rhythmic framework.

2. Analysis of the study data revealed that pitch errors were usually accompanied by rhythmic errors, especially at the bar line. This would suggest a need for increased emphasis upon ensemble experience in the secondary piano program, stressing the importance of maintaining a steady sense of rhythm at the occasional expense of pitch accuracy, if necessary.

3. Although an audio problem was caused by a malfunctioning electronic piano during the administration of the pretest, self-administration of a test by subjects in the piano laboratory seemed feasible and more efficient than testing the subjects individually.

Such use of cassette tape recorders would suggest many possibilities for use in the piano laboratory in order to individualize instruction for the student.

4. Because of the intricate coordination skills required to utilize both hands while performing keyboard music, perhaps one quarter or one semester of instruction does not permit the secondary piano student sufficient time to develop the tactual memory required to reduce the number of eye movements between musical score and keyboard.

It would appear that the type of keyboard sight-reading gained is not as important as the amount of experience achieved during regular periods of instruction longer than one quarter or semester.

References

(1) Jerry Lowder, "An Experimental Study of Teaching Reading Concepts and Keyboard Fingering Patterns to Freshmen College Piano Classes," unpublished doctor's thesis, Indiana University, 1970, 131 pp.

(2) Jerry Lowder, <u>Basic Piano Skills</u> (Worthington, Ohio: Charles A. Jones Publishing Company, 1974).

A STUDY OF TWO APPROACHES TO DEVELOPING EXPRESSIVE PERFORMANCE*

David J. Marchand

Abstract

The purpose of this project was to: (1) study whether expressive performance could be learned; (2) determine which of two instructional methods, entitled Discovery and Expository, would result in greater expressive performance achievement; and (3) determine what effect music experience had upon such achievement. Secondarily, the study also determined what effect the treatments had upon the variables of aural achievement, knowledge of music facts, and vocal skills.

Subjects were college-age nonmusic majors in a music fundamentals program. Three course sections of approximately 30 each allowed comparison of the two noted treatments with a control.

Results indicated that: (1) expressive performance can be learned; (2) technical skills might also be enhanced when expression is emphasized as a learning; (3) the two treatments had similar effects upon aural achievement, knowledge of music facts, and vocal skills; and (4) subjects with higher amounts of experience benefited from the more straightforward, teacher-oriented approach, whereas subjects with less experience benefited from the student-centered, Discovery teaching strategies.

Key Words: aural discrimination, expressive devices, instrumental instruction, music achievement, musical experience, performance ability, teaching method, vocal instruction.

---

* Copyright (c) 1975 by The Music Educators National Conference. Reprinted by permission of David J. Marchand and the Journal of Research in Music Education, Vol. 23, No. 1 (Spring, 1975), pp. 14-22.

Performance has been a major factor in music
education since its inception in the public schools.
Recent discussion in music education literature has
indicated that a reappraisal of performance activities is taking place, one concern being a sus-
picion that performance teaching-learning is too
technique-oriented. A program solely devoted to
teaching technical skills may, as a result, produce
performers who lack expression in their playing or
singing.

It is not entirely clear from the available
literature how one identifies a performance as being
expressive, and how, if at all, such a musical end
is taught or learned. This specific topic is largely
unresearched. Previous projects in the area have
suffered generally from research design problems in
which the subjects of the studies, treated under the
theoretical constructs established by the researchers,
either were not tested at all or were tested under
uncontrolled circumstances.(1)

Competent research dealing with expressive
performance does exist, but these projects were
directed toward evaluating listeners' perceptions of
expressive performance rather than examining the performer as the producer of the effect.(2) Thus, the
purpose of this project was to: (1) study whether
expressive performance could be learned; (2) determine which of two instructional methods, entitled
Discovery and Expository, would result in greater
expressive performance achievement; and (3) determine
what effect previous music experience had upon such
achievement.

Procedures and Design

Relevant literature was examined in order to
arrive at an operational definition of expressive
performance. Although the standard music references,
such as Grove's <u>Dictionary of Music and Musicians</u>,(3)
played a large role in the literature review, the
resultant definition also drew heavily from the
writing of Leonard B. Meyer.(4) In the process of
developing the definition, it became clear that the
most usable form for this project's situation would
be a taxonomy. This provided a more orderly way to
identify and list specific expressive musical

components, such as deviation in rhythm (for example, ritardando) and dynamics (for example, crescendo).

Performance lessons based upon the operational definition were developed and taught, among other lessons, to nonmusic majors in a music fundamentals program at a midwestern university. These performance lessons included both an instrumental experience on a soprano recorder and a vocal experience. Three course sections within the music fundamentals program allowed comparison of the teaching-learning efficacy of the discovery and expository treatments and a control.

Discovery treatment strategies were distinguished by attempts to produce intrinsic learning motivation in subjects, self-initiated problem solving, and subject assessment of achievement. Expository treatment strategies were distinguished by authoritarian teacher behaviors in which subjects were told of the task, provided the content, drilled on the task, and subsequently assessed by the teacher.

The three course sections were respectively designated the discovery, expository, and control groups. The researcher taught the two treatment groups, while the control group was taught by a competent and experienced specialist. There was daily communication between the researcher and the control group instructor to ensure, as much as was possible, that musical content and basic objectives remained similar and controlled for all three sections throughout the project. Aside from the above-stated differences in instruction methods, the only other difference consciously allowed was that the two treatment groups received their performance lessons with additional attention to developing expression in solo performances.

Subjects totaled 89 and were assigned, as equally as possible, to one of the three sections. Although an attempt at random assignment was made, problems (such as the conflicting class schedules of some of the participants) resulted in direct assignment to other groups and thus varying amounts of contamination. For this reason, it was decided to test and compare the three groups before the treatment period in order to assess possible bias.

Pretreatment Measures

Pretreatment data collection included the variables of aural achievement, knowledge of music facts, and vocal skills as well as an inventory of the subjects' previous music experiences:

(1) The Aural Achievement Test: Richard Colwell's Elementary Music Achievement Tests (EMAT) (5) was selected because it seemed the most valid test of this sort for nonmusic majors. Reliability for college-age students has been established at .94.

(2) The Music Facts Test: This measure was constructed by the researcher and included 94 paper-pencil test items. Validity was established both by a panel of experts and by content comparison with music fundamentals texts. Reliability was found to be .96.

(3) The Vocal Skills Test: This measure required that subjects tape record the song America without accompaniment. The performances were judged for tonality, intonation, meter flow, and accurate duration. Two separate adjudications by the researcher resulted in a reliability correlation coefficient of .90.

(4) The Music Experience Inventory: This measure provided a means to translate the amount of prior music experience into quantitative terms that could be statistically analyzed. Inventory information was not only used to indicate possible group pretreatment bias but was also divided into three experience levels--high, middle, and low--and subsequently included in the posttreatment analysis to see what interactive effect such levels of experience had on subjects' expressive performance test scores.

Posttreatment Measures

Posttreatment data collection was primarily concerned with expressive performance achievement, but as a further check on the effects of the treatments, aural achievement, knowledge of music facts, and vocal skills were also measured:

(1) The Expressive Performance Test: Four songs--two for the instrumental part and two for

the vocal part--were selected. Subjects were provided the scores seven days prior to the testing, but
no specific instructions were given for the preparation of expressive performances. Each of the four
songs was analyzed for its expressive characteristics.
These characteristics consequently became the adjudication criteria by which three judges, unassociated
with the project, scored the tape-recorded performances of the subjects. Both the adjudication
reliability (interjudge) and the performance reliability (intersong) were satisfactory.

(2) The Aural Achievement Test: The EMAT was
again administered in its original form.

(3) The Music Facts Test: A total of 145
paper-pencil items, similar in kind to the pretest
but more difficult in nature, were constructed by
the researcher. Validity was established as with
the pretest, and reliability was found to be .88.

(4) The Vocal Skills Test: This measure was
similar in all respects to its pretreatment counter-
part except that the song Aura Lee was used.

Since data on the last three variables were collected pretreatment, testing the subjects on the same
variables posttreatment provided gain achievement
scores for comparison.

Results of the Pretreatment Measures

Results of the pretreatment measures were
examined in terms of central tendency, variability,
and possible significant differences. Probability
levels equal to or greater than .05 were considered
statistically significant in both the pre- and
posttest results.

Table 1 shows the group scores on the four
administered measures and indicates that the control
group possessed subjects with superior aural skills
and with greater knowledge of music facts. Although
the music experience inventory scores did not result
in a statistically significant difference, it was
obvious that the control group had a substantially
greater measure of experience, and this was probably
the cause of its higher mean scores on the afore-
mentioned tests. The two treatment groups did show
fairly equal means throughout the four measures.

178

TABLE 1

MEANS, STANDARD DEVIATIONS, F RATIOS, AND PROBABILITY LEVELS
OF THE PRETREATMENT MEASURES BY GROUP

Measure	Discovery		Expository		Control		F	p
	$\bar{X}$	S.D.	$\bar{X}$	S.D.	$\bar{X}$	S.D.		
Aural Achievement	150.8	19.1	146.4	17.0	160.6	18.0	4.80	.01
Knowledge Music Facts	49.2	17.3	51.0	16.0	59.9	18.1	3.39	.03
Vocal Skills	103.1	4.3	104.2	1.9	104.0	3.4	.98	.37
Music Experience	38.8	32.5	34.2	21.3	49.6	33.5	2.13	.12

In terms of standard deviations reported in Table 1, the expository group was the most homogeneous, with the discovery and control groups indicating comparable score distributions.

It was apparent from the pretreatment results that certain biases did exist among the groups and a perfect, unbiased experiment could not be run. Nonetheless, since the advantages were all focused within the control group, it became reasonably possible to analyze the posttreatment results to some degree of impartiality and accuracy.

Results of the Posttreatment Measures

Posttreatment results are given in two parts. The first part is concerned with the extent to which expressive performance was learned within the three groups and also with the interaction between music experience levels (high, middle, and low) and expressive performance achievement. Obtaining the results necessary for evaluating these questions required the data to be computed through two-way analysis of variance.

After each subject was assigned to one of the three experience levels, the levels were crossed with group mean scores from the expressive performance test. Table 2 shows these data. Here, the three columns of mean scores represent treatment effect upon expressive performance achievement; the three rows of mean scores represent experience effect upon expressive performance achievement; and the nine cell scores represent the crossing and interaction of the treatment variable with the experience variable.

Column mean totals in Table 2 show that the discovery group acquired the largest mean score, closely followed by that of the expository group. The summary of the significance test in Table 3 shows treatment, as a source of variation, attaining an F ratio of 13.61, which is significant at the .01 level. The Scheffé test for paired means disclosed that significant differences existed between both treatment groups and the control group. It was concluded from these results that expressive performance could be learned, with both treatments having similar effects when experience levels were not included as interacting variables.

TABLE 2

EXPRESSIVE PERFORMANCE TEST SCORE MEANS BY
TREATMENT BY EXPERIENCE LEVEL

Level	Discovery	Expository	Control	Row Means
High	26.89	31.35	20.22	24.41
Middle	25.75	20.07	16.33	20.75
Low	18.27	19.49	13.80	17.70
Column Means	23.50	22.24	17.48	

TABLE 3

SUMMARY OF TWO-WAY ANALYSIS OF VARIANCE, EXPRESSIVE
PERFORMANCE SCORES BY TREATMENT BY EXPERIENCE

Source	Sum of Squares	df	Mean Squares	F	p
Treatment	872.39	2	436.2	13.61	.01
Experience Level	1133.90	2	566.9	17.69	.01
Treatment x Experience Level	296.47	4	74.1	2.31	.06
Within	2563.80	80	32.0		
Total	4866.56	88			

As might be expected, the row means totals in Table 2 show that the amount of music experience had a positive relationship to expressive performance achievement. This result appears to correspond with the generally accepted notion that past experience (and achievement) is a fairly good predictor of future achievement. In fact, Table 3 shows experience, as a source of variation, having an F ratio of 17.69 with a significance level of .01.

The data represented by the nine cell scores in Table 2 indicate that there were interactive effects between treatment and experience. Most

181

obvious and of major interest was the disordinal interaction resulting from a shift in mastery of the dependent variable measure between the expository-high cell population and the discovery-middle cell population. Here, the expository-high cell achieved a mean that was 4.46 points greater than the corresponding discovery cell, with the role more than reversed by a mean difference of 5.72 in the middle experience cells. The summary of the two-way analysis of variance in Table 3 reports this source of variation as treatment x experience level with an F ratio of 2.31, which is significant at the .06 level.

The second part of the posttreatment analysis is summarized in Table 4. Aural achievement gain scores were obtained by computing the raw score differences of the EMAT administered pre- and post-treatment. Since the pre- and posttests used in assessing knowledge of music facts and vocal skills were not identical, the pre- and posttest data were first transformed into standard scores and then computed to find gain scores and differences.

Whereas the gain achievements for the two treatment groups were similar on the three measures, the gain achievement for the control group lagged somewhat behind. These results might indicate inferior instruction on the part of the control group teacher, consequently placing the significant differences found among the groups on the expressive performance measure in question. However, this interpretation was rejected since significance tests indicate, in Table 4, very low F ratios for aural achievement and knowledge of music facts. Furthermore, gains were considered less easily obtainable for the control group due to a ceiling effect caused by the pretreatment advantages possessed by this group.

Table 4 also shows that there was a sufficiently high F ratio to indicate statistical significance on gain in vocal skill. Since all groups were similar in this respect pretreatment, the gain by the two treatment groups in relationship to the control group may have been a reflection of their superiority on the expressive performance test, for logic would imply that those who perform expressively must also attain some requisite proficiency in vocal skill.

TABLE 4

MEANS, STANDARD DEVIATIONS, F RATIOS, AND PROBABILITY
LEVELS OF THE POSTTREATMENT GAIN SCORES BY GROUP

Variable	Discovery $\overline{X}$	S.D.	Expository $\overline{X}$	S.D.	Control $\overline{X}$	S.D.	F	p
Aural Achievement	12.8	9.5	10.0	7.3	8.6	7.1	1.5	.21
Knowledge Music Facts	49.5	1.0	51.9	.99	48.6	.99	.75	.47
Vocal Skills	51.2	.74	52.2	.57	47.1	1.1	3.0	.05

Discussion

In this study, there were two primary difficulties--the first being the lack of random assignment procedures and the second being the necessity to utilize two instructors. Both of these undoubtedly affected the control of the experiment to some degree as witnessed, in part, by the pretreatment testing results. However, there are few experiments that are not open to criticism concerning both internal and external validity.(6)

It does appear that expression, as a musical performance objective, can be learned. This musical end is probably brought about through a variety of teaching approaches, much the same as with other performance goals. It might also be that certain technical skills are automatically learned and advanced when students are working to perform in a more musical manner. It would thus seem reasonable that more emphasis in this area on the part of music teachers could have substantial results. Furthermore, published material, such as beginning instrumental method books, should include more expressive musical content and suggested teaching activities than is now the case.

This project failed to turn up any real differences between the two treatment groups on any of the study's variables. Similarities in these groups' gain achievements could be attributed to several factors, including the fact that the same instructor taught both sections. It may also be that there are many different ways to have students learn the same things and that searching for the "perfect method" is a meaningless exercise.

There does seem to be strong indication that one's level of experience may interact with the type of teaching strategies employed. In regard to achievement in performing expressively, the subjects with the greatest experience responded to the more straightforward, lecture-type instruction, whereas the more student-centered teaching strategies benefited those with less experience. In interpreting this finding, the researcher believes that high amounts of experience indicate previous motivation and suggest favorable attitudes and dispositions to further learning. Students with

great experience may prefer a more straightforward
approach, since there is no need to catch their
attention or stimulate their awareness. Conversely,
students who are relatively unsophisticated in the
basic concepts and terminology of a discipline may
respond more favorably to methods that emphasize the
personalizing and concreteness of the learning
task. Finally, although subjects' posttreatment
attitudes were not objectively sought, there was
indication that the discovery group subjects enjoyed
their class experiences to a greater degree than
those subjects in the expository group class.

References

(1) C. T. O'Bannon, "A Study in Developing an
Artistic Interpretation of the Song" (Ph.D. disser-
tation, University of Missouri, 1967); Manley B.
Whitcomb, "Musical Performances on Wind Instruments:
A Study of Interpretive Factors" (Ph.D. dissertation,
Teachers College, Columbia University, 1959).

(2) Edwin Gordon, Manual, The Music Aptitude
Profile (New York: Houghton Mifflin Company,
1965); James Hoffren, "The Construction and Validation of a Test of Expressive Phrasing in Music,"
Journal of Research in Music Education, Vol. 2
(Summer 1964), pp. 159-164; Kate Hevner, "Experimental Studies of the Elements of Expression in
Music," American Journal of Psychology, Vol. 48
(1936), pp. 246-268.

(3) Sir George Grove, Dictionary of Music and
Musicians, Vol. 2 (New York: St. Martin's Press,
1954).

(4) Leonard B. Meyer, Emotion and Meaning in
Music (Chicago: University of Chicago Press,
1956).

(5) Richard Colwell, EMAT: Elementary Music
Achievement Tests (Chicago: Follett Publishing
Company, 1967).

(6) Donald T. Campbell and Julian C. Stanley,
Experimental and Quasi-Experimental Designs for
Research (Chicago: Rand McNally & Company, 1969).

DUTIES AND ACTIVITIES OF MUSIC SUPERVISORY
PERSONNEL IN CALIFORNIA*

Lawrence McQuerrey

In the spring of 1968, the music education department of the University of the Pacific initiated a study to outline a composite job description of California school music supervisory personnel. The 257 California music supervisors listed in the Directory of Music Supervisory Personnel in California--1968 all were sent a letter requesting that they list their duties, responsibilities, and activities (administration, personnel, teaching, inservice, and so forth), enclosing a copy of any duties listed in an administrative handbook or memorandum. They also were sent a form for listing any additional duties. Request forms were returned by 48 percent of the supervisors. The duties and subduties listed in the returns were analyzed, with similar duties abstracted and combined, and duties listed fewer than four times deleted. The resulting responsibility profile contained eighty-two items. Supervisory personnel also were divided into three categories: county, elementary, and unified-secondary personnel.

In February 1970, the eighty-two items of the preliminary survey were incorporated into a second questionnaire. Neighboring music supervisors were asked to offer opinions about the new questionnaire and suggestions for its revision.

The resulting questionnaire was comprised of seventy-six items covering nine areas of responsibility: three items on budgeting, eleven items on materials, two items on facilities, twenty-one items on personnel, eight items on curriculum, seven items

---

on work with students, twelve items on administration, five items on community matters, and seven items on professional matters.

The purpose of this study was to investigate how music supervisors spend their time. No attempt was made to investigate values, purposes, or goals. Each supervisor was requested to indicate whether he spent no time, little time, some time, or a great deal of time on each of the items in the questionnaire. Additional information requested on the survey included the exact title of an individual's position, the title of the person to whom he was responsible, and an explanation of the supplementary duties of respondents who were considered less than full-time supervisors.

The revised questionnaire was sent to the 235 music supervisors listed in the Directory of Music Supervisory Personnel in California--1970. It may be noted that there was a loss of twenty-two supervisors since the 1968 publication. Completed forms were received from 153 of the supervisors. Again, they were divided into the three job categories used in the first study. The respondents included twenty-three county music supervisors, fifty-nine elementary music supervisors, and seventy-one secondary-unified music supervisors.

The answers for each item on the questionnaire were tabulated and percentages computed. The items of the questionnaire then were grouped into nineteen relatively homogeneous categories under the nine major areas of responsibility. Table 1 shows a listing and description of each category with the questionnaire responses presented in terms of percentages.

Some of the data in Table 1 provide material for scrutiny and speculation; for example, almost 5 percent of the music supervisors spend little or no time on the budget and nearly 20 percent do not work with the budget at all. Also, supervisors obviously spend more time purchasing and maintaining materials than they do preparing materials for teacher use. Over 40 percent of the supervisors spend little or no time in articulation or in an organized advisement program. A relatively small percentage of supervisors were involved in funded projects and directed teaching, while a surprisingly large percentage were

TABLE 1

SUPERVISOR RESPONSIBILITIES AND AMOUNT OF
TIME SPENT ON EACH

Area of Responsibility	Functions	Percentage of Supervisors Spending:			
		no time	little time	some time	much time
Budget	Preparing, submitting, recommending, approving budget and music expenditures.	19.2	30.6	36.3	13.7
Materials	Evaluating, recommending, adding, replacing, maintaining, distributing, and inventorying music materials and equipment.	7.6	21.1	41.3	29.9
	Preparing instructional and resource materials, maintaining and ordering library materials.	13.8	32.4	35.1	18.7
Facilities	Assisting in planning new facilities, recommending changes in existing facilities.	15.3	33.9	37.6	13.2
Personnel	Advising and participating in the hiring, firing, recruiting, scheduling, observing, and evaluating of music personnel; preparing and conducting staff meetings and conferences; promoting leadership and morale.	12.4	16.8	39.3	31.5

TABLE 1--Continued

SUPERVISOR RESPONSIBILITIES AND AMOUNT OF
TIME SPENT ON EACH

Area of Responsibility	Functions	Percentage of Supervisors Spending:			
		no time	little time	some time	much time
Personnel	Arranging inservice workshops and clinics; demonstration teaching and consulting; administering summer programs; orienting new teachers.	8.3	15.3	36.4	40.1
	Consulting, visiting, and evaluating classroom teachers; preparing instruction guides; helping with experimental classroom programs.	18.0	23.4	30.2	28.3
Curriculum	Working with principals and district personnel in developing music curriculums; developing goals and assessments; recommending new or revised courses of study (music guides); promoting a balance of music activities.	6.0	15.6	45.7	32.7
	Developing and promoting articulation and coordination in the music testing-advising program.	18.1	24.2	25.3	32.4

TABLE 1--Continued

SUPERVISOR RESPONSIBILITIES AND AMOUNT OF
TIME SPENT ON EACH

Area of Responsibility	Functions	Percentage of Supervisors Spending:			
		no time	little time	some time	much time
Work with Students	Arranging field trips, assemblies, district-wide festivals, clinics, and concerts.	16.6	18.7	31.6	33.2
	Teaching and conducting students.	16.2	15.8	31.3	36.7
Administration	Acting as resource person, music representative to administrative staff; preparing administrative reports and assigned administrative tasks.	4.9	14.8	41.7	38.6
	Formulating and disseminating music bulletins, notices, news releases, policy handbooks, surveys of current music education literature.	11.8	23.9	38.9	25.5
	Coordinating music into total educational program; contacting individuals involved.	4.7	13.7	35.8	45.8
	Planning and implementing funded projects; coordinating use of practice teachers and interns.	39.3	30.2	19.7	10.8

TABLE 1--Continued

SUPERVISOR RESPONSIBILITES AND AMOUNT OF
TIME SPENT ON EACH

Area of Responsi- bility	Functions	Percentage of Supervisors Spending:			
		no time	little time	some time	much time
Community	Coordinating school music programs and concerts in the district or com- munity.	8.8	13.9	43.7	33.6
	Promoting and in- preting music policy to commu- nity; participating and providing lea- dership in commu- nity music activity.	6.5	17.4	47.4	28.7
Profes- sional	Attending and par- ticipating in pro- fessional activi- ties (meetings, conferences) and organizations; assisting in formu- lating music educa- tion policies.	10.0	15.4	39.7	34.8
	Keeping abreast of research and devel- opments in music education; in- forming staff; promoting staff membership and participation.	3.0	14.7	51.6	30.6

involved in community and professional duties. With
the exception of the activities outlined in category
15, most of the music supervisors were involved to
some extent in all of the various activities described in the study. In order to present job
profiles graphically, a weighted mean was computed
for each item of the questionnaire, using numerical
time values. The numbers one, two, three, and four
designated no time, little time, some time, and
much time, respectively. The average of the weighted
means then was computed for the items in each of
the nineteen areas of responsibility. Mean numerical
values are shown in Table 2.

The time allotments of the elementary music
supervisors and secondary-unified supervisors were
similar except that elementary music supervisors
were more involved with classroom teachers and with
actual teaching, and secondary-unified music supervisors spent more time in community and professional
involvement. The activity time allotments of county
music supervisors tended to vary from those of the
other music supervisors. They spent less time on
budgeting and working with students and more time
on personnel and professional activities. The time
alloted for administration duties was similar for
all supervisors. Though the time allotment varied
among the three types of supervisory positions, all
music supervisors appeared to engage in the same
types of activities and duties, as shown in Table
2.

The three supplementary questions included on
the questionnaire provided interesting information
and conclusions. The diversity of titles used by
California music supervisors gives the impression of
a lack of clear structure. Of the sixty titles
listed, forty-five fell under the headings coordinator, consultant, supervisor, director, or specialist. Generalizing from the thirty-four titles
given by the supervisors for the individuals to
whom the supervisors were responsible, it would
appear that music supervisors were responsible
chiefly to district superintendents, assistant superintendents, directors of either elementary or secondary education, unspecified assistants, associate
or deputy superintendents, or other music supervisory
personnel. Additional duties listed by the sixty-
four respondents who were not full-time supervisors
fell generally into the two categories of teaching

TABLE 2

PROFILE OF TIME EXPENDITURES ON SUBDIVISIONS OF
MAJOR DUTY AREAS AS REPORTED BY
SUPERVISORS OF EACH CATEGORY

Areas of Responsibility, Functions	Means for Each Supervisory Category		
	Unified	Elementary	County
Budget			
Preparation, Approval	2.53	2.46	2.14
Materials			
Evaluation, Distribution	3.08	2.96	2.42
Preparation for Teachers	2.54	2.57	2.78
Facilities			
Planning, Recommending Changes	2.54	2.46	2.41
Personnel			
Hiring, Firing, Recruitment, Evaluation	3.04	2.83	2.70
Inservice Meetings, Orientation, Workshops	3.03	3.10	3.40
Classroom Teacher Involvement	2.58	2.75	2.91
Curriculum			
Preparation, Development	3.03	3.01	3.25
Articulation, Coordination, Testing	2.77	2.69	2.64
Work with Students			
Field Trips, Festivals, Concerts	2.82	2.86	2.68
Teaching, Conducting Performances	2.82	3.12	2.50
Administration			
Giving Advice, Acting as Resource Person	3.18	2.95	3.13
Disseminating Literature, Policy, News	2.79	2.75	2.84
Program Coordination, Correspondence	3.29	3.09	3.40
Specially Funded Projects	2.07	1.95	2.02
Community			
District and Community Programs	3.12	2.93	2.95
Presentation of District Policy	3.00	2.91	3.13
Professional			
Professional Organizations	3.04	2.82	3.29
Professional Literature	3.10	3.01	3.30

or supervising in other areas. Half of the part-time county personnel were involved in curriculum areas other than music. Most part-time elementary and secondary-unified personnel were involved in music teaching.

In summary, the diversity of activities and the proliferation of titles registered with the investigator indicate that the music supervisory positions in the public schools would benefit from a clarification of role. Discussion among supervisors has indicated that school administrators are as vague about the role of the various music supervisory positions as are the supervisors themselves. It would benefit music supervisors to study their time expenditures, as categorized and abstracted, in terms of efficiency and effectivenss. They then could arrive, through corporate action, at a statement of activities with value commensurate to the time expended and titles defined in terms of definite professional practice.

INCONSISTENCIES IN THE WRITING OF
JAMES L. MURSELL*

Donald E. Metz

Most music educators know the name James L.
Mursell. Many have read a few of his articles, and
some have even investigated his lesser known chapters and articles in an attempt to become better
acquainted with his point of view. Few would doubt
that Mursell was an important figure in the world of
music education. However, no one has brought to
light the fact that Mursell, for all his stature and
tremendous written output, was quite inconsistent in
his points of view. He frequently contradicted himself and demonstrated uncertainty in areas where
present day readers turn to him for guidance and
insight. Let us examine some of the more interesting
changes of mind in his writing.

Music educators have always been faced with the
problem of choosing appropriate materials for a
given class of students. Listening selections,
especially, seem to vex many teachers, who wish to
be certain that their choice is relevant for their
class. In this regard, Mursell wrote:

> In particular, one should be on one's guard
> against excluding certain compositions be-
> cause one thinks them too "great" or too
> "advanced" for children of a given age.
> After all, who among us gets all that can
> be gotten from the Eroica Symphony or the
> B Minor Mass?(1)

But within five years, he denied this position:

> It is always necessary to choose music with
> reference to the pupil's present capacity

---

* Reprinted by permission of Donald E. Metz
and the Bulletin of the Council for Research in
Music Education, No. 23 (Winter, 1971), pp. 6-11.

for enjoyment . . . . There will be (a very
serious) question about (using) compositions
which project very remote and exalted ways
of feeling, far removed from the present
emotional experience of the pupils, such as
some of the works of Bach, or of Palestrina,
or the later string quartets of Beethoven,
even though they represent some of the
greatest music ever written . . . .(2)

Even the casual reader must sense something
amiss here. Clearly, Mursell was unsure about the
relevance of certain material. At times he had no
objection to occasionally using selections "over the
heads" of the class. He saw such moments as educational, "if handled correctly." (As we shall see,
this language is typically nebulous.) However, the
statement above, made in 1948, obviously took note
of the limits to which this practice could be
taken. Generally, he felt that any work studied,
in listening or in performance, had to be within
the ken of the class--reasonable advice that would
prompt no serious argument. Ultimately, he chose a
conservative viewpoint, easier to justify but less
helpful: "Certainly there is not one and only one
basis for selecting music."(3)

Another area of confusion was whether to teach
for depth or breadth. At first, Mursell sensed
that "what educates the child musically is not so
much the number of songs he has 'read' through as
the excellence with which he has performed them."(4)
But six years after that, he wrote: "it would seem
that extensive rather than intensive experience is
the more desirable."(5) Which statement reflects
Mursell's point of view the best? Probably the
latter, for he continued to emphasize the need for
great variety in class materials in his later books
and articles.

In this same vein, consider the plight of the
novice math teacher who turns to Mursell's book on
Successful Teaching for guidance: "The concrete
and dynamically compelling experiences in and
through which concepts are acquired should be
simple, and they should be copious."(6) But Mursell
considered algebra poorly organized when "too many
examples are introduced and these are superficially
treated, whereas a much smaller number of problems,
each discussed, considered, and studied very

thoroughly would be far preferable." Aware that he
was having semantic difficulties, Mursell <u>attempted</u>
to clarify the point, with this result:

> It may seem that the demand for fewer
> problems is exactly contrary to the idea of
> copious and abundant context. But a few
> problems of the right kind will offer an
> immensely richer context than a great many
> of the purely verbal variety. Thus, once
> more, with the learning of problem solving,
> the evident need is a context that is dy-
> namically compelling, concrete, simple, and
> <u>abundant</u>.(7) (italics mine)

We can sympathize with that young math teacher, for
Mursell's discussion of musical questions was frequently no more clear or certain.

Unquestionably, the most interesting aspect
of Mursell's varying points of view has to do with
the relationship between purely musical values and
those values of a personal, social nature which
somehow accrue through involvement with music. Is
music of value because it can help enlarge and
broaden our artistic insight and sensitivity? Or
is music of value because through it we can improve
our social dispositions, our personalities, and our
understandings of our fellow man? Any attempt to
narrowly categorize Mursell here would be futile.
Research would uncover statements that would speak
to both points:

> Music, in its essence, expresses and em-
> bodies emotion. (It) paints no picture,
> tells no story, stands for no system of
> articulate concepts. It does not directly
> symbolize anything at all beyond itself.
> It is design in sound.

or

> Music is a moral force because of its deep
> effect in modifying social and personal
> dispositions and in opening the way toward
> new patterns of conduct.(8)

Both statements appear in the same book, <u>Human
Values in Music Education</u> (1934). What one must
understand here is, of course, that one statement

speaks of what music is, and the other refers to what music can do. However, Mursell never linked his intra-musical philosophy with his extra-musical outcomes.

One does not deny the case for nonmusical values so much as one inquires how these ends are to be achieved by teaching intra-musically. Mursell's statements in this area are often vague and overly general. Music, as he said, can "discharge the great and central mission of all education, which is to raise the level of human quality."(9) How? Is it because music making develops joie de vivre and camaraderie better than any other undertaking? After all, Mursell was convinced that the arts were important in a democratic education because they "can provide experiences so rich and convincing of what free and orderly association and dealing with one's fellows really means."(10) He came to justify music more and more on the basis of social growth and the personal ramifications of music study. Perhaps we can understand his viewpoint better by examining the following remarks.

In 1927 his philosophy was simple and formal: "Music, indeed, is not a language at all, and essentially it expresses nothing, and contains its own beauty and meaning within itself."(11) By the 1940's, though, he saw it differently: "The fact remains that (the composer) did mean something, that he had some point of human and personal reference, and was not spinning mere abstract patterns to be enjoyed wholly and solely for the sake of their symmetry and elegance."(12)

Let us look deeper at this changing viewpoint and its effect upon his interpretation of the function of the music teacher. In 1927 he said that the ultimate aim of music education must be musicianship and that the achievement of this end came about through the perfection of "skills culminating in proper hearing, in proper rhythmic response, in musical intelligence, and in musical feeling."(13) Such a philosophy leaves no doubt about the kind of methodology needed to develop musicianship. The model chosen was the kind of musicianship exemplified by the expert musician--the connoisseur, if you will. But by 1943 the music teacher had quite a different function. He was now a gentle catalyst. The teacher "is not a representative of music _per se_, but rather a servant of the community whose business it is to promote the acceptance and enjoyment of music by human beings."(14) It is obvious that these two kinds of teachers would develop two entirely different kinds of music students. Again, the broadly based, socially oriented philosophy is apparent as it gradually eased out the more rigorous formalism evident in his earliest writings. It seemed that the shift toward the extra-musical justification was to become permanent. But was it?

For years, Mursell continued to stress the need to see music from many vantage points and to use all of them: "The more we emphasize its aesthetic values, its cultural values, its social values, its human values, the better for the cause we have at heart."(15) And yet, six years after this statement, he denied it:

> In many recent publications on the curriculum and on its objectives, the arts are supposed to have a special bearing on "spiritual values," "cultural values," "personal self-development," or some such category. This, to put it bluntly, is preposterous and dangerously so. It is a complete misinterpretation . . . ."(16)

Convincing as this might seem, Mursell was to reverse his opinion once again.

Shortly after he retired, he contemplated writing another book, one patterned after his _Human Values_ but tempered and guided by an additional twenty years experience and thought. Tentatively titled _Music for Living: Guidelines for Music Educators_, the central thesis was to be this:

> The thought would be that music education should fulfill itself in the actual lives of people, social and personal--in richer enjoyment, fuller and more general participation, more adequate taste, a continuing desire for improvement and for sharing. Music, that is, should be and can be far more than just another subject, but rather a potent force making for better, happier, and more worthy living.(17)

Again, we see the social-personal philosophy of Mursell advocating the very outcomes denied earlier. This kind of reversal plagued much of Mursell's writing. His language varied from specific, clear statements about the need for developing aesthetic sensitivity in and through music, to grossly redundant and confusing ramblings about how music could aid social intercourse, improve one's personality, and help one in times of need. Somehow, music is ennobling, consoling, and strengthening. It somehow imparts something worthwhile to one's character and personality, establishes poise, stability, social grace, and improves one's self-confidence.(18) It can be a "socially potent force, capable of cementing groups toward a common goal, wherein one can rejoice in his sharing of his pleasure with others."(19)

Mursell's ultimate goal was the informed, sensitive, democratic citizen, who enjoyed the arts and the crafts. He made no distinction between the "fine arts" and the practical crafts. "The decoration of a room or the choice of a color scheme for a costume are just as authentic aesthetic processes as painting a picture, reading a poem aloud, or composing a symphony." Any worthy endeavor possessed opportunities for aesthetic development. No subject or course could be considered "superior" in its relation to developing aesthetic sensitivity. From this point of view, we can understand better Mursell's overriding principle: the goal of education is to produce healthy, democratic citizens. Any experiences that could broaden and improve the "human quality" were worthy endeavors. Unless the undertaking could demonstrate its effectiveness in the actual lives of the participants, there could be no reason to consider it important. Thus, Mursell gradually defended music in terms of extra-musical, socio-personal behaviors. Unfortunately, even these outcomes--"richer living," "rewarding life"-- remain amorphous and vague.

The inconsistencies in Mursell's work, as in the work of anyone who publishes as much as he did, can be partially explained by maturity and understandable changes of mind. But the great majority of his reversal statements indicate uncertainty and semantic imprecision. This lack of specificity renders weak a good deal of his work and, to a considerable extent, makes it too hazy for

200

application today. But there remains a quantity of writing, largely forgotten today, which speaks clearly and distinctly about means and ends in music education. A collection of "The Best of Mursell" would serve a useful function.

References

All references are ascribed to James Mursell.

(1) Music in American Schools (New York: Silver Burdett, 1943), p. 150.

(2) Education for Musical Growth (Boston: Ginn, 1948), p. 186.

(3) Music and the Classroom Teacher (Morristown: Silver Burdett, 1951), p. 156.

(4) With Mabelle Glenn, The Psychology of School Music Teaching (New York: Silver Burdett, 1931), p. 55.

(5) The Psychology of Music (New York: W. W. Norton, 1937), p. 349.

(6) Successful Teaching (New York: McGraw-Hill, 1954), p. 73.

(7) Ibid., p. 79.

(8) Human Values in Music Education (New York: Silver Burdett, 1934), pp. 35 and 150.

(9) Ibid., p. 382.

(10) "School Music and the Community," Recreation, Volume XXXVII (1943), p. 405.

(11) Principles of Music Education (New York: Macmillan, 1927), p. 87.

(12) Music in American Schools, p. 157.

(13) Principles of Musical Education, p. 9.

(14) Music in American Schools, p. 7.

(15) "Music and the Redefinition of Education in Postwar America," <u>Music Educators Journal</u>, Volume XXIX, Number 5 (1943), p. 15.

(16) <u>Developmental Teaching</u> (New York: McGraw-Hill, 1949), p. 281.

(17) Personal correspondence dated June 14, 1960.

(18) "Give Your Child Music," <u>Parents</u>, Volume XXIII (May 1948), p. 17, 46-48.

(19) "Music and the Redefinition," p. 11.

THE STORY OF W. OTTO MIESSNER
VISIONARY OF WHAT MIGHT BE*

Samuel D. Miller

Primary to any definitive discussion on W.
Otto Miessner is the fact that his life, talents, and
contributions were all characterized by great versa-
tility. During his long life (1880-1967), he resided
in a number of locales for a variety of reasons--to
study, to teach music in public schools, to be an
entrepreneur, and to teach music in institutions of
higher education. His path of professional activity
was indeed circuitous, covering a large area of the
United States. Studies during his earlier years
took him as far as Germany. Owing to these moves
and the great variety of his endeavors, some of his
activities are shrouded for lack of documentation,
likely discarded or lost along the way. From the
considerable amount of documentation remaining, however, his personal array of talents is well established. He was a gifted composer, a creative
educator, a philosopher and interpreter of his time
with uncanny insight and intuition, a poet skillful
with words, a competent businessman, and perhaps most
important of all a dreamer and humanitarian who was
always creating in his mind's eye pictures of what
might be instead of what was in the state of affairs,
especially where music education was concerned.

This talent for creating, inventing, and
changing things manifested itself in obvious ways
from Miessner's early childhood well into his advanced years. It kept his thinking continually
ahead of his time. Consequently, there exists today
a telling number of creative contributions credited
to him by the music education profession. There are
textbooks; choral collections; a class violin method;
a class piano method; original symphonic orchestral,

---

* Reprinted by permission of Samuel D. Miller
and the Bulletin of Historical Research in Music Education, Vol. 2, No. 2 (July, 1981), pp. 21-34.

choral and piano compositions; several collections
of original songs for children plus several hundred
songs scattered throughout the textbooks upon which
he worked; mechanical inventions for training young
listeners (for example, the "phonoscope"); a mechanical invention to allow young musicians to hear
rhythms played accurately (the "rhyth-o-phone");
filmstrips coordinated with records; the invention
of the first small portable upright piano, commonly
called "spinet" in modern times; visual-tactile aids
for teaching class piano; small musical instruments
for children; and an original tonal system of
monosyllabic mnemonics for solmisation and instrumental study.

Additionally, there are monographs, articles,
speeches, a book entitled <u>A Guide to Symphonic
Music</u>, and the organization of the first public
school band to receive national and lasting recognition in the history of American music education.
Behind each of these contributions there exists an
interesting, colorful story because Miessner himself
was an interesting, colorful individual--always
burning with desire to create, and always experiencing a certain amount of personal turmoil.

At first surveillance, this life and the
diverse products it produced seem to possess no
common thread to hold the parts together. It is
almost as if each facet were an entity in itself.
As with most of us, however, the compelling forces
which took Miessner through life were those shaped
in his earliest years by immediate family ties and
influences and the consequent reactions developed
toward them.

Born in 1880 at Huntingburg, Indiana,
Miessner's early musical environment was somewhat
better than average inasmuch as his father and
grandfather, a German immigrant, were musically
talented. Owing to this, there were homemade
violins, a reed organ, and a hexagonal concertina
in the home. Yet, his reaction to this situation
was the adamant belief that he was denied opportunities to learn and enjoy music. He was provided no
early formal music lessons, his desire for a career
in music was vigorously opposed, and while his
musical talents developed, they did not develop to
the extent that he wished. In fact, as he

evaluated the situation, his love of music was severely frustrated.(1)

As a result of this frustration, he developed early an obsession to help all children grow in a musical environment and to develop their musical potentials to the fullest. His own use of the word "obsession"(2) gives an indication of the importance to him of this aspiration, the strongest of any that guided him. Throughout his life, consequently, all of his professional activities and contributions, in spite of their diversity, must be seen and judged in the light of this dominant obsession. His intention thereby becomes clear--to bring music to all children, to make it accessible in as many ways as possible, and to simplify approaches to the art, recognizing that the steep, stony path taken by the virtuoso is inappropriate for meeting the musical needs of the masses.

Miessner's childhood and adolescent years were marked by certain important memories. His father, Charles, taught violin to classes of students in the evenings, and this was to influence young Otto in later years to be a pioneer in class instruction for all types of applied music.(3) He learned basic fundamentals of music from Skinner's Self-Instruction, one of the many "self-instructors" published in the earlier days of this country. He learned chords and their functions from a cornetist in the Huntingburg town band. By the age of fourteen he was composing his own music and printing it with stamps fashioned from a discarded clotheswringer.(4) His self-taught keyboard abilities developed to at least some extent, for he played Louis Moreau Gottschalk's Last Hope as a piano solo for his high school graduation in 1899.

After high school, he led a rather vagabond existence giving instruction to a small class, traveling from town to town as a photographer taking and selling penny pictures, playing dance music in open air booths, and selling pianos. In January, 1900, with borrowed money and a bundle of original compositions tucked under his arm(5) he entered Cincinnati College of Music to study with Frank Van der Stucken and Arnold J. Gantvoort, a public music specialist.(6) Earning the two-year diploma incredibly fast, by June, 1900, Miessner was now ready to look for his first public school position.

At that time few smaller towns had music teachers in the public schools, but finally he secured a position at Booneville, Indiana, a small town south of Huntingburg. Here he taught singing with the aid of his violin and charts which explained the movable do system. Since there were no books, he daily wrote words and music to the study songs on the blackboard. During his stay at Booneville he also presented a school performance of Mikado and started a coal miners' band. This band was endorsed whole-heartedly by various elements of the town citizenry, since Saturday--the day concerts were given--was payday, and prior to the band's formation many miners had nothing better to do than to squander their earnings and behave in a rowdy manner.(7)

The period from 1905-1909, when he taught at Connersville, Indiana, proved to be one of the most important in his life, for during it he achieved outstanding success as a classroom teacher, conducted many creditable musical performances, wrote some of his first really significant music, organized and directed his own music conservatory, and developed the Connersville school band (1907).

The band quickly received local, state, and national attention. Essentially it developed as a needed remedy to discipline problems caused by a group of boys in music class and was inspired by an open air concert given by John Philip Sousa's famous touring band. Miessner had witnessed the sheer delight of these same boys at this concert, and it seemed only natural to develop a school band to meet their particular needs and interests. The first concert was given December 19, 1907, and the following day, a newspaper review states: "To the audience, [the high school military band's] playing was the greatest surprise of the evening."(8) In March, 1908, it played for the Northern and Southern Teachers' Associations at Indianapolis.(9) Through the March-April (1909) issue of School Music, Miessner himself described to a national audience the details of lessons, practice, and motivation:

> I arranged for fifteen-minute lesson periods with the boys whose parents had consented to buy instruments. These lessons I gave during the noon intermission and after school hours, and within two months I had twelve boys. Their number . . . soon increased to eighteen,

all of whom I taught individually and ensemble in this manner. The boys practiced and attended rehearsals faithfully, lured on by the goal set before them, which was a public concert and uniforms with caps of the high school colors.(10)

Miessner sailed to Europe in May, 1909, to study voice with Alexander Heinemann and composition with Edgar Stillman Kelley, who was at that time a notable American composer. Kelley and Miessner frequently attended concerts given by the Berlin Philharmonic Orchestra conducted by Arthur Nikisch, and during these, Kelley often whispered in Miessner's ear information concerning the shape or design of the music, or points concerning dramatic events. Occasionally these whispered comments disturbed nearby listeners, but being greatly impressed by the importance of knowing such information, Miessner for the remainder of his life worked on inventions and materials to help make music intelligible to the listener. The "phonoscope" record player which had a traveling arrow of light pointing to appropriate spots on an analysis chart as records played was one example of his endeavors along this line, and another among many was the book, A Guide to Symphonic Music. Through both of these, structural analysis of music was passed on to the student.

From 1910 to 1914 he taught music at Oak Park, Illinois, but his final public school teaching was to come years later, between 1956 and 1958, when he was in his late seventies and taught at Fairview and Orange, Indiana. His teaching at these two tiny towns where no young graduates would go was to end in turbulence. "I agreed to go because they needed me,"(11) was his simple reason for accepting these jobs. All went well until 1958 when he was informed by the county superintendent that to continue on, he would have to earn five college credits in music education.(12) By this time, as a music educator Miessner had taught and distinguished himself at summer sessions of the American Institute of Normal Methods (1911-1923) and Chicago Musical College (1924-1931). Moreover, he had organized and directed the music education programs at State Teachers College at Milwaukee (1914-1922) and the University of Kansas (1936-1945).

In other professional achievements directly related to music education, he had taken an active role as editor on three of the most important and successful textbook series ever published in America, The Progressive Music Series, The Music Hour and New Music Horizons. Translations of these were distributed and used widely throughout the world. He had served his profession and earned such esteem that he was placed on a number of important committees of the Music Supervisors National Conference and was ultimately elected its president in 1923. By way of these significant activities he had directly affected the music education of millions of youngsters—many of whom were beyond the borders of the United States.

However, continuance of certification in Indiana in 1958 demanded of him five credits in music education. Miessner's pungent reply was quickly picked up and quoted or discussed in countless newspapers across the country: "I'll be damned if I will go to a University using my textbooks and say 'will you please enroll me in a beginning class for music teachers?'"(13) As a result, he resigned and with pride intact went back to private teaching. The episode culminated in an editorial appearing in the July (1958) issue of The Saturday Evening Post, entitled, "They Wouldn't Let Beethoven Teach Music in Indiana."(14) The controversy was enlivened and pointed out by a number of conservatives categorically attacking professional education at this time. The battle cry of the age was to return to content, to stress mathematics and sciences, and to require fewer doctrinaire methods classes. This controversy was a part of the general alarm and ensuing repercussions experienced by the general populace after the Soviet Union ushered in the space age unexpectedly by successfully launching Sputnik I in October, 1957.

Turning to Miessner's extensive teaching experience in institutions of higher learning, it is necessary to go back to the summer of 1911 when he was invited to join the faculty of the American Institute of Normal Methods, a summer school founded in 1885 by Silver Burdett and Company for the primary purpose of promoting sales of its textbooks by training public school teachers to use them. Since few colleges and universities offered courses for the training of music teachers before 1920, these

208

summer Institutes of two and a half weeks duration, and those offered by other publishing companies, were vitally important to the development of American music education. Until 1924, when he accepted an offer to teach at the summer sessions at Chicago Musical College, Miessner taught at the Western Division Institute held on the campus of Northwestern University at Evanston.

According to numerous advertisements in the Music Supervisors Journal, a diploma in music required the completion of sixteen credit hours and normally took from three to four years to complete. Miessner taught choir, methods, and conducting, and in 1921 he succeeded Edward Birge as superintendent.(15)

During the fall and spring school terms from 1914 to 1922, he served as chairman of the department of music at the State Teachers College in Milwaukee and organized a three-year program for the training of music supervisors which included study in vocal and instrumental music, theory, music history, practice teaching, composition, orchestration, and conducting in addition to school music methods. His philosophy pertaining to the qualities needed by the music teacher were stated in a newspaper article of 1915:

> The supervisor or director of music must be an all-round musician, as well as having a broad general education. The teacher formerly selected because she sang in the village choir or played the piano agreeably will need to have her outlook broadened . . . . It will not be sufficient for the music teacher of the future to have in her possession a notebook crammed with data on methods. The supervisor of the future must be able "to do" as well as "to know."(16)

According to other statements in this article, Miessner was convinced at this early date that an adequately prepared music supervisor must play the piano well, play at least one orchestral instrument, be able to sing, and possess a knowledge of the development and proper training of the child voice. Furthermore, he believed that music supervisors and all other school teachers should have a command of English, an understanding of educational psychology and pedagogy, and an "executive ability to carry out plans."(17)

In 1922, Miessner gave up his position at the State Teachers College, but continued to teach summer sessions at Chicago Musical College. His next major teaching assignment came in 1936, when he was invited to organize and direct the department of music education at the University of Kansas. Prior to that date this institution offered only music education courses for elementary education students. Enthusiasm concerning his arrival ranged quite high, and within a short time he successfully developed both an undergraduate and graduate program.

Former students asked to comment on Miessner as a teacher were exceedingly complimentary--the most frequently used adjective was "inspirational." It is safe to conclude that he enjoyed notable success and was well liked by students and colleagues, not only because of his excellent scholarship, his outstanding musical abilities, and his remarkable number of achievements, but also because of his wonderful ability to inspire, to encourage, and to understand others. Perhaps Genevieve Hargiss gives the most vivid and telling description:

> In Dr. Miessner's classes, his lectures rarely had anything to do with the assignments. He may have prepared some class lectures, but I doubt that we ever heard any of them. He would make a beginning, then the first question or some sudden inspiration of his own would start him talking extemporaneously in another direction. I remember that the period was always over before we realized it had even begun. He was busy with at least a dozen projects at one time, and he shared them all with us. . . . It was his faith in the values of music that inspired his students and made us eager to get into our respective classrooms and begin.(18)

In addition to the chairmanship duties of the music education department, he taught methods, analysis, and orchestra workshop. Retirement came in 1945, when Miessner was 65, and E. Thayer Gaston, one of his first doctoral students, succeeded him as chairman.

Miessner first became interested in national leadership in school music when he attended the meetings of the Music Section of the National Education Association at Asbury Park, New Jersey, in 1905. His former teacher, A. J. Gantvoort of the Cincinnati College of Music, was chairman of one of the music sessions. Early, however, his interest shifted from this organization to the newly formed Music Supervisors Conference, and he became an active member in 1910. Quickly elevating himself to national stature, in 1912 he delivered his first speech to the national meeting at St. Louis, entitled "The Child Voice in Song Interpretation."(19) Although he talked about methods for obtaining beautiful singing from elementary school children, he mainly discussed his philosophy concerning the teaching of children to read music at sight. The principles laid down by him on this subject are significant, for they were used in the reading programs of the three series of textbooks bearing his name.

His rise to acclaim within the organization of the Conference was noteworthy and began with his election in 1919 to the first Educational Council. Among the bulletins written and published by this Council during Miessner's first four-year term were Courses for the Training of Supervisors of Music, Standard Courses in Music for Graded Schools, and High School Credits for Applied Music Study. After his election to a second four-year term in 1923, the year in which the Council's name was officially changed to the National Research Council, more bulletins carrying his name were published: Study of Music Instruction in the Public Schools of the United States; Music in the Junior High School; Standard Courses for the Training of Grade Teachers; A Survey of Music Material for Grammer, Junior and Senior High School Orchestras; and Music in the One-Teacher Rural School.

Through his extraordinary success as a teacher, his Conference activities, his editorial work with Silver Burdett and Company, and his profound personal and scholarly qualities, it is not difficult to see why Will Earhart and others of the Conference Nominating Committee influenced him to accept the nomination for national Conference president in 1923. Subsequently, he was elected president and set as his task the goal of seeing music entered as a curricular offering in all the schools of the nation.

In a short article appearing in the Music Supervisors Journal, he stated that the National Research Council had collected data which proved beyond a doubt that more than one-half of the public schools in the United States did not offer music instruction.(20)

During his term as president, therefore, Miessner attempted to improve this situation by writing a series of three letters which discussed the values of school music. He sent them to 6,100 school superintendents throughout the nation, all of whom resided in cities and towns of over 1,000 inhabitants. These letters stressed the importance of music instruction for every child, and stated that music helps to make a happier school, a finer community, and better citizenship. Moreover, they stressed the fact that the 22,000,000 children of the country should know the joy that comes from acquaintance with music and song. With each of these letters, pamphlets were also enclosed outlining standard courses in music and programs of instruction for classes in violin, piano, and voice. With this accomplished, Miessner had put the basic philosophy, curriculum, and organizational guidelines of music education into the administrative offices of the schools across the land.

The National Conference met in Cincinnati, April 8 to 11, 1924, with Miessner as president. In a review, George Bowen, editor of the Journal, evaluated Miessner's presidential speech, "Music for Every Child" as a "highlight."(21) In it, Miessner vividly expressed his conviction that every child should receive music instruction in the public schools. He told his audience there was a growing demand for practical education--the kind of education that will function in the lives of boys and girls. In the past, he pointed out, "children have been forced to fit the schools; in the future we shall change the schools to fit the children."(22) He maintained that the most important goal of the public schools is to make the child an intelligent, useful, and moral citizen, "intelligent, that he may think clearly and act wisely in private and public matters; useful, that he may serve his fellow-men; moral, and that he may bestow and derive the greatest good and happiness through living." Finally, he referred to music's place in this new educational movement and exclaimed concerning the cost:

Oh yes, I know all about the hue and cry,
"we can't afford this additional expense!"
It is heard throughout the land. It comes
from men who begrudge the schools a meager
billion dollars annually, from men who turn
two billion dollars into tobacco smoke!(23)

In order to emphasize each point Miessner referred to statistical data he had collected. This
information, in the form of tables and graphs,
follows the speech as it is presented in the Conference Yearbook of 1924.

Miessner was elected in 1924 and 1928 to the
Board of Directors, and in 1938, to another term on
the Research Council. After 1944, the year in which
his final term as a member of the Council expired,
he made no noteworthy contributions to the Conference.

Although, according to Bowen and others,
Miessner was an excellent Conference president,
perhaps his most valuable contributions to that
organization were his brilliant, stirring, and
dynamic speeches.

Always one who loved intricate detail, Miessner
stressed and illuminated his points frequently with
research statistics. For example, in his Conference
address of 1918, entitled "Music's Place in the
Public School System," he asserted that the goal of
modern education was to "help the individual live
not only the most complete adult life, but a complete
child life as well."(24) Illustrating the fact that
music was extremely important in the lives of adults
and children he stated that in 1914 over $382,000,000
was spent for church music, concerts, operas, sheet
music, books, phonographs, and theater music. Additionally, the cost of private instruction amounted
to $200,000,000. The total of these two expendi-
tures, he dramatically pointed out, nearly equaled
the amount "spent for our entire educational system
in the same year, including the cost of maintaining
all our elementary schools, high schools, and normal
schools."(25)

As an intellectual subject, as mental training,
he declared, no branch of the curriculum offers a
richer field for study than music. "Music is so
simple," he said, "that the humblest, the most

illiterate peasant, can grasp and retain a melody;
it is so complex that it is worthy of the greatest
intellects of all times." In closing this speech he
went so far as to exclaim,

> let us demand action, legislation, if neces-
> sary. . . . Let us have music taught in our
> elementary schools, in our high schools, and
> in our state universities . . . let us have
> bands and orchestras overywhere, as well as
> singing.(26)

Although there were numerous other speeches--
to the National Conference, to sectional Conferences,
and to educational organizations--the speech delivered
in 1930 to the Conference held at Chicago deserves
special mention, for among other things it demonstrates clearly that in the wake of the depression,
his thoughts were centered on the future. "Man or
Machine-made Music?"(27) was concerned with educational implications to be drawn from the success of
the radio and the "talking picture." After empha-
sizing that these were valuable and could be used "for
the mass distribution of art," he added:

> The mediocre artist no longer has a public.
> Concert Bureaus, Lyceums, Chatauquas are
> vanishing. Only genuine virtuosi-artists of
> international renown will draw paying audiences
> today. It would appear that these, like the
> movie stars, will receive huge salaries, while
> the small-town actor will disappear from the
> scene. Indeed John MacCormack and Lawrence
> Tibbet, Dennis King and Marilyn Miller, today
> are the forerunners of this new era in
> music.(28)

Going further, he made the astonishing prediction for the year 1930, that soon television would
make it possible for Americans to see and hear the
greatest artists at the exact time they perform.
This, he warned, would mean that lesser artists would
find it very difficult to succeed as professional
musicians.(29) Owing to these facts, he insisted
that music educators must strive to teach "most young
performers to play for their own self-culture, expression, and pleasure."(30) Finally, he stated that
in future years the most important duty of the music
teacher would be to raise the level of music appreciation in the country.

It is small wonder that Conference president Joseph Maddy, in a letter to Miessner dated October 8, 1937, invited him to deliver the principal speech for the opening session of the upcoming Conference in St. Louis and further wrote, "In general, your thinking is about ten years ahead of the rest of our contemporaries, and you can point the way better than anyone I know."(31) Most of his speeches, however, returned at one point or another to the phrase, "music for every child," for it expressed the foremost idea on his mind. The reasons he gave for this belief could easily apply to current revisions in the profession. Conference activity was devoted to the development and illustration of these reasons, for he wanted others to become aware of them, to be influenced by them, and, as a consequence, to actively and dynamically join his cause.

Early in his career Miessner expressed the belief that after the toy instruments, which are primarily rhythmic in character, the piano is not only the most practical instrument but also the most important tool for understanding music. To him, it was the best vehicle through which children could experience music completely, that is, with rhythm, melody, and harmony combined.(32) Schools, however, in the early decades of this century typically had large, heavy upright pianos or reed organs. They were not easily moved about nor particularly suited for accompanying children's voices. By 1917, he realized there was a pressing need to develop a small, inexpensive portable piano, one with lighter string tension to produce a softer sound and one small enough to permit a teacher when playing to face and see pupils.

Frank E. Morton of the America Steel and Wire Company drew up the manufacturing plans according to Miessner's own specifications, and Edmund Gram, the Steinway dealer for Wisconsin, agreed to build six of these instruments in his own shop. Five of the pianos were to go to State Teachers College, Milwaukee, where Miessner was teaching, and the sixth to be exhibited in the spring of 1918 at the National Conference.(33) Subsequently, the "Miessner" piano was introduced at the Evansville Conference, and approximately forty orders for delivery when available were received by Miessner.

Quickly thereafter sales of these instruments became so numerous that the capital turnover was four times as rapid as was common for the piano industry during 1918 and a number of succeeding whole years. On one occasion Miessner stated that approximately two thousand "Miessner" (and later his so-called "Monogram") pianos were sold during an average year and "that probably there were fifteen to twenty thousand . . . sold before 1929," when production stopped just before the national depression hit.(34) Throughout the early years the instruments were produced by the Edmund Gram and Jackson Piano Companies in turn. Finally, after he resigned from his teaching position in 1922, Miessner formed his own company and produced them.

Although many piano manufacturers ridiculed these little instruments immediately after their first appearance, the success they enjoyed in public school sales, and unexpectedly, in home and apartment sales, was so impressive, that other companies including Cable, Strohber, Wurlitzer, Schultz, and Steinway, started to produce small uprights also and called them "spinets." After 1909, the year in which overall piano sales were highest in the United States according to the "Census of Manufacturers," piano sales in general continued to drop steadily until the depression. By contrast, however, once the Miessner piano was introduced in 1918, its sales climbed and hit a peak in 1927.

Along with the gradual drop in total piano sales after 1914, there began to occur a general business depression as well. Curiously, however, from 1914 to 1925 sales had doubled in furniture, refrigerators, hardware, tools, clothing, confections and soft drinks, sporting goods, statuary, art goods, jewelry, and tobacco. Sales had tripled in washing machines, automobiles, books, magazines, and newspapers. In a speech delivered to the National Association of Music Merchants in New York City, October 29, 1926, Miessner brilliantly analyzed this situation and brought forth implications for consideration. According to Edward H. Uhl, who commented in the foreword of reprinted copies, "no speech of recent years . . . stirred a meeting of Music Merchants more."

Miessner pointed out that it would naturally be expected that the sale of pianos would be stimulated by increased residential building and the demand for related goods, but that no one with faith in statistics could deny that there was something radically wrong with the piano business. Further, he analyzed:

> It is well called "the restless age." Modern transportation facilities, steamships, railroads, automobiles and aircraft have made the world our parking place. Theatres, movies and public amusement palaces lure the people away from their homes. The postal service, the newspapers, the telegraph and telephone, the player-piano, the phonograph and radio have brought the world into the farmer's front parlor. One set of forces is centrifugal; they take us away from home. Fortunately, the latter forces are centripetal; they tend to keep us at home. (35)

He told the merchants that they must "help bring the love of music into every home." (36)   Then he stated that love for music "must lead to a desire to make music, without which there can be no demand for musical instruments, particularly pianos and other instruments meant for individual playing or participation." (37)   Among the actions he suggested music dealers should take were: (1) to become musical and show an active, personal interest in all things musical; (2) to cultivate friendship with public school personnel; (3) to urge that music be taught in every schoolroom; (4) to give free class piano lessons in their stores that summer; (5) to organize solo music contests and sponsor concerts by children; (6) to co-operate with the schools by lending instruments, printing programs, and selling tickets; and (7) to make interesting window displays of public school musical activities.

During 1927, and in the early part of 1928, Miessner became apprehensive about the total economic condition of the country as he continued to study the Census of Manufacturer's reports. Consequently he kept his inventories low. On a trip west in September, 1928, seeing bankrupt prices marked on overstocks of numerous brands of pianos, he foresaw and predicted the Great Depression and realized that his company with its limited capital could not survive. Upon returning to Milwaukee, he presented and pursued a plan of liquidation which was successfully completed without financial loss by December 31, 1928, approximately one month after the depression unleashed its initial disasterous forces. Although no Miessner pianos were ever manufactured in later years, all small uprights produced to the present day are direct descendants.

Miessner's skillful analysis of causes and impacts of the depression was expressed in, "How the Economic Slump Has Affected the Music Teacher," one of the series of three articles published in 1931.

The present depression differs from all others in that there are not only the usual temporary factors, but, in addition, certain cumulative phases that have never before been present in equal intensity.

Among the temporary factors are those of industrial expansion and overproduction, stimulated first, by world war demands, and subsequently, by super-efforts to keep the wheels turning. The new device of installment selling, aided by mass advertising and high pressure salesmanship, resulted in over-buying by nearly all of us to such an extent that the bubble was fated to burst.

Added to this came the 1929 "money mania," reflected by gambling in stocks on a scale and scope never before experienced, resulting in the "debacle" of last Fall and the "spectacle" of 1930.

The cumulative forces are the unchartered forces, first, of technical unemployment caused by machines displacing human labor; second, new commodities created by modern invention which have reversed the balances of supply and demands in some field overnight, as, for example, in textiles, in fuels, in refrigeration, in transportation, in entertainment; third, in new methods of augmenting the supply of commodities, as, for example, in scientific agriculture, in irrigation and power projects; fourth, the phenomenal growth of industrial mergers and corporate consolidations operating as national chains and displacing the individual entrepeneur.(38)

218

In the third article, "Suggested Remedies for the Prevailing Maladies of Music," Miessner wisely concluded that the American people must come to realize that "self-expression is the law of life,"(39) and that participation in musical activities is most rewarding. He warned that musicians must strive to provide the masses with opportunities to study music through class instruction and that "when engineering and chemistry, law and surgery, sculpture and painting, and all other sciences, arts, and skills are successfully so taught, we are fools to insist that music, only is a sacred exception."(40)

Miessner's interest in writing a class piano method was of course a natural outgrowth of his interest in selling pianos during the 1920's. In spite of this, however, he always thought of himself primarily as an educator rather than a businessman. He had been for years a staunch advocate of the merits of class instruction, since he believed the high cost of private lessons denied many children opportunities to study music. In 1924, therefore, the Miessner Institute, a personal publishing house, brought out the first books of The Melody Way to Play the Piano.(41)

The subtitles and publishing dates of the complete series are: First Book and Teachers Manual (1924); Second Book and Third Book (1926); Teachers Manual for Ampico Piano Rolls, Master Melodies, Minute Melodies, More Melodies, and Solo Melodies (1927); Primer (1930). These were sold and distributed by the Miessner Institute until 1948, when copyrights were assigned to the H. T. FitzSimmons Company.

Melody Way enjoyed its greatest sales period from 1925 until 1930.(42) Special teachers were trained and teaching aids devised; workshops were held in numerous cities; the books were translated and published in Europe, Africa, Australia, and Asia; lessons were even published in many important American newspapers. Melody Way became so popular in this country by 1930, that according to one advertisement, sixty percent of the 557 cities reporting inclusion of class piano instruction in their public schools used it.(43)

The methodology itself was a remarkable reflection of Miessner's profound grasp of the child study movement in education as it might affect music teaching. It began with five-tone scale nursery songs to be sung first by rote, then played back on the black keys, and proceeded toward note reading. Abstract exercises were avoided, and the child was drawn into music through a natural, interesting process. Analyses of chord structures, phrase gestures, and total compositional designs were emphasized and carefully laid out by Miessner. _Melody Way_ classrooms typically contained several pianos, a cardboard keyboard on each desk, and an array of other aids such as chord finders, key finders, and charts.

In 1961, Miessner accepted a cash offer for his royalties in _Melody Way_, thus giving up control of its final destiny.(44) As a creative personal endeavor it was exceedingly important to him, for in this same late year of his life he wrote,

> "I sometimes think that my _Melody Way_
> materials and workshops . . . were the most
> significant contribution. . . . Literally
> millions of children were benefitted from
> these economical class lessons—particularly
> through the great depression years."(45)

Throughout his long life Miessner's mind burned relentlessly with a passion to create new solutions to problems plaguing music educators. Since the days of Guido d'Arezzo music teachers have used mnemonics to teach music reading. Among these are the fixed _do_, movable _do_, letter name, and the number systems. Being dissatisfied with each of these for disadvantages well known by most teachers, he invented his own system in 1931 and called it the "absolute tonal system."

The system consists of euphonious monosyllables derived from letters of the musical alphabet, thus it could be used for vocal or instrumental teaching. The C-major scale syllables are _ca_ (sung "kah"), _da_, _me_ (may), _fa_, _ga_, _la_, _be_ (bay), _ca_. The pitches E and A, not being consonants, were preceded by "m" and "l" respectively. The other letters were followed by "a" (sung "ah"). Miessner maintained that the best sound for sharps was "e" as in "they" and for double sharps the vowel "i" as in "antique." Hence, C-sharp became _ce_ (sung "kay") and C-double-sharp became _ci_ (sung "kee"). Voice teachers often refer to "ay" and "ee" as being bright vowels. In the C-major

scale, he used these brighter vowels on E and B to
mark the tendency tones of both the lower and upper
tetrachords. The darker vowels are usually considered "o" and "u" (sung "oo"), and Miessner used them
to indicate flats and double flats. Hence, A-flat
became lo and A-double-flat became lu.

Among advantages in utilizing the system were:
(1) it was singable at rapid tempi and was euphonious; (2) it yielded but one name for each of the
twelve semi-tones, (3) it could be used in tonal
music, progressing from key to key with the introduction of only one new syllable name after each
key change, (4) it was quite functional in atonal
music, (5) it was an aid to tonal thinking when
taking music dictation, and (6) trained musicians
could find it easy to learn with several hours of
practice.(46)

In January, 1962, Miessner introduced his system to the world of music education in an article
appearing in the Music Educators Journal entitled,
"The Art of Tonal Thinking." Subsequently, extensive
and successful experimentation with school children
was carried out in Dallas under the direction of
Marion Flagg, former supervisor of music, and with
college students in theory at North Texas State
University.(47)

Of the remaining and numerous creative contributions of Miessner, certain compositions and
books deserve comment. Miesnner was very talented
and thoroughly schooled in composition. Over the
years he composed hundreds of children's songs and
lyrics, many of which were contained in the textbook
series. One of the most beautiful and popular of
his songs is "Michigan, My Michigan," known by nearly
every school student in that state.(48) His Six
Song Cycles, meant to be sung to children, were
written in 1907-1908.(49) They were lauded by
Engelbert Humperdinck, Will Earhart, Xavier
Scharwenka, and others. His oratorio Christus was
first played at the Connersville May Festival, 1910,
by the Cincinnati Orchestra under the direction of
Leopold Stokowski.(50) The cantata, Dryad's Kisses,
for children's voices, soloists, and orchestra was
performed by Federick Stock and the Chicago Symphony
Orchestra at Evanston in 1929, and later in 1930 at
Kansas City under the direction of Maybelle
Glenn.(51) Other notable works are Sonata Excelsior

for piano (1917), incidental music for <u>As You Like It</u> (1941), and <u>The Tempest</u> (1916).

In 1944, McKinley Publishers brought out the last two collections of songs composed by Miessner, <u>Sing to Me</u> and <u>Play for Me</u>. These songs were to be taught by mothers or early childhood teachers to little children. After learning to sing them first by rote, children were encouraged to play them on the piano, and finally, in Play for Me, they were introduced to basic notation.

<u>A Book of Choruses for High School Choral Societies</u>, published in 1923 by Silver Burdett and Company, was edited by Miessner, Osbourne McConathy, Edward Birge, and Goerge Chadwick. This book, containing a wealth of material for school vocal groups, enjoyed nationwide distribution and success.(52) The <u>Melody Way to Play Violin</u> was written by Miessner and George Dash in 1928 and was one of the earliest class violin methods published in the United States. The <u>All American Song Book</u>, compiled and edited by Joseph Maddy and Miessner, was published in 1942, by Robbins Music Corporation and was the first comprehensive compilation of standard and popular American song favorites.

Where did the ideas and inspiration for all of these varied and commendable accomplishments come from? Miessner's own answer to the question was, "I don't know . . . from Heaven, I guess." Going on, he commented that the trouble with most people and their hunches was that they didn't do anything with them.(53) His life, in glowing contrast, poured forth an abundance of hunches subsequently acted upon but always with the aim of bringing opportunities in music to every child. This aim was formulated as a reaction to his own childhood experiences, and it never changed; instead it burned even brighter in his later years.

These were spent at Connersville where he resided in a century-old gray house, behind which stood his library-studio-workshop, a converted stable. Here he taught piano and voice to small classes of students and continued to study and ponder on all facets of music history and literature; on the writings of Dewey, Adler, Whitehead, and Santayana; and on everything else in print he could secure in one way or another. The back room of this building was

222

primarily a workshop, and in it he continued to build sets of "melody bells," hand cut brass tubes mounted over a trapezoidal frame which he marketed in wooden cases along with instructional materials.

In this same room he continued his search to find a simple, inexpensive gadget to spot precisely passages of music recorded on discs to aid the layman in studying and understanding shapes and structures in music. The final, exceedingly inexpensive solution he produced and was so excited about was a thin plastic strip which had a hole on one end allowing it to go down over the spindle on top of any disc. The other side of the strip facing the tone arm had a concave shape and was marked off in centimeters. Its lower height allowed the tone arm, which had a simple wire taped on, to pass over and point to the centimeters. With this, his final answer, he began to write analysis charts corresponding to specific records with themes and structures calculated in centimeters. His work on these, however, was sporadic and hindered by the slowing down process inflicted on him by advancing age.

The last National Conference Miessner attended was held in Kansas City, March, 1966. In keeping with his habit of many previous conventions, he rented a display booth, number 316, within the exhibit hall. A large center sign read simply "Otto Miessner, Connersville, Indiana," and to its right a second sign read "Inventions: rhythm master, tachtometer, rhythm record, phonometer, and guides to symphonic music." On the draped table in front lay the advertised equipment, and he eagerly described it to anyone who wandered in, after first taking hold of their arm--a gesture that was nearly his trademark. Although his talk rambled, as one thing reminded him of the next without hesitation, it was never leisurely or aimless, and the zeal and enthusiasm never waned. It was apparent, nevertheless, that he was pressed by the debilitating effects of the passage of time. Moreover, he was undoubtedly burdened by the loss of his wife of many years just a few weeks before.

Miessner died the next year on May 27, 1967, exactly one day after his eighty-seventh birthday. His accomplishments, lively spirit, and human characteristics, however, will long live on vividly in the memories of those who knew him--his friends, former students, and colleagues. These things, rather than the ravages of advanced years, will come to mind. But his accomplishments, in one way or another, will also continued to have a positive effect upon countless numbers of youths for many generations yet to come.

References

(1) Interview with W. Otto Miessner, Connersville, Indiana, 4 August 1961.

(2) Miessner interview, 4 August 1961.

(3) He once asked, "Is medicine taught privately by the best surgeons? Is law taught privately by the best lawyers? If a master surgeon teaches by performing delicate surgeries for a class, why can't music teachers instruct students in class?" Miessner interview, 5 August 1961.

(4) John Beattie, "Meet Mr. Miessner," Music Educators Journal, 42 (January 1956): 24-26.

(5) Among these were "Elsa's Dream," "Hoosier Colonel," and "Rush to the Klondike."

(6) Baker's Biographical Dictionary of Music, ed. Nicholas Slonimsky, 5th ed. (New York: G. Schirmer, Inc., 1958), p. 1686.

(7) Miessner interview, 5 August 1961.

(8) The Evening News (Connersville, Indiana), December 20, 1907.

(9) Program of the May Day Concert, Connersville High School, Connersville, Indiana, May 1, 1908.

(10) See W. Otto Miessner, "Instrumental Music and the Boy Problem," School Music 10 (March-April 1909), p. 18.

(11) Miessner interview, 6 August 1961.

(12) Howard M. Selm to W. Otto Miessner, 17 January 1958.

(13) Among them were The New York Times, The Indianapolis Times, The Dallas Morning News, The Milwaukee Journal, The Louisville Times, The Cincinnati Post, and The Blade-Tribune (Oceanside, California).

(14) The Saturday Evening Post 231 (July 19, 1958): 8.

(15) Alice Gilson, Editorial Department, Silver Burdett and Company, to Samuel D. Miller, 29 November 1961.

(16) Milwaukee Free Press (Milwaukee, Wisconsin), September 19, 1915.

(17) Ibid.

(18) Genevieve Hargiss to Samuel D. Miller, 26 January 1962.

(19) Proceedings of the MSNC (1912), pp. 29-52.

(20) "Salutatory," Music Supervisors Journal 9 (May 1923): 8.

(21) "Conference Highlights as the Artist Saw Us," Music Supervisors Journal 10 (May 1924): 65.

(22) Proceedings of the MSNC (1924), p. 60.

(23) Ibid., pp. 69-70.

(24) Proceedings of the MSNC (1924), p. 53.

(25) Ibid., p. 57.

(26) Ibid., p. 67.

(27) Proceedings of the MSNC (1930), p. 166.

(28) Ibid.

(29) Ibid., p. 165.

(30) Ibid., p. 166.

(31) Joseph E. Maddy to W. Otto Miessner, 8 October 1937.

(32) W. Otto Miessner, "Melodic Approach to Music," Proceedings of the MSNC (1929), pp. 380-381.

(33) W. Otto Miessner to Samuel D. Miller, 17 November 1961.

(34) This figure was given by Miessner himself, August 5, 1961. Occasionally advertisements gave specific figures pertaining to certain school districts. Examples are found in Music Supervisors Journal 9 and 10 (March and October 1923), pp. 9 and 13 respectively. Records of company transactions were destroyed long before 1961.

(35) W. Otto Miessner, Make More Music (New York: National Association of Music Merchants, 1926), p. 9.

(36) Ibid., p. 24.

(37) Ibid.

(38) The Musician 36 (June 1931): 11.

(39) The Musician 36 (July 1931): 7.

(40) Ibid.

(41) Miessner discussed the class piano movement and its merits in "Piano Class Movement," Proceedings of the MSNC (1931), p. 248. Also see Charles Henry McIntosh, This Age of Rebellion (Milwaukee: Miessner Institute of Music, 1928), pp. 30-31, for descriptions of Melody Way class procedures.

(42) Included in a reprint of an address entitled, "Make More Music" delivered to the twenty-fifth annual convention of the National Association of Music Merchants (June 9, 1926), p. 14, Miessner listed 131 cities offering Melody Way classes. During this period there were many lists, mostly in advertisements, of school systems using the method.

(43) Advertisement for The Melody Way to Play the Piano, Music Supervisors Journal 36 (February 1930): 6.

(44) Miessner interview, 6 August 1961.

(45) Miessner to Miller, 6 October 1961.

(46) For a modification of the system see Paul
Roe, Choral Music Education (Englewood Cliffs, New
Jersey: Prentice Hall, Inc., 1970), p. 159, foot-
note. For further information on the system see
"Miessner Tonal Phonetics: An Aid to Tonal
Thinking, Marion Flagg Pamphlet for Teachers" and
two demonstration rental films by Dorothy Inge Smith
and Marion Flagg. All of these are available through
Rhythm Band Incorporated, Fort Worth, Texas.

(47) Marion Flagg to Samuel D. Miller, 3 June
1961. Also see Roe, p. 159.

(48) During the 1950's, Mrs. M. Cedrick
Dowling of Jackson, Michigan, in behalf of the State
Federation of Music Clubs attempted unsuccessfully
to persuade the State Legislature to adopt
"Michigan, My Michigan" as the official state song.

(49) The Evening News (Connersville, Indiana),
April 1, 1907.

(50) Program of May Festival, May 1, 1910.

(51) Miessner to Miller, January 7, 1962.

(52) Gilson to Miller, 29 November 1961.

(53) Aberdeen American News (Aberdeen, South
Dakota), October 2, 1955.

A MULTIVARIATE ANALYSIS OF FACTORS IN THE
BACKGROUNDS OF WYOMING ADULTS RELATED
TO THEIR ATTITUDINAL LEVELS
CONCERNING MUSIC*

Robert F. Noble

To what extent do we do what we say we do?
While they have been enlarged and refined over the
years, the basic objectives of school music programs
have remained relatively constant. Goals such as
"(the) primary purpose of music education programs
is to develop the aesthetic potential . . . to the
highest possible level," "establish working standards
in his [the student's] valuation of music," "be an
active participant in music throughout his life,"
and "musical independence" (15, pp. 1-2) are firmly
supported by most of us in the music education
field. While all these seem to imply application
throughout an individual's life, most evaluations
of objectives' attainment presently are directly at
the instructional level in terms of the school music
curriculum.

True, such objectives contain both cognitive
and affective elements, and the two may be insepara-
ble. As Colwell (3, p. 128) indicated:

> In practical experience, a person rarely
> develops an instinctive appreciation for
> music without knowing anything about it.
> Cognitive awareness heightens the emotional
> response, sharpens the attention, and helps
> to create a genuine aesthetic experience.

We seem to assume a cause and effect relationship, that if, for example, a student is provided

---

* Reprinted by permission of Robert F. Noble
and the Bulletin of the Council for Research in
Music Education, No. 48 (Fall, 1976), pp. 21-35.

true aesthetic experiences, is taught musical understandings and performance skills, becomes musically
independent, and is given standards in valuations
of music he will make "appropriate" affective decisions about music in adult life. While the affective
response is totally the individual's own right, we
expect to shape that response. As Colwell (3, p.
129) further said:

> The responsibility of the school program is
> then to teach the substance upon which under-
> standing is based and to expect [italics sup-
> plied] students to form their own values and
> to experience the aesthetic response as a
> result of what they know and what they hear
> in the music. The task of the school is to
> give students sufficient information and
> understanding to make their own intelligent
> decisions.

The focus of this research is a test of this
assumption. What is the relationship between the
quantitative amount of music education and attitudes
toward music of Wyoming adults?

Because conditions among the target population
could not be controlled nor manipulated, an experimental design seemed infeasible. Multivariate
analysis could show the degree of relationship among
variables.

Statement of the problem. The problem was to
discover the degree of relationship among five variables in the previous musical and personal experience of adults in Wyoming with 11 levels of their
attitudes concerning music. Sub-problems of the
research were:

1. What relationship is there between the extent of previous school music experiences of adults
and their attitudinal levels concerning music?
2. What relationship is there between the
category of present age of adults and their attitudinal levels concerning music?
3. What relationship is there between sex of
respondents and their attitudinal levels concerning
music?
4. What relationship is there between present
urban or rural living of adults and their attitudinal levels concerning music?

229

5. What relationship is there between the
ordered category of present occupation of respondents
and their attitudinal levels concerning music?

Hypotheses. The following hypotheses were proposed for the research, all tested at p<.01:

1. There is no weighting of independent and
dependent variables that will produce a significant
correlation between the new hypothetical variables
established by those weights.
2. Any correlation between the extent of
previous school music experience of adults and their
measured attitudinal levels toward music will be due
to chance alone.
3. Any correlation between the categorized
present ages of adults and their measured attitudinal levels toward music will be due to chance
alone.
4. Any correlation between the sex of adults
and their measured attitudinal levels toward music
will be due to chance alone.
5. Any correlation between category of
present community size and the measured attitudinal
levels of adults toward music will be due to chance
alone.
6. Any correlation between ordered category
of present occupation of adults and their measured
attitudinal levels will be due to chance alone.

Operational definitions. The following
definitions were proposed for agreement in interpretations of hypotheses:

1. Attitudinal level was defined as any one
or more of a possible 11 achieved hierarchical
levels of response, adjudged as appropriate by a
jury, to an instrument designed to measure attitudes
toward music.
2. Category of community size was defined as
an arbitrary placement in an artificial dichotomy,
rural being below 4000 population and urban as being
above 4000.
3. Category of present age was defined as any
one of nine-year spans beginning at age 21.
4. Category of present occupation was defined
as the hierarchical placement of an individual's
occupation according to Hollingshead and Redlich's
occupational scale.

5. School music experience was defined as
the quantitative extent of school class or organizational music instruction received by the respondent
as revealed by his answers to a "Respondent Background Information" form.

Population and sample. The population for
this research were the approximately 200,000 adults
21 years of age and older in the State of Wyoming.
Little was known concerning characteristics of this
population relevant to this research. The educational level in the state is one of the highest in
the United States, but the adult musical opportunities in the state are perhaps more limited than
in any other. There are three community symphony
orchestras and 16 municipal bands; however, there
are only three FM radio stations originating in the
state and no civic operas or professional music
groups (other than rock or country-western bands).
Almost all of the music broadcast by AM radio
stations is in the popular vein. In 1975, 47 percent
(21, p. 2) of Wyoming high school students participated in some school music activity.

For the sample for this research, a small-
sample technique of the NEA Research Division was
used which resulted in a sample of 180. Because of
the unpredictability of response in sampling this
population, an arbitrary oversample of 20 was included for a total n = 200. The researcher decided
on an unrestricted systematic sample using the
telephone book from each Wyoming community. There
was no reason to suspect that nontelephone owners
differed significantly from telephone owners on
either the independent or dependent variables in
the research.

Level of significance. The .01 level of significance was chosen, with a willingness to minimize
the possibility of a Type I error with a resultant
increase in possibility of a Type II error.

Independent variables. Five independent variables were selected for the research. Of chief
interest was the extent of school music experience.
Tested for their relationship to attitudes toward
music were 10 levels of extent of music-learning
experience within this independent variable,
general music in the elementary school, general
music at the secondary level, instrumental music in

231

the elementary school, instrumental music in junior
high, instrumental music in high school, choral
music in junior high, choral music in high school,
performance music in college, and music as a major
or minor in college.

A second independent variable was present age
by category: 21-31, 31-41, 41-51, 51-61, 61-71, and
over 71. This was tested because adults' attitudes
may be influenced by their beyond-school music experiences and maturation.

The third independent variable was community
size, artificially dichotomized as over and under
4000 population. People from rural communities have,
in general, patronized school-music events in a
higher proportion than have people from urban areas.

A fourth independent variable was the sex of
the individual, male or female, a true dichotomy. In
general, more mothers than fathers have attended
school music programs.

A final independent variable was ordered category of present occupation (11, pp. 24-8) among 11
categories in a hierarchy of socio-economic position.
Socio-economic position may affect both listening
and performing opportunities, which, in turn, could
affect musical attitudes.

Dependent variables. A measurement of affective behaviors in music was proposed by the investigator in the original design for this research.
However, three jury members suggested that measurement
of the total affective domain would be impossible
through pencil-and-paper responses alone. Therefore,
the investigator sought to measure attitudes only
toward music (a portion, only, of the affective
domain). For the dependent variables in this research, consequently, respondent attitudes, as
measured by an inventory, were established on a
taxonomy, based on the work of Krathwohl and others
(14) as analyzed for music by Colwell (3, pp. 173-7).
(The 5.0 level, "Characterization by a value or value
complex," was omitted from the inventory.) The 11
levels thus included were:

      1.0 Receiving
          1.1 Awareness (Level 1)
          1.2 Willingness to receive (Level 2)

          1.3 Controlled or selected attention
               (Level 3)
    2.0   Responding
          2.1 Acquiescence in responding (Level 4)
          2.2 Willingness to respond (Level 5)
          2.3 Satisfaction in response (Level 6)
    3.0   Valuing
          3.1 Acceptance of a value (Level 7)
          3.2 Preference for a value (Level 8)
          3.3 Commitment (Level 9)
    4.0   Organization
          4.1 Conception of a value (Level 10)
          4.2 Organization of a value system
               (Level 11)

     At each level, the intent was to measure the
attitude of the individual toward each level component. The levels of attitudinal response theoretically exist in this research on a hierarchical
continuum. Beginning with "awareness," where the
investigator was measuring attitudes of consciousness
of broad forces in music, the hierarchy progressed
in depth and complexity to "organization of a value
system," in which the researcher attempted to locate
a musical value judgment among several possibilities.
In the first 10 levels of response, if the respondent's opinions agreed with those the jury
perceived as "appropriate responses" to four out
of five inventory items measuring a level, the
respondent was adjudged to have "met" that level.
In the highest level, level 11, the respondent had
to be in agreement with jury judgment in five out of
the seven inventory items to have "met" that level.
Inventory items were not grouped together by
hierarchical level; rather, they were rearranged
to avoid patterns in either questions or responses.

Design

     During the inventory-development stage, a
126-item instrument was developed by the investigator. This was submitted to 149 Wyoming adults
for item-testing and to a jury of 18 music education
specialists, of whom half were nationally-known music
education research experts and half public school
music education leaders from Wyoming (see Figure 8).
The jury was asked to: (1) respond to each item of
the instrument as they would see the "musically
literate" person appropriately responding, and (2)
suggest changes, additions, and deletions to the

instrument. The responses were submitted to five factor analyses and orthogonal rotation.

From the factor analyses and jury suggestions, a 57-item inventory was developed for submission to the sample. Five were included at each toxonomic level with the exception of the 4.2 level where seven questions were posed.

Using the telephone books from Wyoming communities (which include farm-ranch numbers) and a systematic process based on community size related to total population, a list of 247 respondents was developed. Each potential respondent was sent two different instruments: a "Respondent Background Information" form and a copy of the attitude inventory. Response to the first mailing was approximately 50 percent, but through repeated mailings, using systematic sampling but to different potential respondents, 200 completed replies were received. Analysis of representativeness of responses indicated adequate geographical, sex, age, and community-size representation.

Analyses of Data

Canonical correlation analysis (7) was the chief test statistic used in this research because it relates several dependent variables simultaneously with several independent variables. In addition, through the coefficients determined, the varying strength of the independent variables and the dependent variables is indicated in achieving the maximum relationship between the two sets. In this research, there were a total of 14 independent variables (10 levels of prior music-learning experience, category of present age, urban or rural living, sex, and the occupation hierarchical level) and 11 dependent variables (11 hierarchical levels of attitudinal response).

Since the prior music-learning experience of the sample was the chief independent variable of interest in this research, the 10 levels of this variable were also analyzed separately from the other dependent variables (but with the same 11 dependent variables) for a more precise examination of their relationships. Since this examination, however, showed strengths of relationships very similar to the first, the original program was used for reporting.

A multiple regression analysis (19, SPSS 5.01) predicting each of the 11 dependent variables from a pool of the 10 levels of prior music-learning experience was also calculated. This analysis included a full correlation matrix of Pearson correlations for all 25 variables.

The canonical analysis produced 10 canonical correlations of which, using Bartlett's transformation of Wolk's lambda criterion (6, pp. 192-3), $X^2 = m \log_e \lambda$ j, only the first two (.66853 and .40637) produced significant X^2 values (calculated in terms of z) at the .01 level. The test of significance showed that the first two canonical correlations led to the rejection of the null hypotheses of zero correlation and implied ability to predict, but the third through tenth failed to be so rejected.

1. <u>Hypothesis 1</u>, that there is no weighting of independent and dependent variables that will produce a significant correlation between the new hypothetical variables established by those weights, was rejected. In the first set of canonical variables, there appeared to be a major contribution in the independent variables of private piano or organ study (-.270); band, orchestra, or choir in college (-.258); and music as a major or minor in college (-.540) and the dependent variables of attitudes in controlled or selected attention (-.273), willingness to respond (-.531); and satisfaction in response (-.469). In the second set of canonical variates, there appeared to be a strong relationship among the independent variables of general music in junior high (-.513); band, orchestra, or choir in college (.492) and music as a major or minor in college (-.392) with the dependent variables of attitudes toward willingness to receive (.456); controlled or selected attention (.350); acceptance of a value (-.396); commitment (-.611); conception of a value (-.284); and organization of a value system (.479).

2. <u>Hypothesis 2</u>, that any correlation between the extent of previous school music experience of adults and their measured attitudinal levels toward music will be due to chance alone, failed to be rejected at the .01 level. Although some evidence suggested that the hypothesis be rejected, the total patterns of evidence could not support that rejection.

FIGURE 1

COEFFICIENTS FOR THE ORIGINAL VARIABLES IN THE
FIRST TWO SETS OF CANONICAL VARIABLES
(ROUNDED TO THREE DECIMAL PLACES)

	Correlation 1 (.701)	Correlation 2 (.446)
Set I		
Piano or organ	-.270*	.112
General music--elementary	.025	.233
General music--secondary	.070	.260*
Band or orchestra in elementary	-.092	-.170
Band or orchestra in junior high	.075	.162
Band or orchestra in high school	-.165	-.018
Choir or glee club in junior high	-.094	-.513
Choir or glee club in high school	-.178	-.083
Performance groups--college	-.258*	.492*
Music as major or minor	-.540*	-.392*
Age category	.118	-.270
Rural or urban	-.157	.002
Sex	-.146	.374*
Occupational level	-.236*	.257*
Set II		
Attitudinal Level 1	.002	-.077
Attitudinal Level 2	.044	.456*
Attitudinal Level 3	-.273*	.350*
Attitudinal Level 4	-.109	.069
Attitudinal Level 5	-.531*	.096
Attitudinal Level 6	-.469*	.079
Attitudinal Level 7	-.064	-.396*
Attitudinal Level 8	-.077	-.377*
Attitudinal Level 9	-.019	-.611*
Attitudinal Level 10	.050	.284*
Attitudinal Level 11	-.036	.479*

* Items in one set which seem to relate to
starred items in the opposite set.

FIGURE 2a.

SIGNIFICANT PEARSON CORRELATIONS OF TEN LEVELS OF MUSIC EDUCATION EXPERIENCE WITH ELEVEN LEVELS OF ATTITUDE

	Level 1	Level 2	Level 3	Level 4	Level 5	Level 6
1. Piano or organ lessons	*	*	N.S.	N.S.	N.S.	.158 s=.001
2. Gen. Music: Elementary	N.S.	N.S.	N.S.	N.S.	N.S.	N.S.
3. Gen. Music: Secondary	N.S.	N.S.	N.S.	N.S.	N.S.	N.S.
4. Inst. Music: Elementary	N.S.	N.S.	.217 s=.001	N.S.	.165 s=.010	N.S.
5. Inst. Music: Jr. High	N.S.	N.S.	N.S.	N.S.	N.S.	.203 s=.002
6. Inst. Music: High School	N.S.	N.S.	N.S.	N.S.	.242 s=.001	.283 s=.001
7. Vocal Music: Jr. High	N.S.	N.S.	N.S.	.238 s=.001	.187 s=.004	N.S.
8. Vocal Music: High School	N.S.	N.S.	N.S.	.196 s=.003	.207 s=.002	.269 s=.001
9. Perf. Music: College	N.S.	.215 s=.001	.176 s=.006	.296 s=.001	.426 s=.001	.400 s=.001
10. Music as Major or Minor	N.S.	.265 s=.001	.173 s=.007	.182 s=.005	.192 s=.003	.212 s=.001

* approached significance: .133 (s=.030)
** approached significance: .146 (s=.020)

FIGURE 2b.

SIGNIFICANT PEARSON CORRELATIONS OF TEN LEVELS OF MUSIC EDUCATION EXPERIENCE WITH ELEVEN LEVELS OF ATTITUDE

	Level 7	Level 8	Level 9	Level 10	Level 11
1. Piano or organ lessons	N.S.	.199 s=.002	N.S.	N.S.	N.S.
2. Gen. Music: Elementary	N.S.	N.S.	N.S.	N.S.	N.S.
3. Gen. Music: Secondary	N.S.	N.S.	N.S.	N.S.	N.S.
4. Inst. Music: Elementary	N.S.	N.S.	N.S.	N.S.	N.S.
5. Inst. Music: Jr. High	N.S.	N.S.	N.S.	N.S.	.233 s=.001
6. Inst. Music: High School	N.S.	N.S.	N.S.	N.S.	N.S.
7. Vocal Music: Jr. High	N.S.	N.S.	N.S.	N.S.	N.S.
8. Vocal Music: High School	N.S.	N.S.	.236 s=.001	N.S.	.308 s=.001
9. Perf. Music: College	N.S.	N.S.	N.S.	N.S.	N.S.
10. Music as Major or Minor	N.S.	.239 s=.001	.347 s=.001	*	**

* approached significance: .133 (s=.030)
** approached significance: .146 (s=.020)

In the analysis of data relevant to hypothesis 1, it was pointed out that the independent variables of previous piano or organ study, performance groups in college, and music as a major or minor in college seemed to be related to the dependent variables of attitudes in controlled or selected attention, willingness to respond, and satisfaction in response. These had the strongest weights in the first canonical correlation.

The evidence from the multiple regression analysis, in which the 10 levels of prior musical-learning experience were pooled and measured with each of the dependent variables, appeared inconclusive. With a table F value of 2.63 for significance at the .01 level, in the analysis of variance from the multiple regression, only the dependent variables of attitudes toward acquiescence in responding ($F = 3.66$), willingness to respond ($F = 9.35$), satisfaction in response ($F = 7.58$), commitment ($F = 4.12$) and organization of a value system ($F = 2.94$) related to the pooled 10 levels of background in music-learning experience, reached significance. Consequently, there is no evidence of predicting attitudes toward awareness, willingness to receive, controlled or selected attention, acceptance of a value, preference for a value, or conception of a value from the pooled 10 levels of musical education.

Testing the sub-hypothesis that: $H_o: B_1 = B_2 = \ldots = B_{10} = 0$ (i.e., none of the 10 levels of the independent variable contributes to our ability to predict each dependent variable), the hypothesis was rejected. Evidences are the following: Performance music in college had a high coefficient in predicting attitudes toward willingness to receive (.323), acquiescence in responding (.309), willingness to respond (.250), satisfaction in response (.260), conception of a value (.220), and organization of a value system (.191). Music as a major or minor had its highest coefficients in predicting willingness to receive (.248), acquiescence in responding (.312), willingness to respond (.591), satisfaction in response (.364), acceptance of a value (.269), and commitment (.360). Only levels 9 and 10 (music experience in college), thus, were strong predictors of any of the dependent variables.

A stronger pattern of evidence, however, seemed to emerge from the following: Using a Pearson r, a significant correlation at the .01 level was obtained increasing in a descending pattern according to the music-education experiential level of the adults, as indicated in Figure 2.

3. Hypothesis 3, that any correlation between category of present age and measured attitudinal levels will be due to chance alone, failed to be rejected at the .01 level of confidence.

The coefficient for the variable of category of present age was only .11751 in the first canonical correlation and -.27036 in the second. In addition, the category of present age produced no significant Pearson r with any of the 11 levels of attitude toward music.

FIGURE 3

PEARSON CORRELATION COEFFICIENTS FOR CATEGORY OF
PRESENT AGE WITH ATTITUDINAL LEVELS
(NONE SIGNIFICANT AT .01 LEVEL)

Level 1	-.051	Level 7	.108
Level 2	.010	Level 8	.089
Level 3	.116	Level 9	.105
Level 4	.081	Level 10	.060
Level 5	-.090	Level 11	-.029
Level 6	.103		

4. Hypothesis 4, that any correlation between the sex of the adult and his measured attitudinal levels will be due to chance alone, failed to be rejected.

The coefficient for sex in the first canonical variate was -.14583 and in the second, .37455. The Pearson r analysis showed a significant relationship only between sex of the respondent and attitudinal level 8 (preference for a value system). However, the relationships with the other nine levels were nonsignificant.

FIGURE 4

PEARSON CORRELATION COEFFICIENTS BY SEX OF
RESPONDENTS AND THEIR ATTITUDINAL LEVELS

Level 1	.031		Level 7	.011
Level 2	.053		Level 8	-.280*
Level 3	.125		Level 9	.029
Level 4	-.041		Level 10	.089
Level 5	.041		Level 11	.157
Level 6	.001			

* Significant at .01 level.

5. Hypothesis 5, that any correlation between category of present community size and attitudinal levels will be due to chance alone, failed to be rejected at the .01 level of confidence.

The coefficient for community size in the first canonical variate was only -.15742 and in the second .00249. There were no significant relationships between community size and any attitudinal levels from the Pearson r analysis.

FIGURE 5

PEARSON CORRELATION COEFFICIENTS FOR CATEGORY
OF COMMUNITY SIZE ACHIEVED ATTITUDINAL LEVELS
(NONE SIGNIFICANT AT .01 LEVEL)

Level 1	-.113		Level 7	.020
Level 2	.098		Level 8	.101
Level 3	.023		Level 9	.044
Level 4	.070		Level 10	-.024
Level 5	.092		Level 11	.053
Level 6	.099			

6. Hypothesis 6, that any correlation between ordered category of present occupation and measured attitudinal levels will be due to chance alone, was rejected.

The coefficients for category of occupation in canonical correlation were the relatively high -.55788 in the first variate and -.44962 in the second. The Pearson r indicated significance between category of occupation and levels 2 (willingness to receive), 3 (controlled or selected attention), 4 (acquiescence in responding), 5 (willingness to respond), 6 (satisfaction in response), 10 (conception of a value), and 11 (organization of a value system).

FIGURE 6

PEARSON CORRELATION COEFFICIENTS FOR CATEGORY OF PRESENT OCCUPATION AND ATTITUDINAL LEVELS

Level 1	.122	Level 7	.118
Level 2	.265*	Level 8	.039
Level 3	.173*	Level 9	.111
Level 4	.182*	Level 10	.170*
Level 5	.192*	Level 11	.178*
Level 6	.210*		

* Significant at the .01 level.

FIGURE 7

INVENTORY ITEMS MEASURING ATTITUDE LEVELS

Level 1--Awareness	Items: 1,2,3,7,26
Level 2--Willingness to receive	Items: 8,15,16,20,30
Level 3--Controlled or selected attention	Items: 19,21,23,27,32
Level 4--Acquiescence in responding	Items: 4,9,13,18,25
Level 5--Willingness to respond	Items: 6,10,11,14,17
Level 6--Satisfaction in response	Items: 5,12,22,24,28
Level 7--Acceptance of a value	Items: 35,36,38,41,52
Level 8--Preference for a value	Items: 29,31,33,34,45
Level 9--Commitment	Items: 39,44,46,47,51
Level 10--Conception of a value	Items: 37,38,42,49,50
Level 11--Organization of a value system	Items: 40,53,53,54(1), 54(2),55(1), 55(2)

FIGURE 8

JURY MEMBERS FOR THE CRITERION INSTRUMENT

Mrs. Mary C. Anderson
Elementary Music Super-
   visor
Lincoln Grade School
Torrington, Wyoming

Donald Bookout, Principal
Wind River High School
Kinnear, Wyoming

Dr. James C. Carlsen
School of Music
University of Washington
Seattle, Washington

Joseph Cassinat
President, WMEA
Riverton Junior High School
Riverton, Wyoming

Dr. Richard Colwell
School of Music
University of Illinois
Urbana, Illinois

Rex Eggleston
Director of Music Education
Natrona County School
   District #1
Casper, Wyoming

Dr. Thomas Kinser
Chairman, Fine Arts
   Division
Casper College
Casper, Wyoming

Dr. Paul Lehman
School of Music
University of Michigan
Ann Arbor, Michigan

Rosalie Lewis
Music Department
University of Wyoming
Laramie, Wyoming

Dr. Gary Martin
School of Music
University of Oregon
Eugene, Oregon

Dr. Carl B. Nelson
Department of Music
State University College
Cortland, New York

Dr. Robert E. Nye
School of Music
University of Oregon
Eugene, Oregon

Dr. Marvin S. Thostenson
School of Music
University of Iowa
Iowa City, Iowa

Rex Yocum
Coordinator of Music
Laramie County School
   District
Cheyenne, Wyoming

Conclusions, Limitations and Weaknesses

   Conclusions. On the basis of the evidence from
this research, the following conclusions appear
warranted, generalizable to the population of adults
of the State of Wyoming:

243

1. While there is a distinct relationship between the amount of music education a Wyoming adult
has had and his achieved levels of attitude toward
music, the actual strength and exact nature of that
relationship is unclear. Adults who have had general
music experience, only, show little relationship from
that experience to their attitudes about music,
Adults show higher levels of attitudinal response if
they have had instrumental and/or vocal experience in
junior high and high school. Comparatively, adults
will show the highest levels of attitudinal response
if they have had music participation in college,
particularly if they have been majors or minors in
music.
2. The age of the adult makes little difference in his achieved attitudinal levels toward
music.
3. The achieved attitudinal levels toward music
of adults are not strongly related to their sex.
4. The adults' attitudinal levels toward music
have no strong relationship to the size of the community in which they reside.
5. There is a strong relationship between the
category of present occupation of the adult and his
achieved attitudinal levels. Individuals in professional fields achieve higher attitudinal levels than
do individuals in a lower occupational level.

Limitations of the research. This investigation
was limited in scope by the following:

1. Conclusions are applicable only to the
target population.
2. Research was limited to the relationship of
the five specified independent variables to the 11
specified dependent variables.
3. Since attitudes cannot be measured directly,
the individual's attitudes were interpreted on the
basis of his reactions to the criterion instrument.
4. Responses to the attitude inventory were
interpreted only as "appropriate" or "non-appro-
priate" on the basis of jury judgments.

Inherent and possible weaknesses. Several
weaknesses seemed apparent in this research:

1. Since validity and reliability of a criterion instrument are critical to the integrity of
conclusions, the latter may be somewhat suspect in

this research because factor analysis only was employed as a basis for inclusion of inventory items.

 2. A specific cause-effect relationship cannot be tested with the analyses used.

 3. The quality of prior music-learning experience, which could affect respondent attitudes, could not be measured, but some of the differential effects of this variable could be expected to be cancelled out due to random selection of respondents.

 4. Because both cross-validation and replication analysis could be important in determining whether the sample contained specific sample error, findings should be cautiously applied. Neither analysis was financially feasible in this research.

References

1. Allport, G. W.; Vernon, P. E.; and Lindzey, G. L. _Study of Values_. 3rd ed. Boston: Houghton Mifflin Company, 1960.

2. Bessom, Malcolm E.; Tatarunis, Alphonse M.; and Forcucci, Samuel L. _Teaching Music in Today's Secondary Schools_. New York: Holt, Rinehart and Winston, Inc., 1974.

3. Colwell, Richard. "Evaluating the Affective Domain." _The Evaluation of Music Teaching and Learning_. Englewood Cliffs, N.J.: Prentice-Hall Inc., 1970.

4. Crickmore, L. E. "An Approach to the Measurement of Music Appreciation." _Journal of Research in Music Education_ 26 (Spring 1968): 239-253.

5. Dayton, C. Mitchell. _Design of Educational Experiments_. New York: McGraw-Hill Book Company, 1970. Pp. 50-53.

6. Dorman, P. E. "Grassroots Accountability." _Music Educators Journal_ 60 (November 1973): 43-46.

7. Dixon, W. J., ed. "B M D 0 9 M Canonical Correlation Analysis." _Biomedical Computer Programs_. 3rd ed. Berkeley: University of California Press, 1973.

8. Finn, Jeremy D. A General Model for Multi-variate Analysis. New York: Holt, Rinehart and Winston, 1974. Pp. 192-3.

9. Greer, R. D., and others. "Adult Approval and Student Music Selection Behavior." Journal of Research in Music Education 21 (Winter 1973): 345-354.

10. Hevner, Kate. "Appreciation of Music and Tests for the Appreciation of Music." Studies in Appreciation of Art. Eugene: University of Oregon Publications, 1954.

11. Hollingshead, August B., and Redlich, Fredrick. Social Class and Mental Illness. New York: John Wiley and Sons, 1958.

12. Kapper, Miriam B. "The Evaluation of Music Objectives." Music Educators Journal 55 (February 1970): 61-63.

13. Klotman, Robert H. "Evaluation and the Process of Change." The School Music Administrator and Supervisor. Englewood Cliffs, N.J.: Prentice-Hall, Inc., 1973.

14. Krathwohl, David R.; Bloom, Benjamin S.; and Masia, B. B., eds. Taxonomy of Educational Objectives: Handbook II: Affective Domain. New York: David McKay Company, Inc., 1965.

15. Leonhard, Charles, and House, Robert W. Foundations and Principles of Music Education. New York: McGraw-Hill Book Company, 1959.

16. Lewy, Ariech. "Affective Outcomes of Musical Education." Journal of Research in Music Education 19 (Fall 1971): 361-365.

17. Lundin, Robert W. An Objective Psychology of Music. 2nd ed. New York: The Ronald Press Company, 1967.

18. Miller, K. R. "Life, Music, and Education." Music Educators Journal 61 (December 1974): 59-61.

19. Nie, Norman H., and Hull, C. Hadlar. "Vernon
    5.01." SPSS--Statistical Package for the
    Social Sciences: Update Manual. Chicago: Uni-
    versity of Chicago, National Opinion Research
    Center, 1973.

20. Rader, Billie Thomas. "The Application of
    Canonical Correlation Methodology with Vocation
    Education Data." Journal of Industrial Teacher
    Education, 51-60.

21. Wyoming Educational Needs Assessment Program.
    Test in Music. Laramie: University of Wyoming
    Center for Research, Service and Publication,
    1975, p. 2.

THE HISTORY AND DEVELOPMENT OF THE AMERICAN INSTITUTE
OF NORMAL METHODS, 1914-1950*

Melvin C. Platt**

The American Institute of Normal Methods was a
three-week summer school operated by Silver, Burdett
and Company to increase the sale of the company's
books and provide pedagogical instruction for school
teachers of music and other subjects. It was established by Hosea E. Holt at Lexington, Massachusetts,
in the summer of 1884 under the name Lexington Normal
Music School to popularize The Normal Music Course,
a school music series which had been prepared by Holt
and John W. Tufts. In the years that followed,
Silver, Burdett and Company purchased the publishing
rights to The Normal Music Course from D. Appleton
and Company, took over the financial operation of the
summer school, and changed its name to the American
Institute of Normal Methods. In 1889, a western
session was opened by Holt at Lake Geneva, Wisconsin;
after two summers there, it was moved to the Chicago
area where it met at various sites until 1929. The
eastern session was also moved from place to place in
New England during the 1890's. From 1900 through
1912, it met at the New England Conservatory of Music
in Boston and thereafter at the Lasell Seminary
(later Lasell Junior College) in Auburndale, a suburb
of Boston.(1)

After Holt and Tufts gave up teaching in the
AINM during the early 1890's, the reins of instructional leadership were passed to Emory P. Russell of
the Boston schools and Frederick A. Lyman of the

---

* Reprinted by permission of Melvin C. Platt
and Contributions to Music Education, No. 2 (1973),
pp. 31-39.

** This article is based in part on portions of
the author's doctoral dissertation, "Osborne
McConathy: American Music Educator"(Ann Arbor:
University of Michigan, 1971).

Syracuse schools. In 1898, Samuel W. Cole, supervisor of music in the Brookline and Dedham, Massachusetts, schools and head of the public school music
department at the New England Conservatory of Music,
was appointed superintendent of the eastern session.
During the sixteen years that followed, he assembled
a distinguished faculty which included Leonard B.
Marshall, Leo R. Lewis, Alice Garthe, Theresa
Armitage, and Osbourne McConathy. The western session flourished under the guidance of superintendents
Robert Foresman (1904-05), Will Earhart (1906-07),
and Edward Bailey Birge (1908-1920). The western
session faculty during the early 1900's included such
well known music teachers as Eleanor Smith, Alice
Inskeep, Stella Root, Thaddeus P. Giddings, and W.
Otto Miessner.(2)

    The major curricular thrust of the institute
from its earliest days was instruction in music and
methods of teaching vocal music to children in
schools. As the institute grew, courses in physical
culture, penmanship, and drawing were added. Although instruction in physical culture lasted only a
few years, penmanship was taught at the eastern session until 1911. Courses in drawing, the most
popular non-music subject taught at the institute,
were offered until 1937.(3)

    In the early years, under Holt and Tufts,
music instruction consisted of a three-summer course
of study in music reading, harmony, and methods based
on The Normal Music Course.(4) As the curriculum
expanded in the late 1890's to include sight singing,
conducting, voice training, chorus, and practice
teaching, the Cecilian Series of Study and Song, a
supplementary song series edited by Tufts, joined
The Normal Music Course as required texts in the
methods course. In 1900, Silver, Burdett and Company
acquired the rights to the Modern Music Series
written by Eleanor Smith under the editorial guidance
of Robert Foresman. For a time, all three series
were used concurrently, but eventually the Modern
Music Series became the only methods books at the
institute.(5)

    In the spring of 1914, Silver, Burdett and
Company issued the first book of The Progressive
Music Series, a new set of school music texts designed to replace the Modern Music Series. For
authors of the new series, the company had turned to

an eminent American composer and organist, Horatio
Parker, and three successful music educators, Osbourne McConathy of Northwestern University, Edward
Birge of the Indianapolis schools, and W. Otto
Miessner of the Oak Park, Illinois, schools. All
four men had previous publications to their credit,
and three of them--McConathy, Birge, and Miessner--
were faculty members of the AINM.(6)

With the appearance of The Progressive Music
Series in 1914, McConathy was appointed superintendent
of the eastern session at Auburndale, replacing the
aging Samuel Cole. Birge, who had served as superintendent of the western session since 1908, was re-
tained in that position until 1921 when he was
succeeded by Miessner. The faculty which taught at
the western session during this period was particularly noteworthy, the most important being Miessner,
Alice Inskeep, Mabelle Glenn, Stella Root, and E. L.
Coburn.(7)

In 1919, McConathy was appointed director of
both the eastern and western sessions, a position
which he held until his death in 1947. As director,
he was responsible for all institute planning which
included the selection of faculty members, changes
in course offerings, and scheduling of classes, and
the securing of food services, facilities for instruction, and residences for both faculty and students.
The day-to-day administration of each session
usually fell to the superintendent and business
manager. Frederick W. Archibald, supervisor of music
at the State Normal Schools at Framingham and Salem,
Massachusetts, succeeded McConathy as superintendent
at the eastern session. However, from 1922 through
1928, McConathy served as superintendent of the
eastern session as well as director for the
institute.(8)

At the time of publication of The Progressive
Music Series, the institute consisted of two depart-
ments--music and drawing. The latter department
(later renamed art department) was always smaller
than the music department, rarely having more than
two instructors. A two-summer course of study was
offered in drawing to accommodate students wishing to
specialize in music and drawing or drawing alone.

A diploma in music was granted upon the completion of a three-summer course of study (a total of

sixteen credits) consisting of daily classes in
methods and practice teaching at the primary, intermediate, and grammar school levels, and harmony,
sight singing, chorus, conducting, and music electives. Voice lessons were offered at an extra
charge. Students were also expected to attend concerts and a series of lectures given at the institute.(9)

Although the curricular requirements of the
eastern and western sessions were very similar, substantial differences existed between the two sessions
in the number and variety of electives available.
The relatively limited number of electives offered to
students at the eastern session may have been the
partial cause and result of its static enrollment,
which averaged around 100 students annually from 1914
through 1924. Concurrently, the western session,
which was held on the campus of Northwestern University, offered a wide range of courses in advanced
vocal methods, supervision, advanced harmony, orchestral methods and orchestration, orchestra, folk
dancing, and educational psychology. The western
session consequently enjoyed its greatest period of
influence with an enrollment averaging almost four
times the number of students attending the eastern
session. In 1921, 455 students studied at the western
session in Evanston (the highest enrollment ever)
while approximately 86 students were enrolled at
Auburndale.(10)

Several other factors contributed to the
success of the western session. First, credit earned
at the institute was applicable toward a certificate,
diploma, or degree at Northwestern University.
Second, the university offered attractive courses
of study in school music, normal piano methods, music
history, music theory, and performance under the
tutelage of noted teachers.(11)

For unknown reasons, the eastern session lagged
behind the western session in becoming affiliated
with a nearby institution of higher learning until
1923. At that time, courses were assigned credit
value and, in an agreement with Boston University,
up to four credits earned at the institute each summer could be applied toward a degree in education or
a music supervisor's certificate.(12)

In the years immediately following the close
of World War I, McConathy and officials at the Silver,
Burdett and Company decided to increase the number of
electives available to students at the eastern session in an effort to increase enrollment and meet
the challenge of universities with enticing diploma
programs in music education. The list of electives
grew in diversity each year, and by 1923, twelve
elective courses covering junior and senior high
school vocal methods, conducting, orchestra, orchestral methods and orchestration, advanced theory,
educational psychology, and folk dancing were being
offered. The courses taught that year were almost
identical to those at the western session.(13)

In 1925, the eastern session, which had followed the lead of the western session in instrumental
music, took the initiative by offering a three-summer
course of study in the field. No space for electives was allowed initially in the course of study
which included courses in harmony, violin, violin
class methods, wind instruments, orchestral methods,
general methods, orchestration, educational psychology, music appreciation, and orchestra. However,
the number of required courses was reduced three
years later to provide for electives.(14)

Concurrent with the gradual rejuvenation of the
eastern session, events took place at the western
session which led to its decline and dissolution.
In 1926, after meeting for twenty years on the
Northwestern University campus, the western session
was moved to Lake Forest College, located approximately twenty miles north of Evanston on the shore
of Lake Michigan. The change in sites resulted from
circumstances surrounding the resignation of Osbourne
McConathy as director of the public school music department at Northwestern University and the appoint-
ment of John W. Beattie as his successor. One of
the conditions under which Beattie accepted the
position was that the relationship between the university and Silver, Burdett and Company would be
severed and that the AINM would be moved elsewhere.
Compliance by the university with Beattie's conditions sounded the death knell for the western
session, which ceased operation after three years
at Lake Forest.(15)

Several factors may have been partially responsible for its decline. Although credit earned at the

institute was recognized by Lake Forest College, the college was not as nationally known or respected as Northwestern University. Moreover, study at Lake Forest was more expensive than at the eastern session. Extra fees were charged for courses in educational psychology and piano class methods, but were included in the regular tuition of twenty-five dollars at Auburndale. The cost of room and board was also higher at Lake Forest. The quality of instruction and living accommodations are unknown factors which certainly could have contributed to the deteriorating situation.

In spite of the efforts made by institute leaders, including Anton H. Embs, superintendent of the western session from 1925 through 1928, the resulting decline in student enrollment caused a reduction in the size of the faculty, which in turn brought fewer students to the institute. In 1929, the western session was officially combined with the eastern session in Lasell Seminary at Auburndale under McConathy's direction. However, the merger existed more in name than in fact. Less than one-third of the western session students came to Auburndale in 1929, and only three former teachers of the western session, Alice Inskeep, Sadie Rafferty, and Alice Jones, taught at Auburndale during the period immediately following the merger.(16)

The availability of a long list of electives and perhaps other unknown factors brought about a steady increase in enrollment at the eastern session during the years preceding the economic depression of the early 1930's. Enrollment statistics for the entire period are not available, but for 1924 through 1927, the enrollment jumped from 105 to 160.(17) During the same period, attendance at the western session was falling rapidly.

As a part of the pattern of growth and change at the eastern session, both the vocal and instrumental courses of study were enlarged from sixteen to twenty credits in 1928, a requirement which was maintained for over twenty years. With the larger curriculum, courses in the rudiments of music and junior and senior high school vocal methods became mandatory for graduation in vocal music in 1928. One year later, more study in conducting and orchestral playing was added to the required list of courses in instrumental music. A required course in eurhythmics was added to the general-choral course of study in 1931, because a program of rhythmic movement for elementary school pupils had been introduced in The Music Hour, a new music series written by McConathy, Miessner, Birge, and Bray and published by Silver, Burdett and Company. With the exception of occasional minor modifications, the requirements of the general-choral and instrumental curricula remained essentially unchanged through 1950.(18)

Like almost every facet of American society, the institute suffered the pangs of financial hardship from the great economic depression. Although enrollment figures are not available during that period, the decline in the number of faculty members --from twenty-three in 1929 to fourteen in 1933-- amply illustrates the difficulties faced by the company and institute leaders. During that time, McConathy, who was teaching at universities in the Midwest and West at the behest of the company, was able to attend the institute only briefly at the commencement exercises in 1930 and 1932. His absence deprived the institute of some excitement and glamour, since he was the only person there with a national reputation of the first magnitude.(19)

Perhaps the most effective action taken to curb the decline in student enrollment and faculty size was the creation in 1935 of a junior division of high school musicians, which was placed under the direction of Francis Findlay, director of the public school music department of the New England Conservatory of Music. Selected students from the New England states were admitted to study at the institute. A limited number of scholarships covering the general tuition were awarded to outstanding young musicians. All students received daily private instruction on their instrument or voice and attended classes in music appreciation, theory, chorus, band, orchestra, and small ensembles. Attendance at concerts given at the institute or by the Boston Symphony Orchestra was required several evenings each week. Many recreational activities, including tennis, golf, and swimming, were also available. The success of the junior division (later called Auburndale Summer Clinic for Young Musicians) is attested by its continuation through 1950. Later directors of the summer clinic were Lawrence W. Chidester of Tufts College (1939) and C. Paul Herfurth, director of instrumental music in the schools of East Orange, New Jersey (1940-1950).(20)

The annual lecture series, an important curricular feature at the institute since its earliest days, received increased emphasis during the 1930's and 1940's. Speeches were given by leading college music teachers, supervisors of music, psychologists, curriculum specialists, and school administrators on a variety of topics in the fields of music history, aesthetics, acoustics, conducting, learning theory, and methodology. James L. Mursell of Teachers College, Columbia University, was the most frequent lecturer at the institute during that period, appearing almost every year for over two decades.(21)

The death of Osbourne McConathy in April 1947 ended twenty-eight years of gifted leadership to the institute and concluded a chapter in the institute's history. He was succeeded as director in 1948 by his close friend and protege, Russell V. Morgan, director of music in the Cleveland schools and professor at Western Reserve University.(22) Morgan guided the American Institute of Music Education (renamed in 1950) through a transitional period wherein the basic curricular offerings of harmony, sight singing, methods, practice teaching, conducting, chorus, and orchestra were replaced by a modern workshop format with concentration on methods, choral and instrumental techniques, and eurhythmics. The workshop idea was inaugurated in 1950 when selected institute faculty members under the leadership of Albert A. Renna presented a one-week workshop at San Francisco State College as a supplement to the regular session in Massachusetts. The following year, the workshop format was introduced at Auburndale and was continued there for one additional summer before the regular three-week session came to an end. Thereafter, Silver Burdett sponsored one-week music education workshops on various college and university campuses in an effort to popularize its music publications and provide music instruction for teachers, a practice which has been continued to the present day.(23)

Viewed in retrospect, the American Institute of Normal Methods, during its first forty years, served as one of the principal avenues through which school music teachers received instruction in music theory, performance, and methodology. Later, with the emergence of baccalaureate programs in music education at colleges and universities, its role changed from an institution offering pre-service instruction to one which provided in-service instruction for music and classroom teachers who wanted to learn about new educational developments, acquire fresh ideas, and improve their teaching and performance skills in a very short period of time. As early as the 1920's, many of the students who attended the institute did not complete the three-summer course of study.

After 1930, the institute gradually became an anachronism in music teacher education, functioning at a time when state departments of education in most states were requiring a bachelor's degree from applicants seeking standard certification to teach in the public schools. Its continued success during that time was due to a number of factors, the most important of which were the high quality of instruction and the variety of practical course offerings. Undoubtedly, the friendly atmosphere, close interaction between faculty and students (both groups lived on campus), relatively small classes, and concentrated study also appealed to many students.

Of the three publisher-sponsored summer schools which operated during the late 1800's and early 1900's, the American Institute of Normal Methods was established first, functioned for the longest time, and enjoyed the greatest patronage by students. Much of the credit for the institute's long and fruitful existence goes to institute leaders such as Edward Birge, Otto Miessner, and Osbourne McConathy. With the assistance of a skilled and dedicated faculty, they were able to mold the institute into a strong pedagogical enterprise, which operated for decades after similar summer schools had been disbanded.

References

(1) [David C. King], "Silver, Burdett and Company: A History from 1885 to 1941," [n.d.], *passim;* and AINM brochures and commencement programs, 1889-1952.

(2) AINM brochures and commencement programs, 1891-1924.

(3) AINM brochures and commencement programs, 1893-1937.

(4) Preparatory and post-graduate courses were also offered after 1895.

(5) King, pp. 58-59, 122-23; and AINM brochures, 1897-1909.

(6) King, pp. 152-55.

(7) AINM brochures, 1908-21.

(8) AINM brochures and commencement programs, 1919-47.

(9) AINM brochures, 1914.

(10) AINM brochures and commencement programs, 1914-24; photographs of the faculty and students of various sessions; and summer school enrollments given in Reports of the Commissioner of Education, 1914, 1916, 1917, and U.S. Bureau of Education Bulletin, 1919.

(11) Northwestern University was one of the first institutions to grant a bachelor's degree in music education (1924).

(12) AINM brochures, eastern session, 1923. Beginning in 1936, study at the institute was recognized by the New England Conservatory of Music.

(13) AINM brochures, 1923.

(14) AINM brochures, eastern session, 1925 and 1928.

(15) AINM brochures and commencement programs, western session, 1926-28; and John Beattie, "Music Education at Northwestern" (unpublished paper), p. 4.

(16) AINM brochures and commencement programs, 1926-23.

(17) Photos of the faculty and students in AINM brochures, eastern session, 1924-27.

(18) AINM brochures, eastern and combined sessions, 1928-50.

(19) AINM brochures and commencement programs, 1929-33.

(20) AINM brochures, 1935-50.

(21) AINM brochures, 1929-50.

(22) Morgan along with McConathy, Mursell, Bartholomew, Bray, Birge, and Miessner, served as co-authors of New Music Horizons, a music series published by Silver Burdett from 1944 through 1953.

(23) AINM brochures and commencement programs, 1946-50.

A LONGITUDINAL INVESTIGATION OF THE RHYTHMIC ABILITIES OF PRE-SCHOOL AGED CHILDREN*

Edward Rainbow

Music has been considered an important aspect in the education of the very young. Organized educational experiences for children ages 3 to 5 are often centered on such musical activities as singing, body movement to music and performing on simple percussion instruments. While musical activities play an important role in the formal education of the very young, music educators have virtually ignored the systematic investigation of the musical abilities of the young child. The statement by Jersild in 1935 is applicable to the situation in 1976:

> Probably because music belongs to the arts, there have been relatively few research studies of the educational aspects of the development of musical abilities in children. Yet literature on the education of young children abounds with discussions and recommendations concerning types of musical experiences which children should have.

Recently published method books discuss in detail and outline a curriculum for the musical development of young children (Aronoff, 1969; Batcheller, 1975; Nye, 1975). The suggested tasks and activities that are to be employed for the development of a child's musical abilities are not

---

* Reprinted by permission of Edward Rainbow and the <u>Bulletin</u> of the Council for Research in Music Education, No. 50 (Spring, 1977), pp. 55-61.

Editor's Note: This research report and the one following which describe a longitudinal study undertaken by Edward Rainbow are relatively incomplete in nature due to an especially tight word-limit restriction.

based upon and supported by basic empirical research. Before early childhood musical experiences can be formulated, the musical abilities and the developmental aspects of those abilities must be known. Such questions as: "What is the nature of the young child's singing and rhythmic abilities?" "What is the role of maturation in the development of these abilities?" "What factors influence the development of musical abilities?" These are only a few of the questions that must be answered if teaching strategies and curriculum are to be properly developed.

An investigation of the related research indicates a current series of longitudinal investigations being conducted at the University of Illinois (Smith, 1960; Boardman, 1964) into the development of singing abilities of children aged 4-8. While rhythmic activities are deemed important in all musical experiences of young children there is a noticeable lack of research into the rhythmic abilities of those children and there have been no attempts to investigate this aspect of musical ability on a longitudinal basis.

This proposed project is addressed to investigating over a period of three years the rhythmic abilities of preschool aged children (ages 3-5). The project has been preceded by a pilot study which indicates what is being proposed is researchable and feasible within the suggested time framework. The first year of the project will investigate the abilities of 3- and 4-year-old children to learn specific rhythmic tasks. The second year will attempt to confirm and support the findings of the first year and to further assess the role of maturation in the ability to learn rhythmic tasks. The final year will be used to investigate evidence developed in the first two years and to develop and evaluate a proposed curriculum based upon the findings.

Purpose of the First Year Project

The purpose of the first year of the project is to determine the ability of preschool aged children to learn specific rhythmic tasks. During the fall semester of the 1975 school year a pilot study (Veenkant, 1975) was conducted in a Dallas suburban school. A group of 40 children ages 4 and 5 was observed in music classes over a period of 16 weeks.

260

An inventory of each student's abilities to do specific rhythmic activities was maintained. The date the child was successfully able to complete the assigned task was noted. From this inventory insight into the relative ease and difficulty of specific tasks was obtained.

Historically, perception in music has been measured by asking a student to demonstrate the ability to do a task. For example, perception of pitch has been measured by asking a student to reproduce vocally a presented musical stimuli. In the case of rhythmic perception a child has been asked to demonstrate perception by reproducing a pattern through clapping or in the case of perception of meter by stepping or marching in time to music.

The pilot investigation produced evidence that, in the case of rhythm, the method of demonstrating rhythmic perception may in itself present a problem. For example, it was noted that many rhythmic tasks were more easily and accurately completed when the child was asked to vocally chant the rhythm than when he was asked to step or clap the rhythm. The ability to chant the rhythm accurately indicates the ability to perceive rhythm, yet the standard method of evaluating perception and teaching the perception of rhythm is centered on clapping or stepping. Perception of rhythmic abilities may thus occur much earlier than proposed by noted authorities and the activities prescribed to develop perception may not be appropriate.

The results of the pilot study also suggested a listing of rhythmic tasks that could be graded on three levels of approximate difficulty from very easy to moderately difficult to difficult. Tasks rated easy were those tasks that could be successfully completed by 4-year-old children with a minimum of instruction. Tasks of moderate difficulty were those completed by most of the children at approximately the mid-point of the semester. Those tasks considered difficult were completed successfully by approximately one half of the children at the conclusion of the semester of musical instruction.

The inventory of the children's ability to do rhythmic tasks was compared with the tasks authors of methods textbooks claimed were essential for young children if they were to learn to perceive rhythm in music. The results of the pilot study suggest that many rhythmic tasks suggested by the authors as being primary in a hierarchy of musical tasks were in fact extremely difficult to complete. For example, Aronoff states that keeping a steady rhythmic beat (by clapping or marching) to music is the first task a young child must learn. Heinlein (1920), this writer's personal observation (1963), and the pilot study suggest that this task may be one of the most difficult tasks to learn and in fact may be a task that most adults cannot do with accuracy.

Specific Problems to be Investigated

Based upon the pilot project, the research completed in the field and the writings of authors in the field, a list of rhythmic tasks has been developed. During the course of one school year (1976-77) these tasks will be taught to groups of 3- and 4-year-old children during regularly scheduled music lessons. The specific problems to be investigated are:

1. To determine how many of the selected rhythmic tasks can be successfully learned by 3-year-old children during the course of one school year.
2. To determine how many of the selected rhythmic tasks can be successfully learned by 4-year-old children during the course of one school year.
3. To estimate the learning difficulty rate of each rhythmic tasks for 3-year-old children and for 4-year-old children.
4. To compare the results obtained through the study of 3-year-old children with the results obtained through the study of 4-year-old children.
5. To compare for each age group the relative difficulty of learning rhythmic tasks when two different modes of response are used. (Vocal chanting vs. the physical response of stepping or clapping.)

The results of the study could be of vital importance to music education for the following reasons:

1. Little empirical evidence exists on the development of rhythmic perception in young children.
2. The construct validity of methodology proposed for use in teaching young children should

be objectively confirmed or rejected.

3. Very few research studies in music systematically observe the actions of a specific group of children over the time span of one school year.

4. Knowledge of the rhythmic abilities of young children and the development of those abilities are directly related to the content of a musical education of older primary grade children.

Method of Investigation

During the 1976-77 school year traditional music classes will be taught to 2 groups of 3-year-old children and to 2 groups of 4-year-old children. The approximate number of children to be systematically evaluated will be 16 in each age group.

Rhythmic tasks to be investigated are grouped into four broad categories: maintaining a steady metric beat, rhythmic echoing, rote rhythm patterns and rhythm patterns presented within a musical context. There are approximately six tasks to be completed in each area. During the course of the initial weeks of the study a pretest will be conducted to determine the ability of each child to successfully complete the tasks. All testing will be audio and video tape recorded and each student will be rated by trained observers on a 5-point scale according to his ability to successfully complete the task. In the scale 1 will indicate the complete inability to perform the task while 5 will indicate the successful and accurate completion of the task.

To insure reliability in rating, video tapings of children doing similar tasks are being prepared and will serve as training aids in developing rate reliability. In addition to the pretest, data on each child will include age in months and an evaluation of motor skills.

Normal music lessons will be taught daily to each class. A video tape camera and recording device will be present in all sessions and it is assumed that the continuing presence of the machine in the classroom would cease to be a novelty and that normal classroom actions could be observed. Rhythmic activities are generally planned and included in all musical lessons with children of this age. The planned activities will be based upon the results of the pretesting of the children and upon

the results of the earlier pilot study. After an
initial 2-week period of instruction, each student
will be video taped in a classroom situation while
specific rhythmic activities are being taught. The
video tapings will be evaluated by a panel of 3
trained judges.

Video tape recordings will be made on a regular
basis for each child (at approximately 2-week intervals) and evaluated by the judges. A developmental
profile will be made for each child noting his improvement or lack of improvement in doing the
specific rhythmic tasks, his consistency to complete
previously learned tasks and the final progress over
the span of one school year.

Using appropriate statistical procedures it
will be possible to compare the abilities of the
children within the 2 age groupings and between the
2 age groupings and to estimate the relationship between maturation, and motor skills and the ability to
do specific rhythmic tasks. It will also be possible
to assess the merits of the two modes of perception
response--vocal and physical.

Consistent with all research with children it
is assumed that older children will perform the
specific tasks more readily than the younger children. It is the hope of the initial investigation
that objective data will be developed that will serve
to confirm theoretical approaches to music learning
or will provide a foundation for a revision of previously held assumption on the development of the
rhythmic aspects of musical learnings. Such findings
are of great importance to the development of an
understanding of how music is learned and how
teaching strategies should be structured.

The second year of the project will be a continuation of the investigation using the same sample
of children studied in the initial project with the
addition of a new class of three-year-old children.
New tasks will be developed to evaluate the abilities
of the 5-year-olds. Experience gained in the initial
investigation may lead to some revision in the tasks
presented to the new group of 3-year-old children.
It is anticipated some refinements in the testing
procedure will also be made.

The third year will bring the addition of a new class of three-year-olds and the elimination of the previous year's class of 5-year-olds. The final subjects under study can be represented by the following figure:

1976-77	A 3 Year Old		B 4 Year Old	

1977-78	C 3 Year Old	A 4 Year Old	B 5 Year Old

1978-79	D 3 Year Old	C 4 Year Old	A 5 Year Old

One group A will be studied over a 3-year span, 2 groups B and C over a 2-year span, and 1 group (D) over a one-year span.

It is hoped that the third year can be used for developing a test of rhythmic task development, the pilot testing of curriculum for preschool aged children as well as the continuation of the observation of the children involved in the entire project.

References

Almy, Millie. The Early Childhood Educator at Work. New York: McGraw-Hill Book Co., 1975.

Aronoff, Frances W. Music and Young Children. New York: Holt, Rinehart, and Winston, 1969.

Batcheller, John. Music in Early Childhood. New York: The Center for Applied Research in Education, Inc., 1975.

Boardman, Eunice. "An Investigation of the Effect of Pre-school Training on the Development of Vocal Accuracy in Young Children." Unpublished doctoral dissertation, University of Illinois, 1964.

Bruner, Jerome S. The Process of Education. New York: Vintage Books, 1963.

265

Gordon, Edwin. The Psychology of Music Teaching.
    Englewood Cliffs, N.J.: Prentice-Hall, Inc.,
    1971.

Greenberg, Marvin. "A Preliminary Report of the
    Effectiveness of a Pre-school Music Curriculum
    with Head-Start Children." Bulletin of the
    Council for Research in Music Education 29
    (Summer 1972): 13-16.

Heinlein, C. P. "A New Method of Studying the
    Rhythmic Responses of Children Together with
    an Evaluation of the Method of Simple Observa-
    tion." Journal of Genetic Psychology XXVI
    (1920): 205-228.

Jersild, Arthur T., and Bienstock, Sylvia. "The In-
    fluence of Training on the Vocal Ability of
    Three-year-old Children." Child Development
    II (1931): 272-290.

Jersild, Arthur T. "A Study of the Development of
    Children's Ability to Sing." Journal of Educa-
    tional Psychology XXV (1934): 481-503.

Jersild, Arthur, and Bienstock, Sylvia. "Development
    of Rhythm in Young Children." Child Develop-
    ment Monographs No. 22 (1935).

Lundin, Robert W. An Objective Psychology of Music.
    New York: The Ronald Press Co., 1967.

McDowell, Robert Harvey. "The Development and Imple-
    mentation of a Rhythmic Ability Test Designed
    for Four-year-old Pre-school Children." Un-
    published doctoral dissertation, University of
    North Carolina at Greensboro, 1974.

McGinnis, Esther. "Seashore's Measures of Musical
    Ability Applied to Children of the Pre-school
    Age." American Journal of Psychology IV
    (1928): 620-623.

Music Educators National Conference. Music in Early
    Childhood. Washington, D.C.: MENC, 1975.

Nye, Vernice. Music for Young Children. Dubuque,
    Iowa: W. C. Brown, 1975.

Pflederer, Marilyn. "Percept and Concept: Implications of Piaget." Music Educators Journal LVI (February 1970): 49-50, 147-148.

Pflederer, Marilyn, and Sechrest, Lee. "Conversation-type Responses of Children to Musical Stimuli." Bulletin of the Council for Research in Music Education XII (Winter 1964): 251-268.

Pflederer, Marilyn. "The Responses of Children to Musical Tasks Embodying Piaget's Principle of Conservation." Journal of Research in Music Education XII (Winter 1964): 251-268.

Rainbow, Edward L. "Pilot Study to Investigate the Constructs of Music Aptitude." Unpublished doctoral dissertation, University of Iowa, 1963.

Seltzer, S. "A Measure of the Singing and Rhythmic Development of Pre-school Children." Journal of Educational Psychology XXVII (September 1963): 417-424.

Smith, Robert Barton. "A Study of the Effect of Large-group Vocal Training on the Singing Ability of Nursery School Children." Unpublished doctoral dissertation, University of Illinois, 1960.

Smith, Robert, and Leonhard, Charles. Discovering Music Together, Early Childhood. Chicago: Follett, 1968.

Veenkant, Diane. "A Pilot Study of the Rhythmic Ability of Four and Five Year Old Children." Unpublished paper, North Texas State University, Fall Semester 1975.

Williams, Harold M. "Studies in the Rhythmic Performance of Pre-school Children." In The Measurement of Musical Development. University of Iowa Studies in Child Welfare, Vol. VII, No. 1 (1932), 32-64.

Young, William T. "A Study of Remedial Procedures for Improving the Level of Musical Attainment Among Pre-school Disadvantaged." Final Report, ERIC, ED 051252, 1971.

267

A FINAL REPORT ON A THREE-YEAR INVESTIGATION
OF THE RHYTHMIC ABILITIES OF PRE-SCHOOL
AGED CHILDREN*

Edward Rainbow

At the Sixth International Seminar on Research
in Music Education this researcher noted:

> Music has been considered an important
> aspect in the education of the very young.
> Organized educational experiences for children
> ages 3 to 5 are often centered on such musical
> activities as singing, body movement to music,
> and performing on simple percussion instru-
> ments. While musical activities play an im-
> portant role in the formal education of the
> very young, music educators have virtually
> ignored the systematic investigation of the
> musical abilities of the young child . . . .

> Recently published method books discuss in
> detail and outline a curriculum for the musical
> development of young children (Aronoff, 1969;
> Batcheller, 1975; Nye, 1975). The suggested
> tasks and activities that are employed for the
> development of a child's musical abilities are
> not based upon and supported by basic empiri-
> cal evidence (Rainbow, 1977).

A research study was outlined that would investigate the role of maturation on the ability of pre-
school children to learn specific rhythmic tasks over
a 3-year span.

During the initial year of the investigations
certain technical difficulties were encountered and
substantial changes occurred in the State of Texas

_____

* Reprinted by permission of Edward Rainbow
and the Bulletin of the Council for Research in Music
Education, Nos. 66-67 (Spring-Summer, 1981), pp.
69-73.

educational system. These unforeseen events led to
a modification of the research problems that had been
proposed in the initial report. It was necessary to
limit the study to children 3 and 4 years of age and
to eliminate the aspect of curriculum development.
Thus the following tasks were undertaken:

1. to estimate the ability of 3 year old
   children to successfully learn selected
   rhythmic tasks during the course of one
   school year;
2. to estimate the ability of 4 year old
   children to successfully learn selected
   rhythmic tasks during the course of one
   school year;
3. to compare the ability of 3 and 4-year old
   children to learn selected rhythmic tasks;
4. to estimate the learning difficulty rate
   for each rhythmic task for each age level,
5. to estimate the effect of training on the
   ability of preschool aged children to
   learn the selected rhythmic tasks.

Rhythmic Tasks

A review of method books that discussed music
instruction for preschool aged children resulted in a
list of 30 rhythmic activities that were recommended
as appropriate for young children. A pilot study
conducted in 1975 led to the reduction in the number
of tasks from 30 to 23. The 3 year study began in
1976 and the results of the first year led to the
elimination of 9 additional tasks. Thus a total of
14 tasks were used during the full course of the
investigation. Five of the tasks required the subject to produce a steady beat to recorded piano
music. Those tasks were (1) clapping hands, (2)
slapping hands on knees, (3) marching, (4) clapping
hands while marching, and (5) tapping rhythm sticks.
The criterion for success in these tasks required
the student to produce 8 consecutive beats in syn-
chronization with the music.

Tasks 6, 7, and 8 required the subjects to
echo vocally words presented in a rhythm pattern.
Words were selected to fit the following rhythm patterns: ♩♩♩♪ , ♩♫♩♪ , and ♩♩♫♩ . Tasks 9, 10,
and 11 required the subjects to immediately clap the
rhythm patterns they had vocalized. In tasks 12,
13, and 14 the teacher clapped one of the above

269

patterns and the children were asked to reproduce the pattern by clapping. In these last 3 tasks verbal cues were not used. All tasks were presented at a tempo that approximated = 104.

Method of Investigation

The entire study was conducted in a cooperative day school in Richardson, Texas, during the 1976-79 school years. Ms. Diane Owens, an experienced music teacher, taught all music classes and assisted this researcher in gathering data. The table presents the number of children in each age group who participated in the study.

TABLE

NUMBER OF STUDENTS OBSERVED AND EVALUATED

	3 Year Old	4 Year Old	5 Year Old
1976-77	27	25	0
1977-78	26	23	4
1978-79	24	25	0
TOTAL	77	73	4

All students had 15 minute lessons 2 or 3 times per week on a regularly scheduled basis. While attendance in the various classes was not mandatory, it was virtually 100 percent in all music classes during the course of the three years of investigation. Daily lesson plans were prepared for each class and rhythmic activities were just one of many activities included. The content of the lessons could be considered a normal sequence of musical events.

The assessment of the children took place within the classroom during the course of the music lessons. A portable videotape recorder was part of the classroom equipment and was used to record the responses of the children to the tasks. All video tapings involved a group of 6 to 7 children and no more than two rhythmic tasks were videotaped during a single lesson.

With the exception of 1976, 3 videotaped evaluations were obtained of each child doing each rhythmic task each school year. The 3 tapings were initiated in the months of October, January, and May. The videotapes of the children were evaluated by a panel of 3 judges. The judges used a 5 point rating scale, 5 points being awarded to a student completing the task to criterion and 1 point being awarded to a student who was incapable of completing the task without numerous errors. The remaining numbers were used to indicate various degrees of success between the two extremes. The judges were consistent in these evaluations during the 3 year period with inter-judge agreement ranging from 79.3 to 100 percent. The average agreement was 94 percent.

Treatment of Data

To assess the relative difficulty of the tasks it was necessary to determine those tasks that were the easiest for the children and those tasks that presented the most difficulty. It was decided that a child would be successful in learning a task if he achieved a mean evaluation on that task of 4.67 or better. A task unsuccessfully learned was a task in which a student received a mean evaluation of 2.35 or lower. Frequency distributions for successful and unsuccessful trials were tabulated for each task and were expressed as percentage of students who were either successful or unsuccessful in completing the tasks.

Analysis of variance for repeated measures was used to compare the ability of the various groups to learn the tasks. When significant main effects were present, a Scheffé test was used to test for significance in the differences among mean scores. Analysis of variance was used to estimate the effect of training on a student's ability to do the selected rhythm tasks. Scores of students who entered the program at 4 years of age were compared with the scores earned by those 4 year olds who had also been in the program when they were 3 years of age.

Results of the Study

Analysis of variance was used to determine if the 3 groups of 3 year old children were similar in their rhythmic abilities. In general, significant differences in mean scores did not exist and the 3 groups of students could be assumed equal in abilities. Tasks that 3 year old children completed

271

most successfully employed a vocal response (tasks
6, 7, and 8). Approximately 50 percent of the 3
year old children could successfully complete these
tasks. Clapping a rhythm pattern after vocalizing
that pattern (tasks 9, 10, and 11), clapping a
steady beat, and tapping a steady beat to recorded
music using rhythm sticks were tasks that presented
somewhat similar degrees of difficulties to 3 year
old children. Approximately 10-14 percent of the
children could successfully complete these tasks.
Tasks involving echo clapping (tasks 12, 13, and
14) and marching in time to music (task 3) were very
difficult. The percentage of students successful in
completing these tasks ranged from 4 to 15 percent
while the percentage of students who were unsuccessful ranged from 52 to 77 percent. Task 4, marching
and clapping in time to music, proved to be the
most difficult task. Less than 4 percent of the
children were able to successfully complete the task
whereas approximately 80 percent were unsuccessful.

Analysis of variance for differences in mean
scores of 3 and 4 year old children indicated that 4
year old children were significantly better than 3
year old children in all tasks except tasks 6, 7,
and 8. The relative difficulty of all tasks was
similar for the two age groups. Approximately 70 to
90 percent of the 4 year old children successfully
completed tasks 6, 7, and 8; 40 to 60 percent were
able to keep a steady beat to recorded music by
clapping (tasks 1 and 2) and using rhythm sticks.
Between 30 to 40 percent of the 4 year old children
successfully completed the echo clapping tasks (9,
10, 11, 12, 13, and 14). Marching in time to music
(task 3) remained very difficult with only 18 to 20
percent of the children having success. Marching
and clapping to music (task 4) proved the most difficult. Less than 15 percent were successful while
55 to 65 percent were unsuccessful.

To estimate the effect of training on scores
of children, comparisons were made between the mean
scores of children who initially entered the program
as 4 year olds and the mean scores of 4 year old
children who had experienced the music program as 3
year olds. While children new to the program scored
lower in their initial assessment, the two groups of
4 year old children were equal in ability at the
time of the second assessment. The second assessment

occurred approximately 4 months after the beginning of the school term.

Conclusions

The results of the study indicated that a majority of 3 year old children investigated could successfully complete rhythmic tasks that used a vocal response. This would support the conclusion that 3 year old children are able to perceive and duplicate rhythm patterns if a proper method of response is utilized. The results of the study would also suggest that vocal chanting is an appropriate means for teaching rhythmic activities in young children.

Tasks involving marching to music and marching and clapping to music, were extremely difficult and the results of the study question the validity of using these activities as a means of teaching rhythmic activities in young children.

The results of the study support similar conclusions regarding 4 year olds. A large proportion of the 4 year old children were successful in vocally reproducing rhythmic patterns. The 4 year old children were more successful in clapping rhythms, keeping a steady beat to recorded music by clapping and using rhythm sticks than were the 3 year old children; however, it should be noted that fewer than 50 percent of the 4 year old children were successful in completing these tasks. A majority of the children found such activities difficult. Marching in time to music is also extremely difficult for the sample of 4 year old children and using this activity as a means of teaching 4 year old children rhythmic or tempo relationships or as means of assessing comprehension of these facets of music would appear questionable.

The results of the 3 year study indicate that the progress of children in learning to do rhythmic tasks is a slow one. In general, significant growth takes place over a 2 year span. This is somewhat similar to what Petzold (1966) noted in the case of growth in auditory perception.

There is a need for empirical verification of teaching theories and theories of music learning. The results of this study lend support to some teaching strategies and serve to refute others that have been proposed by theorists and practitioners. This study investigated a small portion of the complex area of rhythmic perception and ability. Additional studies in this area and other areas are needed if our teaching strategies are to become more than mere speculations.

References

Petzold, R. Auditory Perception of Musical Sounds by Children in the First Six Grades. Cooperative Research Project No. 1051. U.S. Department of Health, Education and Welfare, Washington, D.C., 1966.

Rainbow, E. L. "A Longitudinal Study of the Rhythmic Ability of Preschool Children." Council for Research in Music Education, Bulletin No. 50 (Spring 1977), pp. 55-61.

PHILOSOPHY IN MUSIC EDUCATION:
PURE OR APPLIED RESEARCH?*

Abraham A. Schwadron

The categorization of research designs in
music education into broad classifications of pure
and applied, basic and practical, fundamental and
action, etc. has been considered necessary largely
on nebulous grounds of topical, methodological, and
practical considerations. The difficulties occur
when fields of study overlap--that is, the historical with the descriptive, the aesthetic with
the experimental, or the philosophical with the
practical. Since research in music education spans
many disciplines and research per se requires de-
limitation, the problems of narrow research become
imminent. Phelps notes that "any attempt to assign
arbitrarily any kind of research to one category or
the other is risky at best. . . . Pigeonholing can
be very hazardous. . . ."(1)

Effective research will inevitably exert considerable influence for improvement and modification
on the researcher as well as the profession. Effective, in this sense, may imply something less than
scientific for "the uniqueness of music and art from
other experiences in the school relies on the most
undefinable of its functions."(2) And when research
methodologies become the hallmarks of quality,
rather than the desirability of the work and the
significance of the results, then it must be admitted that a good deal of what is conventionally
called research in music education is little more
than required, time-consuming exercise.

Can there really be pure research in music
education? Does not research in music education

_____

* Reprinted by permission of Abraham A.
Schwadron and the Bulletin of the Council for Research in Music Education, No. 19 (Winter, 1970),
pp. 22-29.

275

imply an applied basis to some degree? To what extent does science provide a point of demarcation?
According to Glenn and Turrentine:

> The true scientist is not concerned with
> value judgments of right or wrong, good or
> bad, but with what is true or false. The true
> scientist accepts the possibility of anything
> but does not accept it as truth until it is
> proven.(3)

In applying this statement of scientific approach to music education the incompatabilities are
self-evident. We are concerned with value judgments,
with right or wrong, and with good and bad. We are
less concerned with true or false than the scientist.
(We preach tolerance for both subjective and objective opinions, with or without scientific proof,
i.e. taste is non disputandum.)(4) We are quite
concerned with attitudes, emotions, understandings,
skills, egocentricities, cultural and historical
determinants, creativity, self-expression, Plato's
"harmony of the spheres," and the happening called
beautiful--a subjective world of symbolic experiences. All these suggest that man is more than
cortical phenomena and endocrinological systems,
and that sympathy and empathy remain important characteristic approaches of art. Like religion, music
moves through that broad gray region of ideas and
accepts the "unproven" or even the unknown on a kind
of pragmatic faith. Further, it seeks constantly
through renewed syntheses of ideas (based on data
from broad fields of knowledge) to modify and refine
interpretations of the good.

It is doubtful where there is provision in the
categories of Glenn and Turrentine (descriptive-
survey, experimental, case study, historical) for
such interpretative research. The pure and applied
classifications, however, are indicated by these
authors as follows:

> Many 'felt difficulties' stem from one's
> own day-to-day activity and need be solved in
> order to proceed with the day-to-day activity.
> The solving of such problems falls into the
> realm of applied [action] research. Other
> 'felt difficulties' do not relate to day-
> to-day activities and need to be solved only
> because they are a source of challenge, in

other words, 'the mountain must be climbed because it is there.' The solving of these kinds of problems can be categorized as pure research.

> Those noted for their successful research . . . are the ones who are sensitive to the difficulties arising out of day-to-day activity . . . .(5)

It is quite probable that the mountain, in many applied cases a more crucial problem, may be related to daily activities in ways not so obvious and must be climbed for this reason. Pure research could serve then to clarify applied and to place day-to-day activity in proper focus. The weakness in the previous statement of categorization is one of over-simplification. Because philosophical and aesthetic inquiries do contend with the mountain one may be led to the misconception that such pure research is not relevant and therefore not particularly conducive to success. If this conclusion is true, we are obliged to inquire why, in the first part of the text, the authors include source readings of excerpts from Plato, Aristotle, Saint Augustine, Luther, etc. --purists by categorical definition, but activists by cultural impact.

When applied, the philosophical becomes practical. The latter takes on consistent meaning and significance from the former, e.g., Plato's Republic, Augustine's Confessions, the Lutheran chorale, Broudy's Building a Philosophy of Education, or music education in the Soviet Union.

Philosophical, experimental, and historical research are grouped by Phelps as pure (basic or fundamental); descriptive and analytical, as applied (action). He distinguishes the two main areas (not without some cautions on the hazards of pigeon-holing) in this manner:

> [Pure research] . . . is based on the accurate reporting of results without any attempt to incorporate practical applications of the findings in the study . . . . Pure research is desirable in almost all fields of endeavor but frequently it is not the type which can produce answers to the questions perplexing music educators daily in the

classroom. <u>Applied</u> . . . research is conducted and reported in such a way that the
investigator included practical suggestions
for applying data of his study to a teaching
situation.(6)

Would research which attempts practical, classroom interpretation of Dewey's <u>Art as Experience</u> or
Langer's <u>Feeling and Form</u>, or Hanslick's <u>The Beautiful
in Music</u>, be considered applied even though the
theoretical basis is philosophical and the method,
speculative? Are "the questions perplexing music
educators daily in the classroom" viewed in proper
perspective? For example, is the problem of youth
music solved by merely gathering data about student
preferences, ranking them, etc., and then applying
the results? Is the question here just the measurement of student preferences or are the truly perplexing problems more deeply-rooted in the why of
music--what Ferguson calls "a fertilizing commerce
between music and human behavior"--and the role of
education in shaping values and preferences?
Philosophical inquiry applied to music education
functions then to clarify the perplexities of daily
problems, to put matters into proper focus, and also
to suggest practical solutions. It is just this
mode of surgical thought and desire for consistency
in both idea and practice that makes categorization
difficult.

The day-to-day consideration as a characteristic of action research is upheld by Pernecky. His
description of this broad category includes not only
a "formal pattern of methodology" and "growth in
the researcher's understanding and concepts," but
also some supported comparative conclusions, three
of which are cited here:

AR [action research] lacks a certain
precision because of inquiries and working
in psycho-sociological conditions. . . .
Results, however, have greater meaning than
in FR (fundamental research) because they are
derived from real situations.

. . . 'Action research is conducted to
improve practices, while FR is usually conducted to establish broad generalization.'

278

'FT is done by outside specialists, while AR is done by people who want to evaluate their own work situation.'(7)

Is music a "precise" art involving a precise form of human behavior? Are not "psycho-sociological conditions" wedded to music and music education and therefore to research in these areas? What is implied by "real situations?" By greater meaning? Similar questions must be raised in regard to the other conclusions as well.

While categorization of this kind is undoubtedly well-intended, the hazards of oversimplification and misconception are imminent. Surely further refinement along such lines can lead to even narrower distinctions of the purely pure and the purely practical. Rather than beat this dead horse, I suggest that we abort categorization and embrace purpose by centering attention on music, mass education, and on the inherent contemporary problems so that the results are far-reaching rather than confined. Paradoxically, the results of so much of the current research remains isolated and, hence, purer than investigators may care to admit. Britton's analysis indicates far better reasons for climbing the mountains than its mere presence:

> Music is an art by definition, and while the arts may proceed by some mysterious internal laws of turbulence peculiar to themselves, they do not do so in accordance with any principles similar to those used by scientists. . . .

> Thus, when one is speaking of the art of teaching a subject which is itself also an art, one is dealing not with scientific facts, but with human feeling.

> . . . I have often been struck by the fact that most of the scientific articles we publish deal with almost purely practical [italics mine] considerations. It is probably time that scientific researchers turned their attention to more basic problems, searching out basic theories, constructing fundamental hypotheses, and in general attempting to establish an intellectual foundation for the research being carried on.

Until we understand better why people
like music, why musical styles change, why
one style is pleasant to some people and unpleasant to others, what predisposes students
to engage in musical activities, what predisposes them to dislike the study of music,
what music is appropriate for children, and
many other similar problems, research findings
will continue to remain applicable only to
highly specialized situations and without
much general validity. Associated with the
complicated problems of the nature of art are
similarly complicated problems of the nature
of human beings and of the societies they
construct.(8)

The real problems in contemporary music education which are daily concerns are to a considerable
extent value-centered. We are coming to realize
that a new or alternate approach is needed for the
construction of value-oriented curricular designs.
The context of this emerging curriculum will focus
on issues relevant to the nature of music and to
the lives of the students. It will lead students
to ask fundamental questions, to engage in in-
triguing musical activities, and to seek answers
based on personal reflection, inquiry, discovery,
and research; it will help them formulate their
values of music on both logical and introspective
levels.

Does it not follow that educators should themselves be encouraged to explore these matters for
both general or practical classroom purposes and the
self-examination of personal value systems, prejudices, tolerances, etc. . . . It seems very odd
that the why of music has been investigated by those
like Dewey, Mursell, Langer, and Meyer and yet
categorically avoided by those directly responsible
for daily musical instruction. To a considerable
extent, our traditional mode of educational preparation may be at fault:

Having been for many years a teacher of
music in search of its many aspects, historical, theoretical, and practical, I have
come to think the question as to where music
sends its hearers and what they see there as
one of considerable importance.

. . . Although our academic plan was intended to break down that legitimate but over-
simple question Why into its several essential
parts, I came to see that our curriculum
(literally, our 'racecourse') led rather to
the mastery of a variety of Hows leaving the
Why to be explored (if at all) in the academic field of aesthetics--another technical
discipline whose forbidding verbiage bars it
from the organized musical curriculum so that
it is generally relegated to a rather minor
position in its more proper field of philosophy
where few music students have either the time
or the inclination to pursue it. A Why,
however . . . lurks behind every How: too
often invisible in the glare of the How, but
still discernible by one who has become
uneasy as to his appreciation of the art.(9)

The question is most applicable to music education. One who is really "sensitive to the difficulties arising out of day-to-day activity" has, in
effect, become uneasy as to his appreciation of the
art and, moreover, his students' appreciation.
Generally, we are adequately prepared to handle
the theoretical, historical, and practical aspects
of music. The aesthetic considerations are notably
absent. Only when a certain maturity of teaching
sets in do the large questions arise as matters of
disturbance: Why am I doing what I am? What do I
believe about the unique significance of music and
man? Why is formal education in music important?
Are my beliefs and practices consistent? Am I so
entrenched in the what and how--and in the quest for
precise measurement--that the why of it all has no
meaning, no interest, or no room? Where are the
solutions to such questions?

It is significant that a number of music departments are now including seminars in aesthetics
for both undergraduate and graduate study. Whether
these are directed to majors in systematic musicology or music education, they should function
primarily to disturb narrow interpretations of the
musical arts and to induce curiosity for further
inquiry.

As tools for research in music education, the
rational processes of philosophy and aesthetics
(viz., deduction and induction) can be utilized not

281

only to examine critically the beliefs, practices, and problems evident in daily teaching, but also to suggest, through analysis and synthesis of validated information, consistent foundations as well as practical approaches.

To realize these results, the research often vacillates from the pure to the applied, from the speculative to the practical, utilizing multiple-derived information to both form and apply ideas. The music researcher who becomes involved in the problems of aesthetic education soon discovers the uniqueness of his position: Like Plato (<u>Republic</u>) he will search for the good on broad and specific planes of reference--the desirable kind of musical society, the role of education; like Colwell(10) he will search for concreteness in order "to objectively identify those elements which contribute to the aesthetic experience;" like Smith(11) he will search for definitive formulae "which will be useful in planning teaching and learning episodes;" like Reimer, he will apply theories experimentally in the classroom.

The music educator can learn to utilize the rational qualities of philosophy without the need for becoming a philosopher. Admittedly, much of what has been considered philosophical or aesthetic research in music education is not as legitimate as philosophers or scientists might interpret it to be. This fact does not relegate philosophical research to a minor position or to a more puristic position. Just as we are learning to apply scientific method we can learn to embrace philosophy on more sys-tematic bases and so realize its research benefits.

It is clear that the meaning of research in music education must undergo further refinement where studies of a philosophical or aesthetic nature are concerned. The primary purpose of research--to open and expand frontiers of knowledge--is at stake. If, as Petzold suggests, "research is not the mechanical manipulation of statistics" but "a creative activity which calls for an intelligent investigation of meaningful problems,"(12) then philosophical research should occupy a recognized station of importance.

Cady's analysis of the four dimensions of re-search--historical, philosophical, descriptive, and experimental--avoids the dilemma of pure and applied categorization. The "gross problem" may cut across any or all of these dimensions. His analysis of philosophical research is noteworthy as a summation of the prevailing trend:

> It seems evident that music educators must assume a broader view of intellect. Only the music educator can compose a philosophy of music education. The philosopher can try but his efforts remain peripheral in meaning. The profession is faced with a need for a basic change, a change in attitudes aimed toward intellectualism and the use of fact and reason for the solution of its problems. This basic change will then produce the quality of philosophical inquiry which will, in turn, provide a philosophical structure within which we can function more realistically, more deliberately, and more effectively. In fact, some of us believe that this is almost a prerequisite to the gamut of endeavors which must be undertaken in music education research.(13)

References

(1) Roger P. Phelps, A Guide to Research in Music Education (Dubuque: W. C. Brown Co., 1969), p. 10.

(2) Max Kaplan, Foundations and Frontiers of Music Education (New York: Holt, Rinehart and Winston, Inc., 1966), p. 45.

(3) Neal E. Glenn and Edgar M. Turrentine, Introduction to Advanced Study in Music Education (Dubuque: Wm. C. brown Co., 1968), p. 90.

(4) According to Ferguson: "that phrase really means that tastes ought not to be disputed, not that they cannot be." (The Why of Music, Minneapolis: University of Minnesota Press, 1969, p. 117.)

(5) Glenn and Turrentine, op. cit., pp. 96-97.

(6) Phelps, op. cit., pp. 10-11.

(7) Jack M. Pernecky, "Action Research Methodology," Council for Research in Music Education, Bulletin No. 1 (1964), pp. 110-111.

(8) Allen P. Britton, "Research in the United States," Journal of Research in Music Education, Vol. XVII, No. 1 (Spring, 1969), pp. 110-111.

(9) Donald N. Ferguson, The Why of Music (Minneapolis: University of Minnesota Press, 1969), p. 4.

(10) Richard J. Colwell, "The Theory of Expectation Applied to Music Listening," Council for Research in Music Education, Bulletin No. 5 (Spring, 1965), pp. 17-23.

(11) Ralph A. Smith, "Patterns of Meaning in Aesthetic Education," Council for Research in Music Education, Bulletin No. 5 (Spring, 1965), pp. 1-12.

(13) Robert G. Petzold, "Directions for Research in Music Education," Council for Research in Music Education, Bulletin No. 1 (1964), p. 23.

(14) Henry L. Cady, "Projections Concerning Change in Music Education Research," Current Issues in Music Education, Volume III (Ohio State University, 1967), pp. 25-26.

THE EFFECT OF THE TELEVISION SERIES, <u>MUSIC</u>,
ON MUSIC LISTENING PREFERENCES AND
ACHIEVEMENT OF ELEMENTARY GENERAL
MUSIC STUDENTS*

Patricia K. Shehan

Research in music education has dealt with
music preferences of children of every age and grade
level, and has been measured using verbal and non-
verbal instrumentation. It has been shown that
students in the elementary grades choose to listen
to more rock music and less non-rock with advancing
age and/or grade level, with a critical change
observable between third and fourth grade
levels.(1) Students become increasingly less
amenable to non-rock music style genres, based on
data for nursery school subjects and second and
third graders,(2) and fourth and fifth grade students.(3) Although the results demonstrated that
the amount of teacher approval received by a
student determines the extent of the student's
free operant listening to the music taught, which
was of a classical nature, preference tests in
these studies found rock music to be the initially
most preferred music before teacher approval was
given. In another exploration of fifth grade
students' musical taste, easy-listening pop music
was the most preferred type, while ragtime, dixie-
land, band march, country-western/bluegrass, and
randomly generated electronic stimuli earned preference scores reasonably comparable to that of
rock music.(4)

It has been the conjecture of music educators that the more one "understands" music the
greater are the chances that one will like that
music.(5) The influence of discrimination on
musical preference was tested using college

* Reprinted by permission of Patricia K.
Shehan and <u>Contributions to Music Education</u>, No. 7
(1979), pp. 51-61.

students who listened to classical and pop music excerpts over a five-week period.(6) Findings indicated that a greater awareness of the components of music effects a greater liking for that type of music. The results of a listening program in contemporary art music for seventh grade general music students point to the importance of familiarity with music through repetitive listening as an important factor in developing positive preferences.(7) However, other studies show no effect on preference due to increased knowledge.(8) The possibility exists that students may react in a negative manner to music they might otherwise enjoy or prefer when confronted with an academic examination. The reaction of humanities classes to the concepts of ballet, architecture, theater, and music was negative, which was interpreted as an unfavorable reaction to the academic situation rather than the pleasurable choice one might associate with the experience.(9)

It should seem that the constant barrage of rock music by the media would be a compelling influence on young people's music preferences because such repeated exposure might increase familiarity resulting in greater understanding, and therefore increased preference for rock music. It follows, then, that exposure to other music might in turn increase familiarity and allow for enjoyment and perhaps preference for other music types. Pairing rock music with less preferred types might also generalize the preference for rock to other types of music. Such pairing is often included as a teaching technique in music instruction. A well-known series, "Pop Hits," uses currently popular songs to teach music concepts which are then transferred to other music types. Classical and rock versions of pieces are sometimes studied together to generate interest.

Music,(10) a series of ten 30-minute programs produced by WETA, Washington, D.C., is a public television series aimed at the introduction of older elementary school children to music concepts and to expose children to a large variety of listening experiences. Funded by the U.S. Office of Education and a grant from the Allied Chemical Corporation, the program format is fast-paced, combining high orchestral quality with comedy skits. It is an attempt, according to its producers, to

286

reach children in grades 6-7-8 with sophisticated tastes in television viewing and music. Viewers are exposed to a wide variety of musical styles--vocal and instrumental, jazz, rock, bluegrass, gospel, Gregorian chant, ethnic, solo, ensemble and orchestral.

The introductory pages of the Guide to Classroom Use in Intermediate Grades(11) explain one purpose of the music series curriculum as focusing "on the cognitive area as a means ultimately of increasing students' affective responses." The relationship between students' repeated exposure to different types of music and their increased preferences for what they have repeatedly heard is suggested in the guide, coupled with the conclusion that repeated exposure combined with instruction on aesthetic listening is the most successful combination of experiences.

Purpose

With a production of a second Music series deep into the planning stages, an assessment of the initial series by student viewers has not occurred. The present study sought to determine the cognitive gain in musical concepts presented throughout the series and the effect of the series on listening preferences with a variety of music types. More specifically, the following questions were investigated:

1. Do achievement test scores differ significantly between those who viewed the programs and those who did not?
2. In general, do preferences for various types of music differ significantly?
3. Is there a significant difference between pretest and posttest preference scores, indicating a preference shift as a result of the programs?
4. What is the nature of the difference in preference among the various types of music presented?

Student attitude toward the series was also investigated as part of the posttest procedure.

Procedures

Three intact sixth grade classes were chosen from a suburban, middle-income elementary school to serve as subjects (N = 72). Subjects in experimental groups one and two received the ten televised Music lessons during their weekly class:

```
Music Is . . .
Music Is . . . Rhythm
Music Is . . . Melody
Music Is . . . Harmony
Music Is . . . Tone Color
Music Is . . . Form
Music Is . . . Composed
Music Is . . . Conducted
Music Is . . . Improvised
Music Is . . . Style
```

A third group acted as a no-contact control group. They did not review the programs, but did complete the preference inventory and achievement test.

The televised lessons were viewed by the two intact classes separately, using a 21" black/white television. Students were instructed to attend to the televised programs. Class instruction in music was limited to the programs during this time period. During the programs, students were not permitted to talk, make noise, or leave their seats. Directions given to students at the onset of each viewing were consistent: "Listen and watch the TV closely. Please keep your comments to yourself. You will be given a chance to share your feelings on these programs at the end of the series."

Measurement Instruments

Subjects in experimental groups one and two were tested on a verbal preference scale used as a pre- and post-treatment measurement. Twenty musical selections of 20 to 25 seconds in length thought to be representative of the musical types were selected by the researcher, and recorded on a reel-to-reel stereo tape recorder. The listening selections of five types of music each served as test items: rock, orchestra, folk, ethnic, and piano (Table 1). These five types were chosen because of their repeated use throughout the series. For each listening item, students responded on a

TABLE 1

MUSIC PREFERENCE INDEX

Item	Type	Composer-Performer/ Title	Duration
1.	rock	Detroit/"Rock 'n' Roll"	:21
2.	orchestral	Copland/Appalachian Spring: "Simple Gifts"	:20
3.	folk	Carter Family/"Chinese Breakdown"	:25
4.	ethnic	Balinese gamelan/"Bumble-bees Sip Honey"	:22
5.	piano	Debussy/Children's Corner: Golliwog's Cakewalk	:20
6.	rock	Chuck Mangione "Maui Waui"	:24
7.	orchestral	Saint Saens/"Danse Macabre"	:24
8.	folk	Carter Family/"Diamonds in the Rough"	:22
9.	ethnic	African Drums/"Drum Talk"	:20
10.	piano	Chopin/"Waltz in c# minor, Op. 64, No. 2"	:21
11.	rock	Aretha Franklin/"Rock Steady"	:22
12.	orchestral	Beethoven/"Symphony No. 3 in E^b," first movement	:25
13.	folk	Morris Brothers/"House Carpenter"	:23
14.	ethnic	Japanese koto/"Sakura"	:20
15.	piano	Schubert/"Impromptu No. 2 in E^b Major:	:23
16.	rock	Fleetwood Mac/"The Chain"	:24
17.	orchestral	Stravinsky/"Petrouscha"	:22
18.	folk	Morris Brothers/"Cripple Creek"	:20
19.	ethnic	Ravi Shankar/"Raga-Manjkhamaj"	:21
20.	piano	Mozart/"Rondo in a minor"	:22

five-point scale: I like it very much (4), I like it (3), I don't know (2), I don't like it (1), I don't like it at all (0). Each musical type was represented by four examples, creating a possible range of 0 through 16 for each type (0 through 80 for the entire scale).

Following the completion of the series, students responded to a twenty-item multiple choice achievement test based directly on concepts listed in the guide, and which were given attention in the program. Four additional questions were used to assess their attitudes toward viewing the television program.

Statistical Procedures

Experimental groups one and two were initially larger than the control group population: (1) n = 30, (2) n = 29, (3) n = 24. A random sample was drawn from experimental groups one and two to equalize the subjects throughout the three groups. Independent t tests were computed with and without the randomly deleted scores, with similar results.

The achievement test reliability coefficient was satisfactory (r = .62) as determined by the Kuder-Richardson Formula 20.

Analysis of variance procedures were used to determine any statistical differences. The Duncan New Multiple Range procedure was used to investigate multiple-comparison.

Results

Question 1

A significant difference was found between achievement scores of viewers and non-viewers (Table 2 and 3). Those student groups that viewed the programs scored significantly higher on the achievement test than the group that did not view the programs.

TABLE 2

ANALYSIS OF VARIANCE
ACHIEVEMENT SCORES

Source	SS	df	MS	F	p
Between Groups	65.79	2	32.90	3.47*	.05
Within Groups	758.16	80	9.48		
Total					

* $p < .05$

TABLE 3

DUNCAN NEW MULTIPLE RANGE TEST
ON ACHIEVEMENT SCORES

Group One	Group Two	Group Three
9.97	9.10	7.75

Note: A solid line connecting means indicates no
significant difference at the .05 level. Any
means not connected are significantly different.

Questions 2, 3 and 4

A three-way analysis of variance was conducted
to study the results of the preference scale. These
results are displayed in Table 4. The data revealed
that:

1. Significant differences in preference for
   the music types among these groups did
   exist (Question 2)
2. There were no significant differences
   between pretest and posttest preference
   (Question 3)
3. The five music types were startlingly different from one another (Question 4)

Question 2--Using a pretest/posttest accumulative mean, the control group of non-viewers
scored more favorably on the preference test, while
those students exposed to the programs scored
significantly lower than the control group (Table
5). Such results might demonstrate general differences in the composite personality of the three
groups rather than the effect of programs upon
preference.

Question 3--By comparing the pretest/posttest
shift, no significant difference was observed
(Table 6). The experimental groups showed an
increase in preference for the music types after
treatment, with the exception of ethnic music
which brought lower scores among all groups. The
control group showed a negative shift in all music
types of the posttest.

TABLE 4

THREE-WAY ANALYSIS OF VARIANCE WITH REPEATED MEASURES ON TWO VARIABLES
COMPARING THREE EXPERIMENTAL GROUPS, PRE- AND POSTTEST, AND
FIVE MUSIC TYPES ON VERBALLY EXPRESSED PREFERENCE

Source of Variance	Sum of Squares	Degrees of Freedom	Mean Square	F	p
Between Subjects	2198.194	71.			
Groups	398.619	2.	199.310	7.642	0.001*
Error	1799.575	69.	26.081		
Within Subjects	7789.300	648.			
Tests	2.006	1.	2.006	.422	.525
Groups X tests	23.503	2.	11.751	2.470	.090
Error	328.292	69.	4.758		
Music Types (MT)	4518.828	4.	1129.707	152.319	.000*
Groups X MT	160.964	8.	20.120	2.713	.007*
Error	2047.008	276.	7.417		
Tests X MT	9.439	4.	2.360	.953	.565
Groups X Tests X MT	16.469	8.	2.059	.832	.577
Error	683.292	276.	2.476		
Total	9987.994	710.			

* Critical level of alpha = .05.

TABLE 5

DUNCAN NEW MULTIPLE RANGE TEST COMPARING MEANS OF
THREE EXPERIMENTAL GROUPS ON PREFERENCE SCORES
(Pretest/Posttest Accumulative Mean)

Group One	Group Two	Group Three
3.979	4.508	5.754

Note: A solid line connecting means indicates no
significant difference at the .05 level. Any
means not connected are significantly different.

TABLE 6

DUNCAN NEW MULTIPLE RANGE TEST COMPARING
PRETEST AND POSTTEST SCORES

Pretest	Posttest
4.800	4.694

Note: A solid line connecting means indicates no
significant difference at the .05 level. Any
means not connected are significantly different.

Question 4--Among the music types, rock music
was found to be the most preferred in all groups,
followed by folk, orchestral, piano, and ethnic
(Table 7). Students' actual range of responses
on the pretest and posttest were as follows:

	Pretest	Posttest
Rock	2-16	3-16
Folk	2-16	0-15
Orchestra	0-14	0-12
Piano	0-14	0-14
Ethnic	0-9	0-8

TABLE 7

DUNCAN NEW MULTIPLE RANGE TEST COMPARING MEANS OF
FIVE MUSIC TYPES ON PREFERENCE SCORES
(Pretest/Posttest Accumulative Mean)

Rock	Folk	Orchestra	Piano	Ethnic
9.604	4.521	3.549	3.486	2.576

Note: A solid line connecting means indicates no
significant difference at the .05 level. Any
means not connected are significantly different.

Because of the significant interaction between
groups and music types noted in the three-way
analysis of variance (Table 4), cell means were in-
spected to note the source of interaction. Table
8 indicates the response of each group to each
music type. All groups were united in their preference for rock music and in their selection of
ethnic music as the least preferred type. For the
experimental groups, there was little variation in
the scores for folk, piano, and orchestral types.
The control group scored significantly higher in
their preference in folk music, due perhaps to the
environmental influences of that population.

TABLE 8

DUNCAN NEW MULTIPLE RANGE TEST COMPARING CELL MEANS
BETWEEN THE THREE EXPERIMENTAL GROUPS AND THE FIVE
MUSIC TYPES WITHIN THE PREFERENCE INVENTORY

Music Types	Group One	Group Two	Group Three
Rock	8.854	10.125	9.833
Folk	3.458	3.667	6.438
Piano	2.458	3.104	4.896
Orchestra	2.729	3.375	4.542
Ethnic	2.396	2.271	3.063

Note: A solid line connecting means indicates no
significant difference at the .05 level. Any
means not connected are significantly different.

Attitude of Students

A four-item verbal attitude scale attached to the achievement test was answered by the fifty-nine subjects in the two experimental groups, resulting in responses supportive of findings in the preference inventory. When students were directed to choose one music type as their favorite, over 80% selected the rock category. An overwhelming majority of students rated the TV series as fair/good, rather than selecting either extreme of poor or excellent. Although many indicated having enjoyed hearing the various types of music on the programs, fewer students were interested in viewing further programs of this type. The following represents the percentage breakdowns:

1. As a means of learning about music, I thought the TV series was

Excellent	13.56
Good	37.29
Fair	45.76
Poor	3.39

2. I enjoyed hearing the different types of music on the programs.

Yes	42.37
No	15.25
I don't know	42.37

3. My favorite type of music heard on the programs was

Rock	81.36
Ethnic	8.47
Orchestra	5.08
Piano	3.39
Folk	1.69

4. I would like to view more of these types of programs.

Yes	22.03
No	38.98
I don't know	38.98

Discussion

The data presented here show findings similar to previous studies in that rock music is over-whelmingly the most preferred music type among sixth grade general music students. It appears that rock music embodies a cultural and aesthetic content that must receive serious attention from the music community. Since most facets of the elements of music can be found in almost any style of music, the study of rock music and other popular types may allow for a growth of fundamental knowledgement of such elements as melody, rhythm, harmony, and form across various musical styles.

Students' exposure to other musical types throughout the ten-program series designed partially for this purpose did not result in a preference change. Musical experiences in school may affect listening attitudes more than preference itself, in that exposure to a musical type may increase tolerance for that type, but does not guarantee preference. Taste is culturally and sociologically influenced and, although educational influences may have a measurable impact on taste, one's preferences are ultimately personal and individual. A student's home environment has a marked impact on the devel-opment of preference, where the degree of exposure to the media of television and radio may be greater than that which occurs in school.

Isolated exposure to ethnic music, a type unfamiliar to students, resulted in decreased pref-erence. Although familiarity may breed preference, the examples of world music presented throughout the series may also have been too diverse and the ex-perience too brief to allow students to feel com-fortable with these unfamiliar sounds. Repeated exposure through the programs led to decreased preference, which supports previous research indi-cating that pleasurable experiences may trigger negative responses when presented in an academic setting.

Although both experimental groups showed achievement test scores that were significantly higher than the no-contact group, this difference was not overwhelming. Lack of a significant pref-erence change for any music type, paired with the small but significant gain, gives rise to some doubts concerning the essential value of televised music lessons. If the projected behavioral responses included the desire to reach students effectively, then greater effort should be spent designing activities and listening experiences that will allow this behavior to occur. Given the considerable time, finances, and staffing involved in producing programs such as Music, it should seem that more thought should be given to the development of pilot programs to test the responses of students.

Television viewing is widespread within our society. Preference may be in part attributed to the influence of the mass media, a conclusion which would seem to encourage the use of special televised programs in the music classroom. Students may show academic gain and preference change when the programming is carefully planned, produced, and tested.

Additional research in the effect of classroom television programs is warranted. In view of this study, a similar investigation to include subjects in an experimental group taught the same concepts through normal classroom procedures is recommended. Further research might also include the series presentation with and without follow-up activities as suggested in the guide. Such investigations may better determine the strengths and weaknesses of televised music lessons.

References

(1) R. Greer, L. Dorow, and A. Randall, "Music Listening Preferences of Elementary School Children," Journal of Research in Music Education 22 (1974): 284-291.

(2) R. Greer, L. Dorow, and S. Hanser, "Music Discrimination Training and the Music Selection Behavior of Nursery and Primary School Children," Council of Research in Music Education Bulletin, Winter, 1973.

(3) R. Greer, L. Dorow, G. Wachaus, and E. White, "Adult Approval and Students' Music Selection Behavior," Journal of Research in Music Education 21 (1973): 345-354.

(4) A. LeBlanc, "Generic Style Music Preferences of Fifth Grade Students," paper presented at
the meeting of the Music Educators National Conference, North Central Divisional Meeting, Indianapolis,
Indiana, April, 1979.

(5) E. Gordon, The Psychology of Music Teaching
(Englewood Cliffs, N.J.: Prentice-Hall, Inc., 1971);
F. MacMurray, "Pragmatism in Music Education," in
H. Henry, editor, Basic Concepts in Music Education
(Chicago: University of Chicago Press, 1958).

(6) D. Bartlett, "Effect of Repeated Listenings on Structural Discrimination and Affective
Response," Journal of Research in Music Education
21 (1973): 302-317.

(7) L. Bradley, "Effect of Student Musical
Preference of a Listening Program in Contemporary
Art Music," Journal of Research in Music Education
20 (1970): 344-353.

(8) Greer, Dorow, Randall, "Music Listening
Preferences," op. cit.

(9) D. Meeker, "Measuring Attitude and Value
Changes in Selected Humanities and Human Relations
Programs," Journal of Research in Music Education
19 (1971): 467-473.

(10) R. Leon, Music: Guide to Classroom Use
in Intermediate Grades (Arts Programming, WETA-TV,
Washington, D.C., 1977).

(11) Ibid.

THE USE OF VIDEOTAPE RECORDINGS TO INCREASE TEACHER TRAINEES' ERROR DETECTION SKILLS*

Melanie Stuart

Abstract

The study evaluated the extent that error detection training (the combination of videotape recordings, slides, textual materials, and class discussions) altered teacher trainees' recognition of specific string techniques or errors, as opposed to the teaching setting in which students used the entire class session to conduct the string orchestra. The data indicated that both error detection training and in-class conducting increased the trainees' recognition of both errors and appropriate string usage. Additional analysis indicated that the error detection training class performed at significantly higher levels than the other group, as measured on the error detection test.

Key Words: audiovisual aids, conducting, string instruments, teaching method, teacher training, videotape recordings.

Among the skills that the music educator will be called upon to use in the classroom is recognizing errors in a performance (Sidnell, 1971, pp. 85-91). Error detection is not an isolated visual or aural process. A large measure of rehearsal procedure is maintained and controlled by the visual aspects (such as recognition of attending, positional problems, fingering discrepancies, and bowing problems), while the aural elements of the music require constant attention.

* Copyright (c) 1979 by The Music Educators National Conference. Reprinted by permission of Melanie Stuart and the Journal of Research in Music Education, Vol. 27, No. 1 (Spring, 1979), pp. 14-19.

The following commentary by Sidnell is an excellent description of the use of error detection skills in music teaching.

> It is of paramount importance that future conductor-teachers of instrumental music performing groups be able to perceive, identify and correct student errors during the rehearsal period. Specifically, the teacher must have the ability to determine instantaneously that the aural stimulus agrees with the visual, and if not, what adjustments are necessary (Sidnell, 1967, p. 1).

It is not sufficient, however, for colleges and universities to identify and list teaching skills. Music instruction in the applied areas provides a strong feedback system. Through the use of private lessons, student recitals, and graded juries, both faculty and students continually evaluate and analyze relevant performance skills. On the other hand, prior to the student teaching setting, teacher trainees have few opportunities to practice or evaluate teaching skills, such as error detection.

Videotaped segments provided teacher trainees with both simulations of rehearsals and portions of live rehearsals. The use of videotaped recordings (VTR) provided a measure of reality within the training, practice recognizing discrepancies, and application of a written analysis as a corrective response (Kersh, 1962; Twelker, 1969).

Method

This study evaluated the extent to which error detection training (EDT) altered the recognition of specific string techniques and errors in position, rhythm, music interpretation, bowing, and intonation. The training sessions were conducted with two intact orchestra clinic classes for four weeks. The students were juniors or seniors who had completed at least one course in conducting, all minor instrument requirements, and had not entered student teaching.

The experimental class spent 20-25 minutes of each 50 minute period working through the EDT materials while the other group (NEDT) spent the entire class session conducting the string orchestra.

300

The error detection training used a combination of videotapes, slides, textual materials, and class discussions to involve the students in recognition of errors while providing models of correct techniques.

All sessions began with a short pretest to introduce the skills within the area of concern. In the bowing section, for example, the task was to identify various types of bowings through aural means alone. After the listening examples the trainees were given the music notation for all examples and the entire class worked through the tapes to associate the aural element with the notation. Videotapes of children demonstrating each of the various bowings illustrated the connection between the aural and visual images.

The last segment of each set of materials was an assignment involving the application of the skills through the analysis of videotaped performances. The trainees were directed through specific questioning to analyze certain measures, each player's performance, and individual performance aspects. In evaluating the performance the trainees were required to assess the bowing used, to identify the type of bowing used, and to determine the bowing and teaching approach they would use for the same passage. A written evaluation of each trainee's analysis was distributed at the next session. This provided information on the correctness and usefulness of the trainee's comments. Cassette recordings containing all the music examples and the videotaped recordings were available in the library for reference.

To assess the effect of the training, a pretest-posttest design using the same test was implemented. The test had three sections: (1) analysis of a string score, (2) multiple choice questions concerning bowing, and (3) analysis of three videotaped simulations of a string quintet performance.

To allow for the accurate evaluation of the test, the VTR segments were carefully staged simulations. The type of error and point of occurrence were predetermined and rehearsed. Finally the completed tape was re-evaluated to assess the accuracy of planned errors and to detect other errors. As the EDT reduced the amount of time the trainees were able to conduct the string orchestra, all students were evaluated on their conducting skills before and after the EDT sessions.

Results

An analysis of covariance (ANCOVA) was conducted on the pretest-posttest scores from the error detection test. The pretest scores were used as a covariate, with the posttest scores serving as the dependent variable. Table I indicates the group means and the information from the ANCOVA.

TABLE 1

MEAN SCORES AND RESULTS OF THE ANCOVA
ON THE ERROR DETECTION TEST

Mean Scores		
EDT = 44.91		NEDT = 28.67

Analysis of Covariance

Source	SS	df	MS	F	Significance
Covariate (Pretest)	319.66	1	319.66	48.06	0.001**
Main Effect (EDT-NEDT)	1322.06	1	1322.06	198.76	0.001**
Explained	1641.72	2	820.86	123.41	0.001**
Residual	113.08	17	6.65		

** Significance level $\geq$ .01

The data indicated that the use of the pretest as a covariate was necessary because the two groups were significantly different on the initial measure. The analysis indicated that a statistically significant difference (in favor of the EDT group) was present between the two classes as measured on the posttest. The "explained" category indicated that a significant portion of the variability evident in the dependent variable was accounted for by the factors (EDT-NEDT).

Because the ANCOVA indicated a significant difference between the groups as measured on the pretest (covariate), additional t-tests were conducted to assess whether EDT or N̄EDT significantly altered trainee behavior from the pretest to the posttest. Table 2 provides results from the t-tests for dependent means. This information indicates that both groups improved statistically significantly over the training period. The ANCOVA indicated, however, that the EDT class performed at a higher level than the NEDT class.

TABLE 2

t-TEST FOR PRETEST-POSTTEST SCORES
WITHIN EDT AND NEDT

Group	Mean	SD	t	df	Proba-bility
Pretest-EDT	21.63	3.85			
Posttest-EDT	44.91	3.45	26.6	10	.001**
Pretest-NEDT	21.77	7.93			
Posttest-NEDT	28.66	6.42	6.5	8	.001**

** Significance level $\geq$ .01

Because the NEDT group significantly increased in the perception of errors without the aid of specific training procedures, it is indicated that error detection skills are enhanced through exposure to the situations in which the skills are required. However, as postulated, substantially greater improvement was achieved through specific training procedures that directed and focused the trainees toward the skills needed to recognize and analyze music errors.

Because the EDT reduced the class period used to conduct the string orchestra, it was necessary to assess the effect of EDT and reduced rehearsal time on the conducting skills of the trainees. The assessment was based on whether the EDT and NEDT groups evidenced statistically different skills on pretest-posttest measures of conducting a string orchestra rehearsal.

The pretest, administered during the second

day of class, required the trainees to conduct the
full string orchestra in order to demonstrate entry
level conducting skills. The pretest was videotaped
and independently evaluated by two raters.

The interrater reliability was assessed
through a post hoc procedure using the Pearson
Product-Moment Correlation ($\underline{r}$). This indicated a
correlation of .70 between the scores of two raters,
which is significant at the .05 level.

Once the interrater reliability was established,
the data from the evaluations were used to conduct a
$\underline{t}$-test to ascertain whether the two intact groups
were statistically different in conducting skills.
Table 3 indicates the results of the $\underline{t}$-test for
independent means.

TABLE 3

PRETEST EVALUATION ON CONDUCTING SKILLS

Group	Mean	t	df	Probability
EDT	40.1			
NEDT	36.2	1.03	17	NS

NS = Data did not evidence statistically significant
     differences at the .05 level.

The data from the t-test led to the acceptance
of the hypothesis that the two groups were not significantly different, as measured on the conducting
pretest, prior to implementing the error detection
procedures.

At the end of the four-week training period
the conductors demonstrated, within the context of
a specific composition, a series of required conducting skills. These conducting sequences were
videotaped and evaluated by the two instructors of
the course (the investigator was not involved in this
assessment). Table 4 indicates the results of the
t-test for independent means that evaluated the conducting across the two groups.

The data indicated that the two groups were
not significantly different in conducting skills at
the end of the error detection training period. The

TABLE 4

POSTTEST EVALUATION ON CONDUCTING SKILLS

Group	Mean	t	df	Probability
EDT	76.36			
NEDT	71.94	1.16	18	NS

EDT group, which had used approximately half of the class time studying the perceptual skills of error detection, was not statistically different from the NEDT group on the skills of conducting. In fact, the EDT group maintained a small advantage on the evaluated conducting skills.

Discussion

The data indicated that both EDT and NEDT significantly increased teacher trainees' recognition and analysis of both errors and appropriate string techniques, as measured on the error detection test. The analysis of covariance on the pretest-posttest measures, however, indicated that the EDT class performed at a significantly higher level than the NEDT class. The conducting skills evidenced by both classes on pretest-posttest measures were not statistically different.

All trainees were involved in perceptual skills training through participation as conductor-teachers of string orchestra rehearsals. Participation in the teaching situation alone (NEDT) generated significantly greater changes on the error detection measure.

It is recommended that the training of error detection skills be approached as a two-fold process, focusing a trainee's attention on specific aural-visual stimuli in conjunction with the trainee's participation as a teacher-conductor of ensembles.

References

Kersh, B. "The Classroom Simulator: An Audio-Visual Environment for Practice Teaching." Audio-visual Instruction 6 (1961): 447-448.

Sidnell, R. G. "The Development of Self-Instructional Drill Material to Facilitate Growth of Score Reading Skills of Student Conductors." Council for Research in Music Education Bulletin 10 (1967): 1-6.

Sidnell, R. G. "Self-Instructional Drill Materials for Student Conductors." Journal of Research in Music Education 19 (1971): 85-91.

Twelker, P. A. "Classroom Simulation and Teacher Preparation." In Twelker, A. P., editor, Instructional Simulation Systems. Corvallis, Oregon: A Continuing Education Book, 1969.

APPENDIX I

ON WRITING A CRITICAL REVIEW

Carroll L. Gonzo

ON WRITING A CRITICAL REVIEW*

Carroll L. Gonzo

The Distinction Between a Critique and a Review

A review of a research project consists of a restatement, in summary form, of the salient features of the investigation, while a critique requires, by definition, that the critic evaluate the merits of the investigator's research endeavors. For a review to be of value to the author who conducted the research and to other researchers and educators who read the review, it should be a critical review which incorporates the important features of the investigation and an evaluation of the merits of the research. The critical reviewer, therefore, must have the ability to abstract a researcher's work and then to evaluate that work in light of accepted research practices appropriate to the type of research, i.e., experimental, descriptive, historical, or philosophical. The following discussion deals with some of the considerations that a critical reviewer should have in mind when writing a review of a research project.

Experimental Research

The format of a research project that is experimental in nature usually includes a problem statement, hypotheses or questions, sampling techniques, review of the literature, procedures for testing the hypotheses, analyses, interpretation of analyses, and conclusions. Although these areas are not mutually exclusive, the manner in which each step is carried out will affect each subsequent step. The examination of experimental research must take

---

* Reprinted by permission of Carroll L. Gonzo and the _Bulletin_ of the Council for Research in Music Education, No. 28 (Spring, 1972), pp. 14-22.

309

into account the scientific precision employed in each successive step in order to make critical and meaningful judgments about the total investigation. A research problem is generally a matter of what seems to the investigator a problem to be researched. In the case of a doctoral dissertation, the nature of a research problem is something the doctoral student and his advisor agree upon. This agreement is, in some cases, subject to a college or university's regulation as to what is an acceptable research topic. Because of these conditions, it is not a simple matter and in some instances not possible to pass judgment on a researcher's choice of a problem. Publications on problem selection agree as to the criteria one ought to consider in choosing a re- search topic. Is the problem of interest to a recognized segment of the academic community? Is the problem original or, if not, does it represent an acceptable replication of a similar study? Does the problem have any theoretical or practical sig- nificance for the field of education? Finally, does the research of the stated problem add to existing knowledge and/or contribute to education in a meaningful way?

The critical reviewer should examine the hypotheses or research questions. Hypotheses help to identify the method of analysis and to determine the procedures necessary for identifying the instruments for collecting the data and for testing the hypotheses. The critical reviewer's task is to point out whether or not these or other similar criteria have been satisfied. If the researcher uses questions rather than hypotheses, these must frame and direct the research efforts.

Having considered the research problem and the hypotheses or questions, the critical reviewer examines the nature of the universe from which the research data were obtained. The universe or popu- lation is defined on the basis of the problem con- ditions, the hypotheses or the questions of the investigation. Here, the concern of the critical reviewer is whether or not the sample drawn from the population was representative, adequate, and free from bias, and whether the population was an appro- priate one for the study.

After examining the sampling techniques, the critical reviewer turns his attention to the methods

310

applied by the researcher. Although a variety of
procedures and techniques, both simple and complex,
are available, the critical reviewer must determine
if the methods used were appropriate to the type of
problem being researched.

The critical reviewer's assessment of the
methodology will, of course, include an evaluation
of any statistical procedures found in the study.
Statistical treatment of the data does not necessarily
make the research good. The critical reviewer must,
therefore, decide if the statistical procedures and
the reasoning underlying their application were
appropriate. Some researchers and, for that matter
some reviewers, have a blind faith in the computer
analysis of research data. The use of the computer
does not make the research any more correct or
scientific than does the use of a calculator or a
host of mathematical experts. The scientific sophistication of any research is rooted in the researcher's
knowledge and his correct use of research techniques
prior to the analysis stage of the research sequence.

The hypotheses dictate the analysis design.
Analysis is not an end in itself. Rather, it is a
means to an end, or the manner in which the results
are generated from the data. The assembly of
results is different from the assembly of data.
The results of statistical tests are generally
reported in tables and the format of the tables
should follow the accepted guidelines found in research journals. The information in the table
should, obviously, be material that was generated
from and is relevant to the problem, the hypotheses
and the data collected.

Finally, the critical reviewer must deal with
the investigator's research conclusions. It is
not an uncommon error for the investigator to
report the results as his conclusions rather than
as an analysis of his results, failing to see that
the results are the facts and the interpretation is
what the researcher makes of the facts. If
appropriate research methods have not been used,
the interpretations can not be valid. The final
section should also contain a synthesis of the
various parts of the research project. The
synthesizing process provides a greater assurance
that important segments of the research are not
inadvertently overlooked. If the research has

carefully recorded each successive step outlined
above, then the investigation could be replicated--a
criterion not to be ignored.

Historical Research

A great deal of historical research has been
nothing more than an aimless and sometimes mindless
codification of source materials about past events.
This particular type of chronicling lacks scholarly
effort and proper research methodology. Good historical research, as in any type of research,
demands the rigor and objectivity of scientific
methods. The function of historical research is to
systematically and objectively find, evaluate, and
synthesize evidence relevant to a specific research
problem in order to establish facts and draw conclusions about past events. Historical research
attempts to explain man's past in a framework that
emphasizes his social, cultural, economic, and
intellectual development. This type of investigation
places more emphasis and value on the evaluation of
the entire effect of a condition rather than on
specific events and conditions that may have been
responsible for its occurrence. In short, the historical research method deals with the broad view of
the conditions and not necessarily the specifics
that help to bring them about.

The critical reviewer takes into account
essentially the same considerations in reviewing
historical research as he does in critiquing scientific research. The fact that the nature of historical data is quite different from data obtained
for other types of research makes historical research
unique and difficult, and this distinction adds to
the considerations the reviewer must concern himself
with when examining it.

When scrutinizing a piece of historical research, the critical reviewer expects that the
investigator will have (1) defined and delimited his
problem, (2) clearly formulated his hypotheses or
questions to be answered, (3) collected primary and
secondary source material relevant to the problem,
(4) subjected his source material to critical evaluation, (5) adequately synthesized the information
contained in his source materials, and (6) through
analysis and synthesis rejected or accepted his

312

various hypotheses and made final interpretations and conclusions.

The critical reviewer will want to point out whether or not the problem selected has sufficient available evidence to conduct a worthwhile study.

In examining the hypotheses, the critical reviewer usually indicates whether the researcher formulated them clearly and precisely in terms of past events. At this point the assumptions are explored to determine whether they are primary and germane to the stated hypotheses.

Even in the case of the historical researcher, the data used are of special interest to the critical reviewer. He expects the investigator to employ both primary and secondary sources. If little or no primary sources were used, the credibility of the research is immediately questionable. These sources are then assessed for validity and reliability. Historiographers are expected to bring to bear external and internal criticism on the materials they have selected thereby providing validity and reliability for this data.

Applying external criticism, the critical reviewer seeks to determine if the investigator has adequately shown that his data are "authentic." Are the data free from inadvertant errors, frauds, forgeries, distortions and/or inventions? Does it appear that the writer has exercised sufficient precaution in analyzing his data for the important question of authenticity? If the criteria of external criticism have been satisfied, the investigation must satisfy internal criticism, which deals with the "meaning" of the source material. The researcher must show evidence that he has sufficiently tested the credibility of his source material. Is the source material of a given contributor free from bias or prejudice? Is the contributor himself a competent scholar?

Finally, a critical reviewer should deal with the manner in which the report was set forth. Generally, the reporting of historical information requires that the investigator weigh his evidence, pull his central ideas and/or points together, attempt to resolve inconsistencies apparent in the data and remain objective in analyzing the data.

Deciding whether a researcher has done these things is difficult and the critical reviewer should be cautious about judgments in these areas.

Individuals who have evaluated historical research have discovered that certain errors tend to occur frequently. For example, the research area chosen for investigation may not have sufficient evidence available to carry forward a worthwhile study or to adequately test the hypotheses. Excessive use of secondary sources of information is also a common error. Other common errors have been the use of a broad or poorly defined problem, failure to evaluate historical data adequately, allowing personal bias to influence research procedures, and reporting of facts without synthesizing or integrating these facts into meaningful generalizations.

Descriptive Research

Research that is devoted to collecting information about prevailing conditions or situations for the purpose of description and interpretation is characterized as descriptive research. This research is carried forward under the same rigorous conditions expected of experimental and historical research, and must meet the same general criteria in terms of research problems and hypotheses, sampling and data collection techniques, data processing, and evaluation.

Although authorities vary in their categorization of descriptive research, all agree that descriptive research can be either qualitative (verbal) or quantitative (mathematical). Most descriptive research falls into one of three categories: (1) survey, (2) inter-relationship, and (3) developmental.

Descriptive research is disparaged by some because it provides the lowest level of scientific understanding. The exploratory purpose that descriptive research serves should not be minimized, however, as information obtained in a descriptive manner often cannot be obtained by any other means.

Among the variety of ways of collecting data in descriptive research are the questionnaire, opinionnaire, and test. The reliability and validity of these instruments, how they were obtained and then reported are extremely important. The credibility of

the results and conclusions of a study hinges on
establishing adequate instrument validity and reliability. The critical reviewer must determine if the
construction of these instruments meets the criteria
for correct instrument format. He should question
the merits of any research that fails to report the
procedures utilized to obtain the validity and
reliability of the instruments used to collect the
data.

If a questionnaire is used to collect the data,
the critical reviewer should determine if the questions are (a) clearly stated, (b) brief and seek
essential information, (c) arranged efficiently and
are readable, (d) objective, minimizing the chance
for bias, (e) in good psychological order, (f) easy
to tabulate and interpret, (g) accompanied by directions that are clear and complete with important
words defined and (h) in categories that provide for
clear answers.(1)

All instruments used in the data collecting
process should be included in the appendices of the
research. The inclusion of this material in the
report allows the critical reviewer to make an
honest appraisal of the investigation and it also
makes replication of the study possible. The inclusion of all raw data in the appendices is considered correct research practice.

The precision with which the researcher uses
statistical analysis in descriptive research requires the same care expected in experimental research. The choice of a specific statistic depends
on the question being asked as well as the nature of
the data. The critical reviewer must determine if
this relationship between the research question and
data exists, and if the investigator has selected
the appropriate statistical analysis. If the research
is descriptive in nature the critical reviewer should
expect to find descriptive statistics. Clearly,
descriptive statistics can assist in quantifying
information in an organized and condensed way that
will make the data conceptually more accesible to the
reader. The critical reviewer will want to determine
if the researcher has confused this function of
statistics as a research tool. Some researchers
make the mistake of using complicated statistical
analyses which are nothing more than mathematical

displays lending little or no relevance to the research question and collected data.

The critical reviewer should also comment on
the researcher's interpretations and conclusions of
the data. Research that contains only descriptions
with no conclusions has little or no significance
regardless of how many pages of description are included. How the researcher interprets the statistical analysis of his data will indicate whether or
not he knows what the figures mean and is able to
convey their meaning to the reader.

Philosophical Research

Philosophical research is unique in the sense
that it is based on a priori reasoning. In a priori
reasoning, sometimes referred to as metempirics, one
arrives at a judgment about something without benefit
of previous study or examination.

It is through this use of rational, reflective
thinking that the philosophical researcher attempts
to arrive at some truth or truths. His objective
data is gleaned from past experience and/or accumu-
lated knowledge. Unlike the experimental researcher,
he is unable to maintain rigid controls in obtaining
his data. Because empirical methods cannot be used
in philosophical research, it is viewed by some
researchers as suspect. Their concern is that empirical research is objective while philosophical
research is subjective and thereby insufficient in
its precision and control to be valid and reliable.
This concern is untenable in light of the fact that
the philosophical researcher employs the scientific
method in much the same way that the empiricists do.
This scientific method was first delineated by John
Dewey(2) as follows: (1) a felt difficulty, (2) its
location and definition, (3) the suggestion of a
possible solution, (4) the development by reasoning
of the implications of the solution, and (5) further
observation and experimentation leading to its
acceptance or rejection. Although this method is
employed by all researchers, step four is particularly important in philosophical research.

Minimizing the value and function of philosophical research is also indefensible in view of the
fact that (1) all research uses some degree of
philosophical reasoning and (2) without philosophical

research scientific research would be meaningless. This symbiotic relationship between empiricism and philosophy can be better understood when one considers the purposes philosophical research serves.

One of the purposes of philosophical research is to determine which activities in education should be continued, terminated or altered. In addition to this, philosophical research can aid in defining or clarifying principles or concepts which then may be useful to educators who are seeking solutions to pressing curricular problems. Finally, philosophical research is a means of examining a variety of existing theories in order to draw conclusions and inferences for the purpose of providing a new or eclectic theory.

According to Villemain(3) the philosophical researcher has several approaches available to him when seeking to achieve one or more of the above purposes. He may decide to "analyze" an educational concept in an effort to render it more meaningful and useful. Or he may wish to "analyze" specific terms currently in vogue so that their meaning might be more accurately served. The researcher could choose, on the other hand, to be "critical" rather than "analytical." For example, there might be specific objectives, concepts or practices in use that need to be investigated in terms of their adequacy of desirability. The investigator attempts to present a critical treatise, the results of which he hopes will prove functional for the profession. Finally, the philosophical researcher may decide to "speculate" about objectives and experiences that may well be significant in the future. Speculation of this sort requires a priori reasoning that would, of necessity, include the "analytical" and "critical" procedures in the collection of the data.

Whatever the philosophical researcher's choice, "analytical," "critical," or "speculative," the end purpose is the same, that is, to determine which practices and objectives to retain, to clarify existing principles and concepts or to synthesize existing theories with the intent of providing a new theory. Once this has been accomplished the empiricist is free to examine the theoretical premises when put into actual classroom practice. In short, the purpose of philosophical research is to provide the theoretical framework for education, while the

317

empiricist's task is to quantify the existing practices in that framework in order to assess their adequacy.

Since the keystone of philosophical research is critical and reflective thinking, the critical reviewer must judge the merits of this type of investigation in terms of the logic and order of the reasoning set forth. The format of the research is scientific in nature because of the method employed and therefore, the critical reviewer should expect to find a problem statement. The manner in which the problem is delineated may take one of two forms. Villemain(4) calls these "inquiry" and "argument" and indicates that although they are separate they are interrelated. The process of "inquiry" generally followed the procedure used in other types of research: problem statement, hypotheses, procedures for testing them, identification of ideas to be introduced, and collection of data.

The manner in which the investigator formulates his hypotheses should be of special interest to the critical reviewer. It is here that the investigator lays his groundwork, through reflective thinking, that allows him to conduct his research. The critical reviewer will want to analyze and evaluate the precision of the reflective thinking in terms of whether it is logical and sequential. Phelps(5) supports this notion and points out that the major thrust of the argument and its attendant sub-headings evolve systematically in terms of their importance to the investigation. He also indicates that the collection of the data and relevant theories, the framing of the assumptions, the setting forth of basic philosophical notions, and the conclusions and their implications will then follow. The critical reviewer should inspect each step for logic and order, and provide a critique that reveals whether the research reflects clear rational thinking leading to defensible conclusions.

Review Format

There are varying opinions concerning the type of format to be followed in writing a critical review. A format that is useful to researchers and readers is one that keeps to a minimum information that has little or no bearing on the research. It is useful to begin the review with an abstract or outline of the research. This approach assists the reader in acquiring the necessary understanding of the content prior to the critical analysis. The abstract should deal with the main points of the investigation and present a general overview of the content. It is helpful if the specifics of the abstract include the statement of the problem, the hypotheses, general methods and procedures, results and conclusions. This information can be short and to the point. While a review should encourage research, not discourage it, this does not mean that the reviewer should not carefully scrutinize the strengths and weaknesses of the investigation. Criticism and analysis should be confined to the research and not the intelligence or personality of the author. Comparing the research to other research in the field, if available, aids in identifying the worth and usefulness of the investigation. If these considerations are taken into account by the critical reviewer, the probability of the review being useful to its readers is greatly increased.

Notes

(1) Joseph Hill and August Kerber, Models, Methods, and Analytical Procedures in Education Research (Detroit: Wayne State University Press, 1967), p. 64.

(2) John Dewey, How We Think (Boston: D. C. Heath and Co., 1933), p. 107.

(3) Francis T. Villemain, Philosophic Research in Education (New York: New York University Press, 1953), p. 3.

(4) Villemain, op. cit., pp. 9-10.

(5) Roger Phelps, A Guide to Research in Music Education (Dubuque: Wm. C. Brown Company Publishers, 1969), pp. 153-154.

References

Borg, Walter R. Educational Research: An Introduction. New York: David McKay Company, Inc., 1963.

Dewey, John. How We Think. Boston: D. C. Heath and Co., 1933.

Hill, Joseph and Kerber, August. Models, Methods, and Analytical Procedures in Education Research. Detroit: Wayne State University Press, 1967.

Phelps, Roger. A Guide to Research in Music Education. Dubuque: Wm. C. Brown Company Publishers, 1969.

Sax, Gilbert. Empirical Foundations of Educational Research. Englewood Cliffs, New Jersey: Prentice-Hall, Inc., 1968.

Shumsky, Abraham. The Action Research Way to Learning. New York: Teachers College, Columbia University, 1958.

Smith, Henry L., and Smith, Johnnie R. An Introduction to Research in Education. Bloomington, Indiana: Educational Publishers, 1959.

Van Dalen, Deobold. Understanding Educational Research. New York: McGraw-Hill Book Co., 2nd ed., 1966.

Villemain, Francis T. Philosophic Research in Education. New York: New York University Press, 1953.

Wiersma, William. Research Methods in Education: An Introduction. Philadelphia: J. B. Lippincott Co., 2nd ed., 1969.

APPENDIX II

ABOUT THE AUTHORS

HAROLD F. ABELES, Associate Professor of
Music Education, Indiana University, Bloomington,
Indiana.

HERSCHEL V. BEAZLEY, Instructor in Music,
Imperial Valley College, Imperial, California.

SUSAN R. EISENSTEIN, Instructor, Pace University, Chappaqua and Croton-Harmon (N.Y.) Public
Schools, and Member, Board of Directors, Ossining
(N.Y.) Council on the Arts.

JAMES L. FISHER, Principal, Catoctin High
School, Frederick County (Maryland) Public Schools.

HAROLD E. FISKE, JR., Associate Professor and
Chairman, Music Education Department, University of
Western Ontario.

MARY E. FRIEDMANN, Associate Professor,
Department of Music Education, Cleveland State
University, Cleveland, Ohio.

CARROLL GONZO, Associate Professor, University
of Texas, Austin, Texas.

PAUL HAACK, Professor, Art and Music Education
and Music Therapy and Associate Dean, School of
Education, University of Kansas, Lawrence, Kansas.

GEORGE N. HELLER, Associate Professor, Music
Education and Music Therapy, University of Kansas,
Lawrence, Kansas.

HOWARD G. INGLEFIELD, Chairman, Music Department, University of Wisconsin, Whitewater, Wisconsin.

ESTELLE R. JORGENSEN, Professor and Chairman,
Department of School Music, McGill University,
Montreal, Canada.

DONALD S. LEVI, Research Assistant, Department
of Housing Preservation and Development, New York
City.

JERRY LOWDER, Associate Professor and Head of Group Piano Instruction and Pedagogy, The Ohio State University, Columbus, Ohio.

DAVID MARCHAND, Professor of Music, Chairman of the Music Department, Towson State University, Towson, Maryland.

LAWRENCE H. McQUERREY, Professor and Chairman, Department of Music Education, University of the Pacific, Stockton, California.

DONALD E. METZ, Professor of Music Education and Acting Chairman, Music Education Department, College-Conservatory of Music, Cincinnati, Ohio.

SAMUEL D. MILLER, Professor and Chairman of Art and Music Education, The University of Houston, Houston, Texas.

ROBERT F. NOBLE, Professor of Educative Foundations, University of Wyoming, Laramie, Wyoming.

MELVIN C. PLATT, Professor of Music and Coordinator Graduate Studies in Music, University of Oklahoma, Norman, Oklahoma.

RUDOLF RADOCY, Professor, Art and Music Education and Music Therapy, University of Kansas, Lawrence, Kansas.

EDWARD RAINBOW, Professor of Music, North Texas State University, Denton, Texas.

ABRAHAM SCHWADRON, Professor of Music and Chairman, Music Department, University of California at Los Angeles.

PATRICIA K. SHEHAN, Associate Professor, Music Education, Washington University, St. Louis, Missouri.

MELANIE STUART, Assistant Professor, Michigan State University, East Lansing, Michigan.

INDEX OF METHODS USED IN COLLECTING

AND ANALYZING DATA

INDEX OF METHODS USED IN COLLECTING
AND ANALYZING DATA

The page number is the first page of the article employing the particular method, technique, or statistical approach.

Analysis of Covariance, 299

Analysis of Variance (various designs and applications), 9, 20, 29, 174, 259, 285

Barron Independence Scale, 105

Canonical correlation analysis, 228

Case Study, 119

Chi-Square test, 29, 128

Colwell Elementary Music Achievement Test, 174

Correlation (various applications), 9, 20, 29, 60, 105, 174, 228, 285, 299

Counter-balanced experimental design, 29

Crown-Marlowe Social Desirability Scale, 105

Descriptive Research, 9, 20, 60, 119, 128, 186, 228, 259

Duncan New Multiple Range Test, 285

Experimental Research, 29, 105, 163, 174, 285, 299

Factor Analysis, 9, 228

Historical Research, 45, 94, 195, 203, 248

Hoyt Analysis of Variance interjudge reliability, 9

Interjudge reliability, 9, 20, 29, 60, 259, 299

Kassarjian Inner-Otherdirectedness Scale, 105

Kuder-Richardson Formula 20-21, 9, 285

Likert-type rating scale, 9, 20, 105, 285

Longitudinal study, 259

Multiple Regression, 60, 228

Newman-Keuls test, 29

North-Hatt Occupational Prestige Scale, 105

Pearson Product-Moment Correlation, 20, 29, 105, 228,
        299

Philosophical Research, 71, 146, 195, 275

Post-hoc comparisons (following analysis of variance),
        20, 29, 174, 259, 285

Pretest-Posttest Control Group Design, 105, 163, 174,
        285, 299

Primary Sources (historical inquiry), 45, 94, 195,
        203, 248

Questionnaire, 128, 186, 228

Reliability (in test, scale, or measure), 9, 29, 60,
        105, 174, 285, 299

Scheffé test, 20, 174, 259

Secondary Sources (historical inquiry), 45, 94, 203,
        248

Spearman-Brown split-half formula, 20

Split-half reliability, 20, 105

t-test, 60, 105, 163, 285, 299

Validity (in test, scale, or measure), 9, 20, 174,
        228